the medium is the rear view mirror

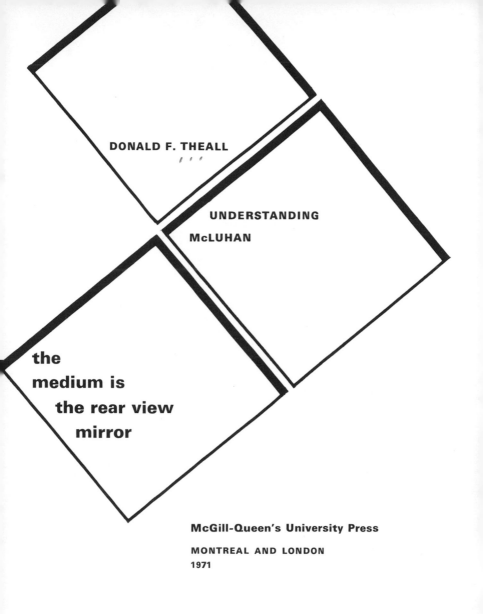

DONALD F. THEALL

UNDERSTANDING

McLUHAN

the
medium is
the rear view
mirror

McGill-Queen's University Press

MONTREAL AND LONDON
1971

Permission to quote from the following is gratefully acknowledged: *The Eternal Present* by S. Giedion, number six in the A. W. Mellon Lectures in the Fine Arts, Bollingen Series XXXV: Volume 1, *The Beginnings of Art* (copyright © 1962 by the Trustees of the National Gallery of Art, Washington, D.C.); Volume 2, *The Beginnings of Architecture* (copyright © 1964 by the Trustees of the National Gallery, Washington, D.C.); reprinted by permission of Princeton University Press. *Finnegans Wake* by James Joyce, by permission of The Society of Authors as the literary representative of the Estate of James Joyce, and The Viking Press, Inc. "In a Station of the Metro" from *Personae* by Ezra Pound, copyright 1926 by Ezra Pound, reprinted by permission of New Directions Publishing Corporation, and by permission of Faber and Faber Ltd. from *Collected Shorter Poems.* "The Love Song of J. Alfred Prufrock" from *Collected Poems, 1909–1962* by T. S. Eliot, by permission of Faber and Faber Ltd. and Harcourt Brace Jovanovich, Inc. "Playboy Interview: Marshall McLuhan," *Playboy* magazine (March 1969), copyright © 1969 by HMH Publishing Co. Inc. "The Taste of Space" from *Poems: New and Collected* by A. J. M. Smith, reprinted by permission of Oxford University Press. *Toward a Marxist Humanism: Essays on the Left Today* by Leszek Kolakowski, translated from the Polish by Jane Zielonko Peel, copyright © 1968 by Leszek Kolakowski, published by Grove Press, Inc.

© McGill-Queen's University Press 1971
ISBN 0 7735 0093-6 cloth; ISBN 0 7735 0106-1 paper
Library of Congress Catalog Card Number 79-135417
Printed in the U.S.A. by
Vail-Ballou Press, Inc.
*Designed by Robert R. Reid
and Susan McPhee*

TO JOAN My Calypso, Circe, Minerva, Penelope

McLuhan put his telescope to his ear;
What a lovely smell,
he said, we have here.

'The Taste of Space'
by A. J. M. SMITH

contents

This book only came to be through an accidental conversation. Over cool drinks on a warm summer day, Dr. Hugo McPherson, then Canada's Government Film Commissioner, questioned my statement that I would never be guilty of perpetrating a book on Marshall McLuhan. Out of the problems raised in that conversation, I began writing a short paper for personal perusal and realized that the subject occupied my mind enough to lure me into writing a study of the works and influence of the Toronto specialist in culture and technology. For that initial conversation and for subsequent conversations I owe particular thanks to Dr. McPherson.

PREFACE

My greatest debt, of course, is to Marshall McLuhan himself, with whom I worked as a graduate student and as secretary of his first Culture and Communications seminar. If, as the book indicates, our interests have developed divergently, it was through his role as a masterly teacher that I, like many other students, first received my initiation into combining an intellectual life with pursuing the study of English in a university.

For many years Arnold Rockman and I discussed McLuhan, his exasperations and values. Professor Rockman offered many suggestions about the current book and provided even more help by being a constant source of stimulating conversation about those areas in which this work is involved.

For constant encouragement and suggestions received from Dr. John Grierson of McGill University, whose knowledge of the communications field is a vast resource and whose criticisms have been invaluable, I wish to record my thanks.

Other colleagues at McGill have been helpful in many ways, in reading the manuscript, in providing information about specific points, or in lightening the duties of a department chairman so that he might have the time to think and write. I should particularly like to thank Professor D. C. Frye, Professor A. E. Malloch, Professor Darko Suvin, Professor B. Weems, Professor I. Gopnik, and Professor Istvan Anhalt for various kinds of assistance, discussion, or inspiration, reassuring them that the weaknesses in the book are mine and their own contributions have been positive. While teaching a special media institute for three summers, I exchanged ideas and arguments about McLuhan with Professor Peter Ohlin, Mr. Mark Slade, and Mr. Terry Ryan. These conversations kept an interest aroused over the period of years in which McLuhan was becoming a myth.

The year before writing this book I directed a thesis for Mr. John Fekete on McLuhan, and the constant discussion of his work was a great help. Other graduate assistants, Mr. A. Rynd and Mr. R. Blumer, provided aid in various ways; Miss L. Alper assisted in checking endless quantities of material.

For their aid in typing the manuscript I should like to thank my secretary, Mrs. Elizabeth Boon, and my research secretary, Miss Hazel MacIntyre, who accepted vast amounts of responsibility for the mechanical production of a sometimes labyrinthine manuscript.

Part of my research was supported by the Humanities Research Fund of McGill University, which also assisted in the preparation of the final manuscript, and by the Canada Council. This work has been published with the help of a grant from the Humanities Research Council of Canada, using funds provided by the Canada Council.

A successful experience in bringing forth a book requires a special kind of wife and a dedicated editor. First, to my wife Joan, who assisted at all stages with ideas, suggestions, reading and re-reading of the manuscript, and just perpetual patience, it is impossible to give proper credit. In Mr. Darrell Dickie of the McGill-Queen's University Press, an author encounters that rare type of editor who understands and empathizes and whose every office improves the work.

Even second-rate science fiction today uses the name and concepts of Marshall McLuhan. A recent example, Koontz's *Fall of the Dream Machine,* looks to a future where the control of media over man has reached the apocalyptic all-pervasiveness that McLuhan predicted. In that society, his real name forgotten, the doctrines of the prophet McLooan still live on. Koontz accepts McLuhan's premises and uses them, but he rejects the positive nature of the vision that McLuhan presents, using it in a completely opposite way to create an imaginary world where man is robotized by the productions and effects of media—a world that he relishes destroying with considerable bloodshed and violence. From Ferkiss' *Technological Man* to such popular writing, McLuhan has set off a great debate, but the debate is one that should have been quite familiar to his literary colleagues since it has been implicit for a long time in the world of the arts, of the utopian thinker, and of the humanities.

INTRODUCTION

Why a book on McLuhan? Partly because his insights are by no means as startling as some may think, except that so many of us have lost touch with the world of the arts and the humanities. Partly because, while his quixotic conclusions may ultimately mislead and even do harm, the basic body of knowledge to which he points is vitally important to survival today. When even such imaginative social scientists as C. Wright Mills can categorically reject the method of the artist in coming to know about society, the vacuum is bound to be filled by activities such as McLuhan's.

But a book on Marshall McLuhan encounters a large number of perils, not least of which is the range of material that McLuhan chooses to cover. This imposes a problem of decision as to what constitutes the essential aspects of McLuhan's method—a problem he himself makes more difficult by at least implying it is not a method, but perhaps an anti-method using probes and insights and not worrying about any type of coherence in the process. Yet his roots are in the arts and the humanities and there is a way in which these days we all uncomfortably feel that advertising and media are applied arts and humanities. A graduate dean of a senior university (a senior scientist) recently suggested to me that probably there should be a tax on the advertising industry to support research in the humanities. Whether this is a fully comfortable thought, there is considerable truth in the close interrelationship and it is a truth that McLuhan has seen, even if sometimes through a rather foggy lens. Consequently, this study accepts the strong emphasis that McLuhan himself puts on the arts and the humanities as a way of Understanding McLuhan.

But it is more than a way of Understanding McLuhan, because, even if McLuhan is wrong, there is a very considerable intellectual effort to be made in understanding the importance today of an aesthetic in a world of social and political upheaval. That upheaval began with a revolution in life style in the more developed cultures. That revolution is an aesthetic revolution which has had vast implications for social and political problems. This is an area in which McLuhan is deeply involved, although he is sometimes totally apolitical and when he is consciously political he is usually quite conservative. McLuhan's fascination to so many people from so many areas of activity is tied up with the problems of this revolution. To look more carefully at the sources of his ideas and where they may lead could easily provide some insight into the ways in which appropriate engagements between the humanities, the arts, and the sources of unrest and power in the society should relate.

As early as the publication of *Explorations*, and especially *Explorations Eight* which he called *Verbi-Voco-Visual Explorations* (reprinted in a somewhat revised form by Something Else Press, 1967), he used the principle of the collage to put together type faces and other visual materials. This use of printed collage goes back, McLuhan himself suggests, to Mallarmé's *Un Coup de Dés* and has strong affinities as well with Wyndham Lewis' use of headline type in the Vorticist publication, *Blast*. The principle of the collage is vitally important in the arts today, having close affinities with movements involving the concepts of serendipity or chance, i.e. arrangements of objects, and the like. The earliest collages in the twentieth century involved conscious planning and produced such works as Kurt Schwitters' *Merzbild Einunddreissig* (1920) which can be compared in some very rough analogy with the way that Eliot arranges fragments into a poetic canvas in *The Waste Land*, pointing out "These fragments I have shored against my ruins." Collage provides a technique for bringing together disparate and heterogeneous objects in such a way that they comment on one another.

McLuhan's own work uses principles of juxtaposition and raises many of the philosophical questions which must ultimately be answered about the techniques and strategies implicit in the collage technique, though it is safe to say many of the answers provided so far have been over-facile. They do not really penetrate the way relations between objects, or objects and concepts, illuminate rather important aspects of the social scene itself. The question is raised with even greater urgency by contemporary multi-media techniques, but it is hardly answered by the slick determinism and dogmatism that can be concealed behind the juxtapositions of epigrams in a writer like McLuhan.

What the collage does raise is the question of the operation of serendipity through association. Juxtapositions of phrases, objects, or concepts which phrases or objects symbolize, trigger a variety of responses in different people. As think groups such as Synectics, Inc. have learned, such associative mechanisms are closely related to processes of discovery. Consequently, the judicious selection of materials to trigger associations can in itself become a reasonably powerful heuristic device and people have used McLuhan this way in much the same way as the *I Ching* or meditations on the *Pensées* of Pascal or the *Aphorisms of Yoga* may also have been used. Wisdom through proverb and aphorism is an old and haunting aspect of human knowledge as one discovers in the Wisdom Books of the Bible.

To the extent that McLuhan's work seems intimately related with these currents, he has become attractive to some contemporary artists such as the group published by Something Else Press. They obviously read him as if he were random, whereas there is a series of motifs by which any group of McLuhan documents are woven together. From the business community's point of view McLuhan's thoughts are in many ways really rather safe in contemporary terms, such as his 1970 suggestions to a committee on education that the role of ETV is to bring together all of the great figures across the continent and make them accessible within a single classroom, a concept that Ford and Encyclopaedia Britannica have worked with since 1950. The strategy that McLuhan employs, like the strategy of advertisers, appeals to a variety of audiences in different ways. This is a natural outgrowth of the technique that he employs and of the way that he popularizes thoughts that have been in circulation for the last half-century or so. But he not only involves the people who find him a source of agreement or reassurance, he also involves those who hold him in considerable skepticism, if they wish to reach an audience of a more general kind in the media area. He will be quoted (even if negatively) by most individuals wishing to show an inner awareness of the complexity of the media scene. References to what he has to say turn up in major anthropologists and sociologists, in futurists, in government officials, and among executives—all of which merely intensifies the myth of McLuhanism. He therefore becomes the objective correlative of what he preaches, a fact he himself illustrates again and again in references to himself in his latest work *Culture Is Our Business*. (This work is not dealt with in the text since it appeared after the text was already prepared for the printer, but see Appendix 1.) He is not only an important index to our age, but allowing the way that anomie has become a sign of the times, he reveals within his activity what might very well be some real insight and wisdom about the current situation. If there is, the sources that he uses in the arts and the methods by which he achieves his insight may actually be more important than anything he has to say himself. For this reason the artist may find him valuable, though not for the reasons McLuhan would most like or for the reasons which the business, financial, and media community have found him fascinating.

In using the principle of collage he has contributed to the development of an important new form, the essai concrète, which this study discusses, and he may well also have provided the same function (though from a different point of view) for this period as Addison performed for the bourgeoisie in the eighteenth century.

If people like Ferkiss are right in asserting the birth of a new man, and this appears likely even if their own reasons are wrong, for the youth see themselves as new men, then McLuhan's kind of relation in this process may not be startlingly different from Addison's relation to the new merchant and business classes. For some his success at this point might be the most questionable aspect of his activity, but whatever the point of perspective, the figure of a contemporary substitute for Mr. Spectator of eighteenth century England is important in terms of the history of sensibility, the history of media, and social history.

All that this study can be is the itinerary of coming to see what McLuhan means, as written by someone who shares much of his background and interests both in literature, art, and tradition and in modernity and popular culture. Such an assessment requires a kind of balance between an honest attempt to see what is really legitimate and interesting in McLuhan and a willingness to confront the most serious criticisms that can be brought against him without allowing the negative criticism to completely mislead the reader about what McLuhan himself is and does. Consequently the book is written in the spirit of an awareness of the social and political issues involved in aesthetics as well as the way in which McLuhan potentially distorts sources as he creates his own popular myth, just as Addison did. Those who read an account of this type expecting critical diatribe of the sort found in something like *Sense and Nonsense in McLuhan* will not find what they want, but there is little value in reducing exposition to an excuse for presenting either ideology or philosophy when the best way to do that is in other studies which should develop if this study succeeds. Those who expect the adulation that McLuhan finds in Culkins and others who contributed favourable accounts to *McLuhan: Hot & Cool* or *McLuhan: Pro and Con* will be disappointed, since this book insists on thinking about McLuhanism rather than living it as a religion or even as a basic way to embrace all contemporaneity.

A man like McLuhan has wit, erudition, and the ability to cross not only academic fields, but fields in the professional community and the academic. He has a fund of history and a sense of tradition which few possess these days. He represents a willingness to confront the present and yet not to reject the past. Yet he often approaches this area with the stance of a huckster, the techniques of a propagandist, the strategies of a con man.* Though as he himself suggests these somewhat reinterpreted might legitimately be defended as being within the realm of an artist, he denies the role of artist and insists he is a philosopher who sometimes may seem anarchist-humanist, sometimes contemporary Thomist, and sometimes an apologist for Madison Avenue. The real problem is whether or not he can be seen as sacrificing the gifts of academic insight and social responsibility that are the peculiar responsibilities of the "intellectual" which by all accounts he must be, or whether he can look the other way while achieving a specific end, thus creating a world like that of the media where the end justifies the means. This dilemma I do not attempt fully to resolve, but if it were true that there is an academic and intellectual who could reach the populace the way McLuhan has, and if he were willing to use the privilege of the inconsistency of the artistically oriented writer to conceal the fact that at times he sacrifices academic integrity and social responsibility as he sees it for popular effect (employing paradox as concealment more than as revelation), then it might well be said of him as it was said of Addison by Pope:

> Who must not laugh if such a man there be
> Who would not weep if Atticus were he. . . .

* The use of phrases like *con game* and *con man* is meant to remind the reader of the interest that many intellectuals like McLuhan had, in the early fifties, in a book by sociologist David Maurer entitled *The Con Game.* Maurer's study examined the life and ways of a group of criminals with a strong artistic style, the confidence men. As such it invoked the artistic interest that had been shown in this figure by Thomas Mann and Herman Melville as well as by Mark Twain. It is suggested that McLuhan, who showed great interest in Joyce's analysis of the artist-son, Shem, as a counterfeiter—"Jim the Penman"—in *Finnegans Wake,* was actually aware of the way that the traditions of the artist as liar (Plato, Sidney), as counterfeiter, and as con man could all coalesce about the role of the artist as involved in the playing of a game, the creation of fictional forms. Obviously there are different ways in which poets and those who see themselves as carrying on quasi-poetic activity would interpret this role in actual practice. Much of McLuhan's practice of such artistic legerdemain seems to focus on this image of the artist as counterfeiter or con man.

list of abbreviated titles

CB	Counterblast
COB	Culture Is Our Business
DL	The McLuhan Dew Line
GG	The Gutenberg Galaxy
FW	Finnegans Wake. By James Joyce
LC	The Literary Criticism of Marshall McLuhan. Edited by Eugene McNamara
MB	The Mechanical Bride
MM	The Medium Is the Massage
M:HC	McLuhan: Hot & Cool. Edited by Gerald Stearn
M:PC	McLuhan: Pro and Con. Edited by Raymond Rosenthal
UM	Understanding Media
VP	Through the Vanishing Point
WP	War and Peace in the Global Village

Editor's Note: Since the great majority of references in the text are to the works listed above we have dispensed with the apparatus of footnotes and have adopted the following conventions. Following a citation, the abbreviated title and page number are written thus: (CB 124). When several quotes from the same work follow closely the first reference, only the page number appears in parentheses, e.g. (124). Works cited which have no abbreviated title are handled similarly, e.g. (*The Historical Novel* 104).

It was common enough in the early fifties to speak of the influence the big foundations were having on university research. Ford, for example, especially in the behavioural sciences, was spending large sums of money for projects of dubious intent, if not of dubious merit, according to critics within the universities. But in the world of the patron, as in most human planning, serendipity plays a part larger than we sometimes suspect.

One of the most important projects grew out of what was, by foundation standards, a rather small grant from the Ford Foundation to a relatively unknown group at the University of Toronto. But that small grant of $40,000 produced not only the periodical *Explorations*, which was one of the more interesting intellectual events of the decade, it produced what France has come to call *McLuhanisme* —the pop philosophy of the guru cum prophet cum philosopher cum promoter cum popularizer cum pseudo-artist, Marshall McLuhan. The *Explorations* period, as students of McLuhan know, was the crucial point when the McLuhan mind moved into the orbit of *The Gutenberg Galaxy* and *War and Peace in the Global Village* and *Through the Vanishing Point* of the present to somewhere, perhaps in Kubrick-Clark terms, beyond Jupiter in a turned-on 2001 vision of tactile colours, a film which incidentally McLuhan has described in the November 1968 issue of his *Dew Line* as nineteenth century.

Of course Ford should not be praised or blamed for Marshall McLuhan, but in one of the ways in which money is a medium of communication, Ford first communicated to others that McLuhan (who was then a maverick among English professors) might well be worth something. It is certainly unlikely that anyone in 1953 ever imagined how the mass age message of McLuhan might monopolize media meditations unless he had happened to know the history of the arts and of the study of literature in the twentieth century and had a very fertile imagination. Those who knew McLuhan believed it could, because he was a man with

1

Beyond Jupiter

a wit, an imagination, and a sense of marvel capable of amazing. My particular Gutenbergish (partly because of publishers' budgets or publishers' conservatism) approach to McLuhan will place him in a series of developments where he appears like the twentieth century Addison he really is. Addison was a popularizer working in a rather new medium. He realized the important role that the periodical essay, as a mode of early mass education, could play in developing a new code of manners and morals during the transformation of an aristocrat-dominated society into a mercantile one. The *Spectator Papers* provided documentation of the phenomenon as well as contributing to this process which Addison strongly supported. In his way, Addison contributed to the change of taste, sensibility, manners, and morals in eighteenth century London.

McLuhan, who has now moved back to a regular periodical "multi-media" newsletter, the *Dew Line*—recapturing a form he tried in a much more modest way in the early fifties in a little multilithed sheet called *Network*—parallels Addison for what is commonly becoming known as "the McLuhan Generation." The parallels could be pushed some distance. If in terms of promoting literacy, mechanism, and mercantile culture Addison attacked the pun and the language of ambiguity (Johnson, following Addison, after all accused Shakespeare of "losing the world for a quibble"), McLuhan extols the pun and worships the master punster of all time, James Joyce. The contrast, in fact, reads a little like a McLuhan analysis of culture—the visual, linear-oriented, Gutenbergite, Addison (who incidentally supported standardized typography and attacked the sixteenth century versions of typographical poetry), against McLuhan (who writes quasi-concrete poetry made up out of the works of others such as Joyce or as in a recent *Dew Line* out of his own ideas—"Breakdown as Breakthrough").

If one wishes to weave further such patterns, the whole thing might come out of an observation that Wyndham Lewis, a former friend and mentor of McLuhan, made in *Men Without Art*: "When Addison introduced the word 'genius' to take the place of the word used up to that time, 'wit,' he did us all a disservice. Wit, as a generic term for all those possessed of an excellent judgement, would tend (apart from the advantages resulting from its

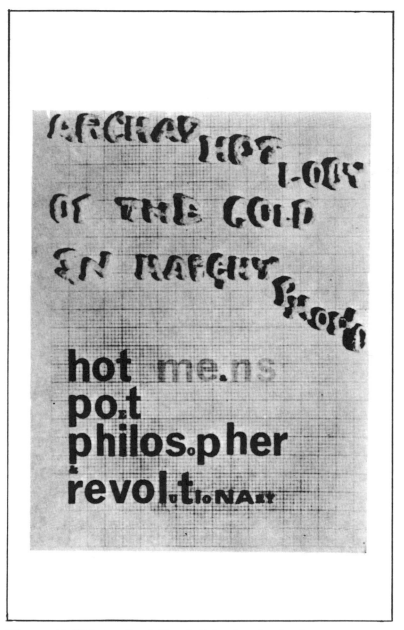

less pretentious sound) to marshal the gifted upon the *laughing* side of the world. But that little change of a popular monosyllable made all the difference . . ." (109). McLuhan backs those who brought wit back into the twentieth century and is himself fond of humour, laughter, and the use of cartoons and of jokes. "The pun," says McLuhan, "is a major example of breakdown—as breakthrough since it draws attention to the nature of language itself as multi-levelled."

And that simply brings us to where McLuhan is at. As he writes "the tale of the tribe," there was the gradual growth of the Cartesian world view when print mechanized the fragmentation of the phonetic alphabet. The phonetic alphabet was linear, says McLuhan, and print further accelerated the exclusiveness of linearity. Where new cultures like America's grew up, he argues citing de Tocqueville, they were so influenced by this linearity that de Tocqueville could argue that America did not understand Cartesianism, it lived it. Ben Franklin, the American most influenced in a literary sense by Addison, was for McLuhan a key revealer of the American sensibility. Franklin, who placed morality on a linear bookkeeping basis, symbolizes this practical Cartesianism. The twentieth century, McLuhan argues, has inherited electricity (though to my notice McLuhan has never spoken of Franklin as having planted the seeds of destruction of his own culture). Anyway, electricity, beginning with the telegraph and moving through a series of technological metamorphoses, finally arrives at the TV set and the computer which create a multi-dimensional, multi-levelled world that can only be handled by the pun. The linearity of print should be abandoned and the multi-dimensionality of the new electric media accepted. Accepted not embraced, because as researchers (Observers, Mr. Spectators) of the multidimensional century, it is not desirable to decide on values until we have understood what is going on. Just as Addisonian sensibility is replaced by a new sensibility, Addisonian morality is replaced by a willing suspension of moral judgement.

Now there are a number of objections to this kind of account:

1) McLuhanites would say it was linear and, of course, it is. They would argue that you cannot "analyze" the matters they discuss by linear methods. And they are right, for the whole story

that McLuhan is trying to tell is like any human story (though they would also say a story-line is irrelevant) and deals with a multi-faceted existence and therefore requires a multi-linear approach with the lines weaving in and out.

2) My own critical conscience would tell me it was too simplified and simple minded. Yet the temptation is there, because McLuhan has a technique by which he continually compares and contrasts opposites—a quasi-philosophical polarization of reality. This means that such patterns as ear vs. eye, phonetic alphabet vs. speech, Cartesian logic vs. multi-dimensional thinking, linear vs. mosaic, and the like are part of his natural mode of expression.

3) What McLuhanism is about in spite of its weaknesses is far too important to be written off in this rather superficial way. The very fact of McLuhan's central role as a cultural myth suggests that he is deeply involved in some essential problems which will reveal either something about the culture or something of lasting human insight. This is why he can sell to the businessman and the avant-garde artist as well as to many, though not the majority of, academics. Whether McLuhan is in some lasting sense right or wrong, the businessman is interested in where we are and the way it is. The artist wants to probe the sensibility of his time and finds any irritant an important stimulus to his own processes of discovery. McLuhan, whatever else, never fails either to stimulate or irritate, for his name has become a household word, the subject of *New Yorker* cartoons, a person politicians want to be in touch with, and a rallying cry for many varieties of movements.

Why examine McLuhan? In the first place, he has been and still is a most sensitive recording instrument in locating the major figures and the major currents of his day. He was interested artistically in advertising in the late thirties and he early spotted the importance to general consideration of cultural problems which emanated from Joyce, Klee, the Bauhaus, Giedion, and many others. His sensitivity is not only contemporary, for he early recognized the importance of the history of rhetoric and the trivium to contemporary communications problems. By 1950 he had realized the importance of the new cybernetic metaphors with which we have since lived. In the second place, his role can be compared with Addison's and that is indeed an important role in a society.

Third, he is, as will become evident, a poet-artist manqué, aping the best of his generation and creating a new kind of essay form for his pop and minimal and conceptual art renditions of the very different visions of James Joyce. Fourth, he is a technological determinist in philosophy and this is an important (in fact, crucial) position to understand today if we are not to substitute a philosophy about the existing relations of production with a philosophy about the deterministic nature of technology. Fifth, whatever else, he is a myth and myths are always important as ways of understanding. And sixth, he is not an American, he is a Canadian; something which after a moment's reflection startles everyone unless they are willing to give some credence to his own theory which provides the title of his journal—that Canada, land of the DEW line, provides a natural anti-environment to the United States and hence an early warning system of what is going on in that environment. That is the presumed purpose of McLuhan's *Dew Line*, which, originally published as a monthly at $50 a year, has now come down to six copies for $25 a year. (Is Canada perhaps half as effective a warning system this year?)

All these would be sufficient reasons to look at McLuhan, but as Tom Wolfe, the American critic, has said, "What if he is right?" No one is all right, but there seems little doubt that McLuhan has right insights and that these must be "grokked" (the only way to seem not to be using linear language) by sensing where they form part of our present sensibility and understanding of the environment. It is possible to discover a great deal in McLuhan without necessarily accepting the general theory that weakens a great deal of his work. If he has been one·thing in the past, he has been a great teacher to many of those who encountered him. He carries into his writings this same ability to intrigue the mind by presenting many of the processes of his own thinking in action. Great teachers, on the whole, do not indoctrinate but provide insights which can be commented upon and developed.

What may bother most of us at an initial exposure to McLuhan is that his view of modernity is one that seems to move in the direction of being exclusive rather than inclusive in nature, as when he deals with what the contemporary period or the near future might be. If we move from print and a visual orientation to television and computers and an audio-tactile orientation, it suggests that we are going to move from one position to its polar opposite, that we will exclude linear logic, visual emphases, and strong commitments to print in favour of multi-dimensional intuition, audio-tactile emphases, and strong commitments to a new oral culture. Admittedly McLuhan describes this world as multi-sensory, which would seem to suggest inclusiveness, but his method of describing the earlier change from audio-tactile to visual would seem to suggest exclusiveness. Such categories may well themselves be called linear by those who, like McLuhan, feel all categories are to disappear. But in spite of this most of us feel that inclusiveness cannot in itself be exclusive if the inclusiveness in question, as the McLuhanites insist, is a totality or total field, this apart from whether or not the particular operation of the senses allows for quite the degree of specialization or fragmentation that McLuhan's analyses suggest.

What McLuhan seems to require is some kind of paradoxical logic akin to that implicit in the way in which Hugh Kenner (one of McLuhan's literary disciples) has suggested the Stoic Comedians (Flaubert, Joyce, and Beckett) are supposed to have created their literary structures. Interestingly enough this rage for paradox has roots in McLuhan's early interest, as a Roman Catholic, in G. K. Chesterton, a master of the paradox.

But such paradoxes are founded in some naïve versions of Hegelianism and therefore can be related to a nineteenth century point of view. Yet it is also, in a different way, an inheritance from the Renaissance, a period in which McLuhan did most of his early scholarly work. It leads to the ways that McLuhan seems to say one thing and then somewhat later quite its opposite—both equally dogmatically. As a technique it also dominates the way that he puts together his aphorisms, those short pithy statements or maxims for which he has become famous. To say "the medium is the message," for example, seems to contradict the distinction between medium and message as well as between form and content. In trying to make sense of the paradox implicit in it, however, the mind is forced to meditate upon the complex relations between medium and message, between form and content, and even about the nature of the code in which messages are "informed" or communicated. McLuhan in such formulae crossbreeds the talent of the copywriter with that of the epigrammatist to create a unique, contemporary type of poetic aphorism.

Interestingly enough, it has lately been demonstrated that a great deal of talk about communications, or communications about communications, is bound to get involved in this type of paradox for the simple reason that one is talking about two levels of discourse simultaneously. One is the actual level of communication and the other, the communication about the communication. This is equally true of a phrase like "the medium is the message," for it too is a medium with a message which seems to work at cross-purposes. But then McLuhan would go further and pun and suggest that here we could also have the "medium is the massage," with the covert suggestion that the "medium is the mass age." Such overlayering is meant to indicate the way in which any message is also a massage, and perhaps even more properly so in a mass age which, with its environmental difficulties, also is a "mess age" (CB 23). Whether we can accept this or not, it forces a kind of intellectual participation in filling in the details of the prose and becomes what McLuhan describes as "cool" rather than "hot."

All the dynamics of this kind of style are bound up in McLuhan's own intellectual quest, his history, and his relations within a social network. Obviously his sense of paradox and aphorism arises from his literary background; his sense of an adman's style goes back to *The Mechanical Bride,* and the whole problem of relation between medium and message to his interest in Thomistic philosophy or New Criticism. We must start understanding "media" by understanding McLuhan.

McLuhan is a medium and quite possibly a medium who is the message. His style and his intellectual technique both justify this title and they both coalesce with his method. In the first place they create the form which McLuhan presents to his public, and secondly, they are the result of an attempt to read the signs of the future in the world about him as if they were signatures of some being or intelligence. Besides, McLuhan is a master of metaphor and uses the metaphor to probe and to prophesy.

2
A
Do-It-Yourself-Creativity-Kit

Two senses of medium coalesce here, but both of them are characteristic of modern interests which McLuhan pursues. Medium in its more frequently used sense is intimately tied up with his first book, *The Mechanical Bride*, and he is recognized as one of the first thinkers to take media such as radio and newspapers seriously. Medium, in the other sense, is tied up with cabalistic and esoteric ways of seeing the poet or artist, as held by *Symbolistes* like Mallarmé or later poets like Yeats. Here the poet is receptive to, or able to read in a magical way, secrets hidden from the average man. Sometimes, as with Yeats, such insights went as far as to suggest the important difference between oral poetry and poetry geared to the printing press, or so deep as to create a total symbolic system of a socio-psychological nature out of apparently spiritual visions.

Understanding McLuhan is a process of retracing and reconstructing the evolution of his form and style; his method; his uses of history, poetry, art, and philosophy; and his *engagement* with the worlds of popular culture and technology. Tracing back the roots from which the exfoliating growth of McLuhanism blossoms forth, the explorer discovers deeply traditional sources in humanism, in literature, in history, and in philosophical thought. McLuhan early schooled himself in the history of rhetoric (the art of persuasive speech in its broadest sense) and the disciplines traditionally associated with rhetoric—grammar (the art of language) and logic. His earliest activity was as a student of English literature (he wrote an M.A. thesis on Meredith, who incidentally was one of Joyce's early enthusiasms) and he established a competence in English literary history and its classical backgrounds. Following this he studied the Renaissance in depth as a continental milieu.

Gradually his interest shifted to contemporary literature and to the viewing of contemporary literature in the wide context of the older and newer contemporary arts and the evolution of contemporary thought in the sciences and philosophy. In all of these interests there coalesced a strong commitment to "humanism," and through a religious conversion, to a "Catholic" theology. His movement into the sphere of popular culture grew out of his interest in presenting traditional humanistic arts to young students in North America. As he examined their cultural objects—ads, comic books, radio programmes, the press, etc.—his interest (partly under the influence of Norbert Weiner's "communications" revolution) shifted to the means of distribution as much as the object. From that point to an interest in culture and technology is a small step.

Again the McLuhanite may say all this is not very relevant, as McLuhan himself suggested on a broadcast with Goldmann ("The Open Mind," WNBC, May 1966) when questioned about his traditionalism and his Catholicism (quoted in M:HC xvii). But, after all, *The Gutenberg Galaxy* is a book about history, filled with erudition and presented with academic paraphernalia. It examines in some detail Shakespeare, Bacon, Rabelais, Alexander Pope, and Joyce among others—a list which reads rather like the interests of a humanist. From this background McLuhan, in fact, develops his method. The very base from which McLuhan moved into a consideration of the mass media provides him with a unique quality of imagination to bring to the study of cultural objects. One of the simple reasons why McLuhan has come to be so important is the widespread lack of qualities of imagination.

As the McLuhan comet was working its way to ascendancy in *The Gutenberg Galaxy*, C. Wright Mills was extolling to American sociologists the virtues of de Tocqueville and Taine, both figures who also interest McLuhan. To the question: "Were de Tocqueville or Taine alive at this time would they not be sociologists?" Mills replies in the words of a London *Times* reviewer who had written:

> Taine always saw man primarily as a social animal and society as a collection of groups: he could observe minutely, was a tireless field worker and possessed a quality . . . particularly valuable for perceiving relationships between social phenomena—the quality of sprightliness. He was too interested in the present to be a good historian, too much of a theorist to try his hand as a novelist, and he thought of literature too much as the documents in the culture of an age or country to achieve first-class status as a critic. . . . His work on English literature is less about English literature than a commentary on the morality of English society as a vehicle for his positivism. He is a social theorist before all else. (*The Sociological Imagination* 17)

This same quality of "sprightliness" in Taine is one way of describing the quality of McLuhan's wit. While he is not a literary historian, novelist, or, in the narrow sense, a critic like Taine, literary and artistic interests are his major starting point. (His analysis of *King Lear* may be interesting yet fail to be good criticism.) Mills argues that Taine remained a "literary man" partly because of the inadequacies of the nineteenth century's zealous search for laws. In such a situation as Taine's era of the nineteenth century, according to Mills, art often comes to the aid of the social sciences; though he argues that art today is inadequate to this task:

> In the absence of an adequate social science, critics and novelists, dramatists and poets have been the major, and often the only, formulators of private troubles and even of public issues. Art does express such feelings and often focuses them—at its best with dramatic sharpness—but still not with the intellectual clarity required for their understanding or relief today. Art does not and cannot formulate these feelings as problems containing the troubles and issues men must now confront if they are to overcome their uneasiness and indifference and the intractable miseries to which these lead. The artist, indeed, does not often try to do this. Moreover, the serious artist is himself in much trouble, and could well do with some intellectual and cultural aid from a social science made sprightly by sociological imagination. (*The Sociological Imagination* 18)

Like Mills, McLuhan is interested in the sociological imagination; unlike Mills he finds it in writers such as Joyce. But McLuhan also is a kind of artist, a *new* kind of artist, and within one sphere he is trying to provide such sprightliness of imaginative approaches. If there is a general need of a "sociological imagination," perhaps McLuhan tries to deal with that specific area of sociology involved with communications and technological structure, providing what he might call a "communications imagination."

What are the major influences on McLuhan's imagination? Rather than attempt to discover them serially, it is possible to allow these influences to appear in the process of discussing the way in which McLuhan's imagination manifests itself in his works. Since the very nature of imagination is closely linked to metaphor, and metaphorical or analogical thinking, perhaps the best point at which to begin is with the importance of metaphor and analogy in McLuhan's thinking. The importance of the metaphorical method of exploration can easily be overlooked even though such important scientific investigators as Donald Hebb have clearly shown that metaphor (i.e. analogy) is the basis of even scientific exploration (*The Organization of Behavior* 18).

Metaphor occupies a special place for a literary mind and especially for someone who has been a student of the history of rhetoric. Prior to McLuhan, the studies of George Herbert Mead and Kenneth Burke demonstrated the importance of symbolic and metaphorical thinking in man's social development. The contemporary age has resurrected the sense of metaphor Aristotle had set forth in his *Poetics* where he argued that metaphor was the true mark of genius. The most extensive form of metaphor according to Aristotle was metaphor by analogy or proportion. The sense of importance about the subject had been clearly impressed on the literary mind of the thirties by I. A. Richards' *The Philosophy of Rhetoric* where Richards discusses at length theories of metaphor and their relation to a contextual theory of meaning. Both from McLuhan's interest in Thomistic philosophy, with its emphasis on "analogy," and from his interest in the New Criticism which had been inspired by Richards, he became habituated to thinking in proportionate relations. Such a way of thinking can lead one to discover that the form is to the content as the medium is to the message, or that the dynamics of skimming over the water on a surfboard can be compared to the process of skimming over the intellectual problems of a culture, such as in the work of Descartes or Heidegger.

For McLuhan, as his early literary studies on Joyce would suggest, the world is a network of such analogies—the result of a book of nature which has been patterned by some overall intelligence. The fact that they are perpetually revelatory provides a peculiar power to McLuhan's work whether or not one accepts the basis from which it emanates. After all, the use of metaphor shows a quickness in seeing relationships which is close to the basis of whatever we describe as creativity.

But McLuhan's metaphors are not merely comparisons or analogies coming out of the past. They are constantly related to the network of feeling of the present. For example, take "rear-view mirror" where one of the vital safety factors in a car and the process of utilizing it are compared to the way in which we examine present cultural phenomena. In *War and Peace in the Global Village*, McLuhan discusses how he uses the rear-view mirror of Pound and Joyce. Even titles like *The Gutenberg Galaxy* exploit the contemporary metaphor and his works abound in the application of contemporary crazes like "surfboarding" to intellectual activities such as philosophizing or theorizing about education: "Heidegger surfboards along on the electronic wave as triumphantly as Descartes rode the mechanical wave" (GG 248). Here there is not only the metaphor itself employing a covert analogy, but also an explicit analogy in which Descartes' relation to his age and its mode is similar to Heidegger's relation to his age and its mode. The point of the analogy is an exposé of the inadequacies of Descartes for an electric age. Whether we agree with McLuhan's facility or not, the technique when it is successful provides a poetic discovery. If TV is "cool" as radio is "hot," all of the interplay of hot and cool (in both senses of the words) becomes open to us.

The character of McLuhan's metaphor is not only rooted in the use of modernity, but in the employment of comparisons which are calculated to shock and to puzzle. They are characteristic of what the seventeenth century described as "wit." That wit produced the metaphor of the metaphysical poets, such as Donne's comparison of a pair of lovers to a pair of drawing compasses:

> Our two soules therefore, which are one,
>   Though I must goe, endure not yet
> A breach, but an expansion,
>   Like gold to ayery thinnesse beate.
>
> If they be two, they are two so
>   As stiffe twin compasses are two

("A Valediction: forbidding mourning")

Thus an adaptation of the witty conceit of a metaphysical poet's mind transported into a modern setting becomes an ideal vehicle of communication for McLuhan.

McLuhan's interest in the metaphysical poets' wit grew out of his interest in Eliot's theory that they were the last poets to have a united sensibility (i.e. a sensibility where thought and feeling are united). In fact, not only did the "metaphysical wit" have an influence on McLuhan as it did on most literary critics of his generation, but Eliot's now discredited doctrine of the "dissociation of sensibility" (i.e. that a unified sensibility disappeared around the time of Milton and Dryden) influenced the way McLuhan sees print (i.e. moveable type) as creating or causing a fragmented man, and therefore a kind of dissociated sensibility.

What makes the technique of analogy work, as Arthur Koestler has shown (*The Act of Creation*, passim), is that the seeds of creativity are implicit in the witty metaphor. The very process of having to explore the relationship makes the person participate in a recognition of similarities and differences. By the time one finishes exploring McLuhan's notion of the rear-view mirror, the real insecurity of our age about the concept of history, and its relationship to the processes of acceleration in the world around us, is as apparent as the revelation of technological power implications is in Kubrick's satire on the Bomb.

At their best, McLuhan's metaphors become the basis of new theories. Whether we agree with what he calls "hot" and what he calls "cool," the theory of participation involved and its relation to effect are vital to understanding communications. The metaphor forces a fuller kind of exploration because, as McLuhan himself argues, it is a depth technique.

In McLuhanese, his metaphors could be described as providing a "Do-It-Yourself-Creativity-Kit." In this way, even the initially less adequate metaphors can be useful for meditation which will lead to some kind of creative insight. The insight in McLuhan's books is not always his but the reader's, generated by the metaphors which create a pseudo-synectic group-think method for participation. To accomplish the task of giving the metaphors more impact, McLuhan has crossbred the world of advertising with the world of poetry.

A great deal of McLuhan's later prose style developed out of his study for *The Mechanical Bride*. There, as he tried in his subheadings to "one-up" and hence reveal the meaning of the ads, he played with a style and technique similar to that of the ads themselves. One ad showing a young woman standing at a window with her hand out in the rain has the copy: "There's deep consolation . . . serene through shower or heavy rain . . . for those who know the casket of a dear one is protected against water in the ground by a Clark Metal Grave Vault" (MB 15). McLuhan quips on this: "How dry I am?" / "I cried until they told me it was watertight" / "The more the burier, said Digby O'Dell?" (referring to the mortician in a radiocomedy series) / "More stiffs are turning to the watertight brand?" (MB 14). This is "wit" deliberately built on the ad world, a *Dunciad*-like re-creation of the word by playing with its uncreation. This mode of wit reveals certain premises of consumer society as cliché as well as interrelating diverse modes of expression. But the same technique presented with a different object can involve theories of cultural criticism. The opening presentation in *The Mechanical Bride* is a front page of the New York *Times*, where McLuhan treats the layout as "front-page cubism." A phrase such as "front-page cubism" is characteristic of the crossing of contemporary interest, copywriting sense, and analogic witty metaphor. It becomes in later books such things as "Francis Bacon, PR Voice for the *moderni*, had both his feet in the Middle Ages" (GG 183), or "War as Education: . . . Education as War: . . ." in *War and Peace in the Global Village* (96, 148).

Advertising and poetry have often been compared, and there is even a cult within the advertising world that views the copywriter as poet or the creative man as artist in the same way that Pohl and Kornbluth satirized in *The Space Merchants*. This is where Mc-Luhan's insistence that advertising is a modern form of rhetoric is useful. Just as the line between the creativity of rhetoric and the creativity of poetry was difficult to draw in the Renaissance, so the advertising man, the visual artist, the film maker, and the poet all share the same, or part of the same, universe of expression. What makes the difference between the "rhetorical" adman and the artist can only be defined in terms of depth and intensity. Pop art has explored part of this paradox in terms of the way context and mode of contemplation can transform straight "pop" material into art. Those who, like McLuhan, wish to stress the continuum between the various worlds of expression will argue that everything becomes art once it has ceased to be the "junk" of the present moment. Without pursuing the various implications of art, junk, and pop culture, it is possible to see that McLuhan (much as the advertiser) exists somewhere between a poet and a rhetorician.

McLuhan, perhaps unwittingly, is a kind of pseudo-poet. In a sense he himself suggests this when, in an interview with Gerald Stearn (M:HC 301–2), he contrasts himself to James Joyce who has traversed the same ground more intensely. The term pseudo-poet is not meant pejoratively, but to define a direction toward a fundamentally poetic goal. After all, for McLuhan who sees the arts as early warning systems, this is quite a creditable ideal. The very strategy of the McLuhan type of aphorism comes fundamentally from poetic (or at least artistic) sources. In the *ABC of Reading*, Ezra Pound told his audiences that "Literature is News that STAYS news" (29), that "Artists are the antennae of the race" (81). This is pure McLuhanese, using the language of journalism to create special effects.

But there is more to it than that, for Pound and McLuhan are both engaged in the production of contemporary aphorisms or epigrams. The aphorism, which forms the base of most epigrams, is a rhetorical device closely associated with one of the main currents of influence on McLuhan's technique and behind the development of the McLuhanesque form. Bacon as PR man for the *moderni* developed, in the early print era, the essay form which used as its major mode of development of form, the aphorism. McLuhan, as PR man to the tribal *moderni*, has carefully studied Bacon, as the extensive discussion in *The Gutenberg Galaxy* reveals. Perhaps in some way he even sees himself as a modern Bacon, an electric age version of Bacon, establishing the basis for a new intellectual movement. Like Bacon, McLuhan is trying to "read" the Book of Nature (which for him includes technology, history, and the total contemporary world), or rather, in post-Gutenberg electric age terms, to make manifest the total environment. Yet, there is an interesting similarity here, which may suggest there are analogies between different technological ages. Just as Bacon moves from reading the Book of the Spirit to reading the Book of Nature and sees nature as something that can be exegeted and analyzed, McLuhan examines the environment as if it were some type of artifact—a new nature turned art, paralleling the nature that Bacon's day thought had become a work of art. This new environment when contemplated by multi-level, non-linear strategies renders forth its dynamics, just as Bacon discovered his nature through reading the natural world as if it were a book. Would it be fair to say that McLuhan sees the world as if it were a TV show and that his discussion of war differs little from his discussion of *2001?*

What is at stake here is fundamental to what McLuhan achieves. His method is an ever-growing extension of *The Mechanical Bride*—an attempt to "read" (in the Baconian and new critical sense, i.e. the exegetical sense of the word) cultural objects. From the *Bride* to *Understanding Media*, these objects may shift from precise ads or comics or pop literature to the effects of actual technological devices, but the strategies are essentially the same. The problem, if there is one, is that TV as a cultural object is something rather different from a particular TV or radio programme.

The particular strategy, however, is an inheritance from the exegetical literary traditions of the past filtered through Bacon to the New Criticism of the present. McLuhan's involvement at Cambridge during a time when I. A. Richards' *Practical Criticism* was producing the new *explication de texte* of Empson in England, or Brooks' New Criticism in the U.S., considerably reinforced an aspect of his rhetorically conditioned background. The use of such exegesis for moral criticism of culture had evolved from the so-called Cambridge School and its leader, F. R. Leavis.

In England, interestingly enough, the Cambridge School gradually generated a parallel interest in communications and media in Raymond Williams who moved from an analysis of *Culture and Society*, through a discussion of *The Long Revolution* brought about by the mass arts, to a critical study of media in *Communications*. Another English outgrowth was the development at Birmingham of the Centre for Contemporary Cultural Studies, under the direction of Richard Hoggart who, in *The Uses of Literacy*, examined the sociology of popular arts with relation to British working class society. Both Williams and Hoggart argue, in fact, for the use of the literary imagination in sociological analysis in ways surprisingly similar to C. Wright Mills. The difference of all three of these individuals as compared with McLuhan is their strong commitment to some modified Marxist position as the only position consonant with the growth of the new society that must emerge from that long revolution. But then also, all three share, distinct from McLuhan, a commitment to an ethically viable social science, while McLuhan adopts the more "objective" attitude of the behaviourist.

Even if McLuhan and the McLuhanites argue that there is a radical difference between their ways of making the environment manifest and Bacon's "readings," the similarities are as important as the differences. Besides, the Baconian attitude opens other interesting questions about McLuhan's method, style, and form. The Baconian essay, as McLuhan himself points out, was devised as "words presented for use" in distinction to "words presented to persuade." Fundamentally, Bacon wanted to enable people to follow the patterns of his thinking about a subject and then to be able to go on to use the "essay" for further weighing and examination of the problem. From this the view that Pascal held of the "essay" tradition as a *peinture de la pensée* (a painting of the mind in action) possibly arose. Such might be the result of crossing Bacon with Montaigne who had seen the "essay" as a presentation of the self. In all of these writers, though, the essay is tied to the aphorism and to the relatively discontinuous presentations of aphorisms. In fact, Pascal creates his work out of the arrangement of discontinuous *pensées* in which he stresses the importance of arrangement of units and of the principle that words differently arranged mean different things.

Headlines and ad copy are by nature epigrammatic and aphoristic. They also are quite attractive to McLuhan's sensibility. But the modern sensibility has been "turned on" by aphorisms or epigrammatic-like writing as well. The Japanese haiku made popular among English poets by Pound and Yeats; the condensed juxtaposed imagery of the post-symbolist; the poetry, and the aphorisms of Eastern writing (Yeats rather early translated *The Aphorisms of Yoga*), all appealed in the twenties and thirties and have been elements at some time for some part of contemporary youth (beat or hippie) culture of the late fifties and sixties. It is not difficult in such a milieu to cross-fertilize the aphoristic headline with an "essay" type of presentation. This, after all, is the mode of presentation of the *Bride, The Gutenberg Galaxy,* and (allowing for the short chapters) *Understanding Media*. A rather more complex combination of presentation still organizes itself in brief individual units in *The Medium Is the Massage* and *War and Peace in the Global Village*. Perhaps the term essai concrète (see Appendix 2) could be coined for this particular mode of presentation, making it analogous to concrete poetry (a form McLuhan also plays with). In any case, the possibilities of radical discontinuity within the essay form (quite distinct from Bacon's relatively discontinuous but always sequential dialectic) provided a way of fusing the aphoristic and the discontinuous method.

Discontinuity, as opposed to flow, is one of the characteristics of an electric age according to McLuhan, a theme that has been picked up by members of the McLuhan coterie in management circles (viz. Peter Drucker, whose latest volume is *The Age of Discontinuity*). Certainly more radical modes of discontinuity have been one mark of the twentieth century. As the quantity of information to be handled increases astronomically, juxtaposition, in which it is implicit that many possibilities can be simultaneously suggested, becomes a natural mode of composition, e.g. the condensations in multi-image and multi-screen film. McLuhan in his writings associates this with the creation of symbols—the throwing together of things to create new meanings. Such discontinuity, which seems a feature of all the early twentieth century arts, has a natural attraction in film because of the possibilities inherent in "framing" pictures and montage. It is also a natural outgrowth of news presentation in newspapers and in television.

Bacon used his aphorisms in a style that develops in terms of a *pro et contra* movement (which perhaps suggests some of the genius of the Penguin collection of criticism *McLuhan: Pro and Con*). This dialectic movement, inherited from the schoolmen—the earlier *moderni*—provides a way of moving from point to point as Bacon seems to have considered the mind did. In a way it is a precursor of Hegelianism. McLuhan does not precisely move by way of *pro et contra* but he does move by way of division by opposites into what is ultimately a kind of pro and con movement. Consequently the entire universe of McLuhan is always dualistic—visual vs. audio-tactile; continuous vs. discontinuous; script vs. print; phonetic vs. non-phonetic alphabets; hot vs. cool; ancient vs. modern; war vs. peace. This passion for dualities is natural enough in human thought, but it can lead to rather gross oversimplifications as well. In any case, the condensation of the essay form almost seems to welcome the investigation of sharp dualities even among some of the more continuous kinds of essayists. Addison, for example, worked in terms such as true and false wit, primary and secondary imagination, Ovidian and Horatian styles of letter writing. This dualistic bias is a major feature of the McLuhan style and of the McLuhan method of analysis.

The aphorism and the dualistic style both appeal strongly to memory. Consequently, there results the adman stance and the role of intellectual investigator which McLuhan can easily combine. But the essay style as a recording of the mind in action also has strong affinities with poetry. The marriage of poetic technique, advertising technique, and the essay form provides the basis of McLuhan's mode of presentation.

Each part of the Do-It-Yourself-Creativity-Kit then becomes a kind of meditation with Marshall McLuhan that ties in closely with the theory of teaching that is behind McLuhan. St. Thomas Aquinas (and McLuhan is avowedly Thomistic) held that the only way to teach was to lead the student's mind through the processes of one's own mind—a retracing of the processes of cognition (which McLuhan argues characterizes symbolist poetry as well as Thomistic pedagogy). Each essay follows precisely this process, even including the mental chaos with the resulting irritation to the minds of some of McLuhan's readers. Here, of course, McLuhan's thesis about the similarities of the mediaeval and the modern seem to hold, for it is by the use of a technique from the Middle Ages translated into modern terms that McLuhan achieves a "cool" prose medium—one that engages and forces participation and completion rather than providing closure.

The use of substantial quotations is characteristic of McLuhan's mode. *The Gutenberg Galaxy*, among other things, is an excellent anthology on print and its effects. But this again is a part of the essay tradition and even one of its faults. Ben Jonson in *Timber: or, Discoveries* (585-6) wrote:

> Some that turne over all bookes, and are equally searching in all papers, that write out of what they presently find or meet, without choice; by which meanes it happens that what they have discredited, and impugned in one worke, they have before, or after, extolled the same in another. Such are all the *Essayists*, even their Master *Mountaigne*. These, in all they write, confesse still what bookes they have read last; and therein their owne folly, so much, that they bring it to the *Stake* raw, and undigested: not that the place did need it neither; but that they thought themselves furnished and would vent it.

The mediaeval tradition of sentences cited from the authorities and quoted and commented upon, and the Renaissance use of commonplace books in which writers collected quotations from various authors for further use, made writing a medley of material from various sources. Jonson himself in *Timber*, in fact, does something similar, though suggesting that there is a right and wrong way to do it. McLuhan, too, quotes, anthologizes, and borrows, turning his texts like a mediaeval schoolman and yet frequently trying to retain some of the total feel for the sources from which they came. If McLuhan sometimes seems to be in the process of digesting his own reading, he would claim this is one of the processes of the mind that he is trying to manifest. His borrowings he views like a poet's borrowings, which should evoke the whole of the source in part, and fuse it to a new structure of thought and feeling.

Interestingly enough, these parallels between McLuhan's position and Bacon's reflect part of his own analysis of Bacon in *The Gutenberg Galaxy*. Bacon stands with one foot in the Middle Ages and one in the Renaissance: McLuhan stands with one foot in the electric age and one foot in the world of literacy. Though their worlds are radically different, their problems are similar and they both combine elements of the temperament of humanist and scholastic. McLuhan as a popularizer may be closer to Addison, but the strategic position in which he is located is close to Bacon. After all, McLuhan could be described as a PR man for the with-it moderns, who has one foot in the world of mechanism and literacy. If Bacon read nature as a book, McLuhan views the landscape of the electric age as a television documentary.

The McLuhanite and the modern can condemn this type of investigation of where McLuhan's method and style come from as irrelevant, since to them it is *what* is and not *how* it came to be that really matters. Yet this is obviously inadequate, for the very forces that McLuhan uses exist at present by virtue of the very fact that he uses them. Besides, they form a common tradition not only for McLuhan but for that area of the literary tradition which most interests him. Paradoxically McLuhan, like Eliot, makes history important by making it here and now. Besides that, however, McLuhan also makes history important by making it the way of understanding the "now." Without discussion of the Greeks, of the Middle Ages, of the Renaissance, and of the intervening centuries, it would not be possible to see what actually is happening in the current period. McLuhan's inadequacies, and they are great and serious and will have to be revealed eventually, are not identical with those of many of the modern enthusiasts who embrace his point of view. In fact, it is always somewhat paradoxical to see the type of following that he really has—the avant-garde, the rebel, the youth—and it is also a tribute to the peculiar power of a prose poet manqué who has discovered a new form, the essai concrète.

The evolution of the essai concrète is an excellent example of how McLuhan's analyses and McLuhan's method and mode of presentation evolve together. McLuhan discovered that the modern equivalent of the aphorism was to be found in the headline and in advertising copy. In 1915 one of his major influences, Wyndham Lewis, had used the headline as mode of composition for a periodical called *Blast*, which launched the Vorticist movement. Since there are close affinities between McLuhan and Vorticism (with which Pound, as well as Lewis, was associated), McLuhan explored the form in the fifties in a pamphlet called *Counterblast*, a reversal in one way of Lewis' pro-visual, pro-typographical analysis of the new audio-tactile world in *Blast*. Yet like *Blast*, McLuhan in his work was fascinated with the image of the vortex—he ends his first volume of essais concrètes, *The Medium Is the Massage*, with a presentation of Poe's vortical image from *The Descent into the Maelstrom* where the mariner saved himself by "understanding the action of the whirlpool." This stands for the technique that moderns must adapt as "a possible stratagem for understanding our predicament, our electrically-configured whirl" (MM 150).

McLuhan's use of the press and its evolution as a means of discovering a new type of book format is a result of his awareness of the aesthetics of the press's role in our society as it had developed from Mallarmé. Ezra Pound in his aphorism that "literature is news that stays news" provided a basic insight into the influence of the form of the press on aesthetics, a theme that McLuhan had traced in an article on "Joyce, Mallarmé and the Press." The newspaper world is, as Karel Čapek says, a "world like that of the wild beasts [which] exists solely in the present." For McLuhan, the "actualized realism," which Čapek discovered to be "the ontological system of newspapers [which in itself was] eternally expressing new realities in a stabilized and unchangeable form" (LC 12), becomes an entirely new form when it is placed in a literary context without a dateline. From the newspaper format of the earlier *Counterblast* and the use of modified headlines in *The Gutenberg Galaxy*, it is only a step to the magazine-like format of *The Medium Is the Massage* and the extensive use of gloss and marginalia in *War and Peace in the Global Village*. In the *Galaxy* McLuhan associates gloss and marginalia with the oral culture of the Middle Ages and with the increased load placed on memory by such audio-tactile cultures.

In this way each page becomes a mosaic that must be multi-levelled. Its affinities with surrealism and dadaism on one hand, and gloss, marginalia, and illumination on the other, show the way that the McLuhanesque method marries the present and the past. It follows the Joycean mythic method—the simultaneous juxtaposition of the phantasmagoric and the sordidly realistic, the mythic and the present, which Eliot said placed Joyce in aesthetics on a par with Einstein in physics.

But McLuhan crosses Bacon and the magazine format, marries the mediaeval and the surrealistic, as part of what is an essentially Addisonian programme. The contemporary Addison would certainly, if committed to the audio-tactile, abandon the continuities and embrace the discontinuities and would fall in love with typography and the pun which so thoroughly horrified the eighteenth century essayist. Possibly he would even, as McLuhan has done, wed the short format of the scholarly or magazine article (to which the producing academic is early forced to accommodate) to the format of the book as a collection of post-Gutenberg articles, notes, and queries.

The "probe" has become a favourite piece of jargon among the McLuhanites, for McLuhan does not expound or explicate, he probes. The nature of McLuhan's "probe" though is found in the pun. The pun, like the subtitle of the chapter on "Movies" in *Understanding Media*—"The Reel World"—brings together two different ways of grasping reality. "Reel world" here is taken from a Joycean pun, "Roll away the reel world, the reel world . . ." (FW 64), which crosses the "mechanical-artificial" nature of film with a reminder of the world of reality. Harold Rosenberg once described it as an example of McLuhan's indulgence—this is just not so, for it is typical of the heart of McLuhan's method. McLuhan turns all of the literary techniques for crossing different kinds of discourse into different ways of grasping reality and uses all of them most effectively as devices to probe media.

3

Probing Through McLuhan:
Understanding Media

Since the pun is his beginning point, he can say that he is Joycean and that part of his wisdom comes from *Finnegans Wake*. His view of the pun is a "breakdown as breakthrough." The pun "breaks down" the normal movement of language revealing something that has been "repressed" or "numbed." The pun is also characteristic of the way that language can render up reality by breaking down some expected movement and providing a breakthrough into some new area. As a discovery technique both pun and metaphor have been examined by Arthur Koestler in *Insight and Outlook* and *The Act of Creation* as the archetype of the creative act. This theme, like McLuhan's, comes out of Joyce and Freud.

One thing that McLuhan's activity with pun and metaphor proves is that today's businessman is really looking for poetry. As long as the poetry comes by way of a short piece of prose and does not present itself as "art," it fascinates. The ad world has turned some businessmen partly back into the Renaissance man seeking poetic visions of reality. If McLuhan said such things, he would say this is part of the "retribalization" of the contemporary world.

In any event, it means he can "play" poet covertly using the most basic strategies of a poet and a form that is potentially poetic—witness how the "essay" quickly turned itself into the verse essays of Dryden and Pope.

McLuhan takes the tools of the "poetic" and translates the poetry of Joyce, Eliot, Mallarmé, and of artists like Klee into his essay form. What businessman (or for that matter academic or practising artist from another area) will take the time to read James Joyce? McLuhan even tells his audience repeatedly that it's all in Joyce—language, fashion, war, education, telephone, radio, cinema, television, even the idea of "bits" of information. For example his quip on movies—the "reel" world—makes Joyce more accessible by translating from the Menippean satire of *Finnegans Wake* into essay.

Yet this would not exclusively make McLuhan popular. What does make him popular is his formula for uniting two things that our civilization is worried about—the alienation of the self and the alienizing influence of technology. How this works may be seen in a recent *Playboy* interview where McLuhan himself associates his technique with the essay (and by implication with a "poetic" type of activity):

> My work is designed for the pragmatic purpose of trying to understand our technological environment and its psychic and social consequences. But my books constitute the *process* rather than the completed product of discovery; my purpose is to employ facts as tentative probes, as means of insight, of pattern recognition. . . . I want to map new terrain rather than chart old landmarks. (*Playboy* 54)

Without the "pragmatic purpose," businessmen and academics from non-artistic fields would probably disregard McLuhan. But with this purpose present they can go exploring with him in the electric age in which they live. To enlist their involvement McLuhan has to link his "pragmatic purpose" to those basic concerns. The particular area of communications technology provides a neat bridge, since it links up easily with his own artistic background and it involves both the expression of the self and the transforming power of technology.

The magic of his motif—"the medium is the message"—comes specifically out of these three factors: it relates to the world of the arts (language of expression) and it involves the receiver (the self or individual) and the sender (the mode of transmission or technology). Besides, it plays with some kind of ambiguous interpenetration of receiver and sender. Working from this motif, McLuhan tunnels in two directions:

1) towards technology in general by treating any technological achievement as a medium which is then a message. As McLuhan says: "You've got to remember my definition of media is broad: it includes any technology whatever that creates extensions of the human body and senses from clothing to computers" (*Playboy* 56);

2) towards the person by seeing technology as an extension—an outering (or "uttering")—of the self. In this dialectic however, the technology, the medium, always seems more important than the human person. McLuhan's major interest is in how the medium affects the person, not how people affect media. This bias gives rise to one of the most important of his concepts—each medium causes a different relationship between the human senses, a different ratio.

Now all of us, as Tom Wolfe has suggested, have been aware that TV or the telephone or the computer is affecting us, as well as the world in which we live. This is a part of what provides the feeling of intense "alienation" from the environment. But there has been little or no genuine investigation of, or even speculation about, the question of how these different technological modes of transmission actually do affect our relationships. McLuhan, having started with the problems of communication in modern poetry and the effect of cultural revolution in the Renaissance, uses his experience and knowledge as a way of opening up such speculations. Since he is the first man to have successfully turned society on to this question, there is little doubt of his historical importance.

Rather than instructing people or adopting a criterion of certainty, McLuhan speaks as Bacon suggests some poets do—in parables and cryptic aphorisms, suggesting rather than saying. He even exhibits concern about the possibility of speaking more directly: "I'm trying to get my audience involved in perceptions.

So I use their language. The language of their environment. . . .
I expect my readers to do more work than I did. But I'm offering
them opportunities, roles of initiative" (M:HC 296). He himself
admits that communication between people is extremely difficult
and extremely rare. McLuhan on communications is McLuhan at
his best:

> Actually, communication is an exceedingly difficult activity. . . . If
> there is the slightest tangential area of touch, agreement and so on
> among people, *that* is communication in a big way. . . . commu-
> nication is *making*. The person who sees or heeds or hears is en-
> gaged in making a response to a situation which is mostly of his
> own fictional invention. (M:HC 293)

Modern poets are the ones who are really trying to communicate
by introducing ways of discussing multi-relationships:

> You cannot discuss multi-relationships on a single plane, in a single
> form. That's why the poets of our time have broken all the planes
> and sequences, forming a cubist prose. (M:HC 293)

Communication is difficult, only attainable for the few, and only
to be achieved with considerable work.

McLuhan's probes are meant to be ways of communicating a
process rather than a product, and to achieve this they must be
ones which deal in terms of multi-relationships. But here difficulties appear. A "pragmatic purpose" and disinterested probing are
not necessarily easily, or even desirably, married. There is nothing
wrong with probing for a purpose as long as the probe does not
pretend to be a pragmatic principle. Yet McLuhan's magic cannot
work without transforming the probe into the pragmatic principle.
If Eliot has Prufrock saying, "I have measured out my life with coffee spoons," this is a way of probing a fictional character and may
have significance for other individuals. If McLuhan says "The
medium is the message" or "All media are metaphors," these become imitative of tools of analysis, especially if they are used to
reject other ways of probing—such as examination of what the
media transmits (which incidentally is not content as he suggests,
but a combination of form and content unless you are willing to
consider the canvas and chemical portion of the paints as the

28

medium and everything else as the "content" in a painting). McLuhan must expect his reader to handle language in a much richer and more complex manner than usual, for it is necessary to keep shifting the way various words, or sets of words, enter into the process.

McLuhan is describing an existential encounter. For, if a medium is an extension, and all extensions create alterations of what the person has been, then any media situation has profound existential significance. In fact, the medium in its interplay is a process, of which McLuhan says:

> The medium, or process, of our time—electric technology—is reshaping and restructuring patterns of social interdependence and every aspect of our personal life. It is forcing us to reconsider and reevaluate practically every thought, every action, and every institution formerly taken for granted. (MM 8)

Here the statement is about external alterations. The language is interesting: electric technology reshapes and restructures us and forces us to reconsider and reevaluate. But this naturally is linked to the deeper effect of media. It not only transforms society, it transforms the self by transforming the ratio within the sensorium. McLuhan holds that each medium has certain sensory biases which relate to the portion of the person that is extended. The phonetic alphabet, as an extension of the eye, is intensified by print; television, as an extension of touch, reverses the values of the print world.

There may seem to be difficulties at times. Consider an "artificial" example: If the wheel is an amputation of the foot, then why not consider the printing press an amputation of the hand, so that print extends the hand the way the wheel extends the foot. Then print could numb touch by replacing the touch of the hand in the act of writing; and print could become frozen gesture replacing the tactile "handtouch which is speech without words" (FW 174). But then print would favour "touch" and be "tactile," or would it? Implicit in my piece of McLuhanese is the beginning of a chain of McLuhanite meditation (or McLuhanacy depending on how you value the activity). But probably if McLuhan's method is followed it would fit his universe and would ultimately be rationalized in terms of a dialectic interplay between "touch" and "vision."

For the moment accepting the McLuhan method, the ratio of the senses is altered by each technology so that the man conditioned to print has a visual bias, the tribal man an audio-tactile bias. All media alter the sensory mix and result in forcing changes on the individual. The relation assumed is that of passive consumer to active process. Media process the person by accelerating internal and external change; the person appears to have little to do with the processing except to try to understand and then control it by a "superior arrogance," as McLuhan describes it.

If the acceleration of the unfolding of this is noticeable, it is because the mobility of McLuhan's metaphors (owing to the fact that his prose must always be in process) is essential to its working at all. One area of his appeal is that many people know that static descriptions are not very useful—McLuhan quips, "If it works, it's obsolete"—and are seeking methods that will allow for thinking about process. But here is where it becomes so difficult to deal with McLuhan. Raymond Williams, who has pointed out that if *The Gutenberg Galaxy* worked as a book it would be self-annihilating, observes: "And here, I think, especially as literary scholars . . . we encounter great difficulty. I mean that to think in terms of active configurations when we have left the poem and entered the rest of the world is almost mindbreaking" (M:HC 189). Yet this is precisely what McLuhan tries to do—to turn the whole world into a multi-media poem—and in fact he says that satellite technology has made the world itself cease to be nature and become a work of. art: "From that moment [the moment of the first satellite] all terrestrial phenomena were to become increasingly programmed artifacts and every facet of human life now comes within the scope of the artistic vision" (WP 178).

McLuhan's assertions in *War and Peace* go even further, for discussing the process of "going" and "returning," the process of transformation in the *I Ching*, McLuhan declares:

> One of the peculiarities of an electric technology is that it speeds up this process of transformation. Instant and total rehearsal of all pasts and all processes enables us to perceive the function of such perpetual returns as one of purgation and purification, translating the entire world into a work of art. (WP 183)

This should not be such a startling new vista to a Renaissance scholar like McLuhan, for he is certainly very familiar with the tradition in which people like Thomas Browne and the Metaphysical Poets could view the world as the art of God the creator and hence as a "work of art." Admittedly, McLuhan is saying today it *has* become a work of art, but certainly that is what the earlier proponents of this view were also saying. (Perhaps when Nietzsche declared the death of God, man had to wait for the second coming of the satellites.) Despite the earlier view, what McLuhan is trying to say is that now since the world is enveloped by man, it is a content and not itself a form; the change has caused the world to be a massive junkyard and it has become an object of contemplation. Historically however, or even non-historically and structurally from a contemporaneous point of view, the "wit" of McLuhan's presentation is based on a rather elusive change.

Yet McLuhan is trying to do precisely what a long hermetic tradition has always proposed—to read the symbology of the earth as a means of finding a "gnosis." Bacon saw his world as a "book" because the book was a prestigious art form. McLuhan substitutes a more with-it art form as his model of the universe, but still viewed so that the "tasks above are as the flasks below" (Joyce's statement of a hermetic doctrine of correspondences) (FW 263). McLuhan should be praised for manifesting, through new art forms, aspects of our earthly existence. McLuhan is not only an artist—a poet manqué—but an important apologist for the artist and artistic points of view. In such a position McLuhan is reading the language of the outer world and relating it to the "inner." One way of achieving this translation is reading the language of the media and relating it to the structure of the sensorium, as McLuhan does in his ratios between media effects and their alteration of the proportionate relationship between the senses.

Now, however, McLuhan's strategy forces us to confront the reconciliation of the artist with the social theorist, for certainly McLuhan plays both these roles. What is often overlooked is that, in playing both roles, McLuhan is consciously playing the role of a "fool." Apart from his own use of the town fool of Vancouver in *The Medium Is the Massage*, the whole title of that work is a put-on about McLuhan. Presumably if one thing should be sacred it is the dictum which is synonymous with McLuhanism, "The medium is the message." Yet in McLuhan's world even this is a matter for playfulness.

McLuhan is consciously a clown or court jester (a role which in one sense he consciously occupies in Canada with respect to his advising of the Trudeau cabinet). His most outlandish statements that contain some kind of wisdom in their folly relate to the role of the mediaeval or Renaissance fool. Consequently, at one of the high ritual moments of Western society—the moon shot—McLuhan can declare of the astronauts, the heroes, that they are "nobodies" and yet describe the ritual, which has enthralled everyone, as "the greatest educational television programme of all time." This is not very different from Tom Wolfe's descriptions of the way that McLuhan handles "the great" (M:HC 15).

If the electric age is, as McLuhan says, a time in which everyone is playing roles, is it not proper for a scholar of the Renaissance drama to play the role of a traditional "fool"? When Erasmus, one of McLuhan's interests in *The Gutenberg Galaxy*, wrote a work called the *Encomium Moriae* (the Praise of Folly), he played with a series of paradoxes to produce a learned interplay of wisdom and folly. If we look at the erudition of *The Gutenberg Galaxy* it is not too surprising to think that McLuhan might be trying to translate that particular activity into the contemporary electric age. With his fondness for reverse parallels then, the paradoxes of McLuhanism would be the opposite of the paradoxes of Erasmianism, with the new "folly" introducing the age of the electric network as the old had introduced the age of print.

Something of this spirit plays behind so much that McLuhan seems to value in Rabelais, Cervantes, Swift, Joyce, and others. Part of the enthusiastic response to his work may well be a response to the humour that runs through it and to the obvious commitment to humour on the part of the author. Yet such a stance leaves a perpetual ambiguity about just where McLuhan stands re McLuhan. Certainly it is a factor that must be involved in any assessment of McLuhan and one that colours McLuhan the man enough to provide the kind of figure which Tom Wolfe has discussed (M:HC 31–48) as puzzling businessmen in New York and San Francisco. Is there the possibility that there is, implicit in

McLuhan's activity, a theory which sees the managerial class as the patrons of the new humanists, a group unable to depend on the support of the academy and yet not willing to play for mass acclaim in the more simple ways?

If McLuhan adopts the role of a clown, it is the role of a very learned clown, for he is as much an erudite as an entertainer. *The Gutenberg Galaxy* alone, without his Joyce scholarship and general literary scholarship, would be enough to establish his erudition. And it remains a running theme throughout his work, involving the scholarly frame of reference of *War and Peace* and the total commitment to university criticism implicit in *The Vanishing Point*. If he is a humanist, he is a humanist who wishes to talk to the schools and therefore, like Bacon, is also a bit of a schoolman —in two senses. The mixture perhaps means that there is some sort of upside-down historical parallel in his mind between our age and the sixteenth century when print invaded the consciousness of Europe. If so, playing roles and using strategies similar to the men of those times is the only way to reconcile the discordant and conflicting opposites into some creative achievement.

What our analysis of McLuhanism next requires is that we confront some of his direct problems and then his works. In confronting the works it is necessary to view them as a mixture of art and social commentary, remembering the way the elements of a mediaevally committed Catholic, a clown (or learned fool), and a scholar (and possibly schoolman—in the traditionally scholastic sense) are congenial roles which come together to form the kaleidoscopic character of Marshall McLuhan.

In the Middle Ages, as we noted earlier, the practice of commenting upon the texts of the masters was a standard technique for the advancement of knowledge. Works such as St. Thomas Aquinas' *Summa Theologica* were the subject of an ever-expanding set of comments and criticisms. McLuhan, perhaps unconsciously, has provided something not too dissimilar for our own age. The very crypsis and apparent contradiction that mark *The Gutenberg Galaxy* and *Understanding Media* invite further discussion and commentary on McLuhan. One of the ways that many enthusiasts advise us to read him can only generate the habit of using his aphorisms as take-off points for further commentary and development. McLuhan's works, then, are a contemporary *Summa Technologica*.

4
Enmeshed in a Web of His Own Making

The particular way in which McLuhan succeeds and fails becomes rather critical in spite of his own protestations that he is only presenting probes and does not necessarily believe in them. What makes McLuhan successful and what makes him partly valid? How does he succeed as social commentator, as critic, and as artist?

McLuhan has in so many ways challenged or upset the standards that the "literate" world has built up that it becomes difficult to speak critically of him without being part of what he attacks and therefore disqualifying oneself to McLuhanites as having the right to talk meaningfully about his work. This would matter very little if all McLuhan were as meaningless as Finkelstein makes it in his *McLuhan: Sense and Nonsense;* but Finkelstein's insistence on a certain limited type of rationalism blurs many of the issues involved in the McLuhan world. What exasperates most of McLuhan's critics is the entirely new criteria that his world presents. For example, it has been rather characteristic of humanist criticism to stress a certain "refinement" in sensibility. In *The Gutenberg Galaxy*, McLuhan actively associates such refinement with the "print" medium and with a print bias. Therefore, when turning to *Understanding Media* or *The Medium Is the Massage*, critics discover what is often an extremely crude sensibility. They have the choice of overlooking it or seeming to impose standards that are just not part of McLuhan's world. Perhaps there is a parallel and partial defence in the "rock" movement. Frank Zappa of the "Mothers of Invention" has spoken of how the "Mothers" introduce their audience to the whole world of music and turn them on to Stockhausen, Bach, electronic music, and Ravi Shankar. McLuhan similarly turns people on to Joyce and Mallarmé, Rabelais and Cervantes. In an age of transformation, refinement and crudity as categories for criticism are themselves extremely crude and possibly totally inept critical tools. But the way that McLuhan uses this confusion of values makes for frustration and anger among those who are not committed to him.

As our exploration of McLuhan progresses, some serious problems are emerging. McLuhan himself tells us that "the medium is the message" and that it is a prime error in theory to "ignore the function of the form as form" (UM 267). This clearly suggests that McLuhan himself must be writing in such a way that the overt message means a great deal less than the method and technique of expression which constitute his medium of expression (or form). But if this is so, what about the individual elements within the McLuhan presentation? When he says that media are "hot" or "cool," that certain images are of "high definition" or "low definition," how far does he expect that the reader will believe him or even care? Terms such as "hot" and "cool," "time" and "space," "visual" and "tactile," all relate to systematic bodies of information about the structure of human processes. Statements in Loewenstein's *The Senses* (a book McLuhan uses) are not probes, but descriptive and analytical statements codifying a body of scientific knowledge. Within this area statements about the visual, the tactile, the kinesthetic have meanings which McLuhan would describe as linear, and which are a kind of content.

Since McLuhan naturally is true to his own principles, the language he uses is not meant to be linear. This implies that single sentence statements are not meant to be "read" in the usual way, but to be regarded as multi-faceted probes. Such a view appears to create the paradox where it is not right to identify "the medium is the message" as a McLuhanesque principle, since this would create a dilemma that could only result from misunderstanding McLuhan. Yet McLuhan himself as well as many of his followers do seem to take some statements such as "the medium is the message" as principles, although if McLuhan were actually to regard them as such it would create the dilemma of McLuhan apparently misunderstanding his own medium (unless he is willing to accept the actual paradoxical nature of this problem within his own theories and style). The mosaic approach, which McLuhan says is the only approach to the simultaneous, being "a multidimensional world of interstructural resonance," does not permit a reader to attribute a univocal meaning to any single unit. McLuhan's playing with his own motif in the title of *The Medium Is the Massage* underlines this. A mosaic emphasizes the way in which all of the elements are important in achieving a total effect. Admittedly the use of "journalese" or "telegraphese," and especially of ad-like rhetoric that McLuhan employs, tempts people constantly to associate him with his tags in the same way as highly quotable poets have been associated with views they did not necessarily embrace, e.g. Shakespeare's "Neither a borrower nor a lender be."

But McLuhan's essay method is founded on the "mosaic" and for him one of the best places to discover the mosaic in action is in the contemporary press. There "the daily communal exposure of multiple items in juxtaposition" provides the "complex dimension of human interest" (UM 204). What he means by "the press" is the layout and juxtaposition of articles, headlines, and the like, which, as early as *The Mechanical Bride*, he associated with the techniques of symbolist aesthetics, viz. "Why is a page of news a problem in orchestration? / How does the jazzy ragtime discontinuity of press items link up with modern art forms? / You never thought of a page of news as a symbolist landscape?" (MB 3).

If McLuhan performs a function for the present age analogous to Addison's in the eighteenth century as popularizer of a new image (while reversing the values of Addison's point of view) this is precisely the stance that he must take. In discussing the press, McLuhan says that Addison and Steele discovered "a new prose technique to match the form of the printed word," the technique of "equitone" (UM 206). Equitone maintains a single level of tone and attitude towards the reader throughout the entire composition, avoiding the variety of pitch and tone of the spoken word. McLuhan points out that today Addison and Steele's equitone must be abandoned, for its relevance was destroyed when the telegraph "broke language away from the printed word" giving birth to "headlines, journalese and telegraphese" (UM 206). The literary community is in error in still being committed to "mannerisms of supercilious equitone that mime typographic uniformity." Mosaic provides a way of creating a new style which has affinities with headlinese, telegraphese, and journalese—ways of breaking down the equitone; another of McLuhan's breakdowns as breakthroughs.

McLuhan, as medium, is the message that to read his message as message is a mistake. Yet he constantly appears to be engaged in evolving a map of a structure which is to guide his audience. The fact that this aspect of McLuhan is simultaneously present with the mosaic is part of what constitutes one of his worst flaws, part of what makes him merely a popularizer and permits him to carry out a basic misreading of James Joyce, the very man he holds up as the major modern mind for understanding media.

To begin to understand where McLuhan becomes enmeshed in a web of his own making, it is important to hold in abeyance his own clown-like and poetic strategies for side-stepping errors of fact and reconciling all apparent contradictories. The difficulty starts with the very theory of dramatic interaction which he feels dominates the world. If, as Harold Adams Innis felt, Addison and Steele were "tempering animosities" in the process of making the newspaper "a purifying and constructive force of value to the divine and the philanthropist as well as the politician" (*Bias of Communication* 145), McLuhan in contradistinction generates conflict and tension. His preoccupation with "conflict" is apparent in that one of the two concluding sections of *Understanding Media* is about weaponry and one of his recent works, *War and Peace in the Global Village*, is about "war." In fact, our point in history, according to McLuhan, is distinguished by the conflict between the mechanical and electric technologies, and "To live with both of these technologies is the peculiar drama of the twentieth century" (UM 342). In the social sphere this means that "Today we appear to be poised between two ages—one of detribalization and one of retribalization" (UM 344).

Dramatic conflict appeals to McLuhan's critical sensibility because he developed as a literary critic during the early days of I. A. Richards' influence at Cambridge—an influence that created the "new criticism" led by Cleanth Brooks in the United States and marked by such works as Empson's *Seven Types of Ambiguity* in England. A large portion of the literary milieu of the time followed T. S. Eliot in emphasizing a revival of a poetry based on wit, tension, and paradox that brought once again into vogue such groups as the Metaphysical Poets. The critical vocabulary involved terms such as "tension," "resolution of conflict," and (going back to Coleridge) "reconciliation of opposites." Wit and paradox are favourite McLuhan devices, being associated as they are in the new criticism with a more inclusive way of seeing reality.

The history of the return of this movement to Hegelianism is well known, since its dialectic nature is rather apparent. If media are art forms, as McLuhan argues—and by this naturally he means the media as technological devices, not what is presented in or through the media—they are susceptible of the modes of analysis that one uses in approaching poetry. A view of the world as a conflict rising out of a dialectic interplay is congenial to McLuhan's whole sensibility. His strategy, and he attributes the source of it to H. A. Innis (though obviously it is deeply rooted in areas that interested him long before he met Innis), is a strategy of interface. For example, in an introduction to one of Innis' books McLuhan says:

> Innis . . . changed his procedure from working with a "point of view" to that of generating insights by the method of "interface" [referring] to the interaction of substances in a kind of mutual irritation. (*Bias of Communication* viii)

Even in discussing the technique in the context of the history of political economy and attributing it to Innis, he locates it in a literary context: "In art and poetry this is precisely the technique of 'symbolism' (Greek—*symballein*—to throw together) with its

39

paratactic procedure of juxtaposing without connectives." This turns out to be the natural mode of dialogue as opposed to written communication and thus to be essential to the "mosaic."

The use of "interface" can lead to the rather remarkable insights McLuhan claims to generate, such as his insistence that radio, which on one side is a "tribal dream," also simultaneously develops into a way of providing privacy for the teenager:

> The ear is hyperesthetic compared to the neutral eye. The ear is intolerant, closed, and exclusive, whereas the eye is open, neutral and associative. Ideas of tolerance came to the West only after two or three centuries of literacy and visual Gutenberg culture. (UM 302–3)

At the moment it is not the adequacy of such a statement, but its construction that is important. The "insight" develops by counterpointing eye to ear, auditory to visual, in a conflict of qualities which supports both the analysis that radio provides a "closed" world for the teenager and a heated-up world of new tribalism capable of producing a Hitler. As an added factor, the issue of "tolerance" can be raised and paradoxically related to the rigid, lineal culture of print associated with the eye.

Now one thing is evident from what was said earlier: this should be read in conjunction with other elements in the discussion and in the whole work. Another thing is also evident: the crypsis and the surprise of the statement are bound to engage the reader's mind and to generate a whole series of queries about the relationship that radio has had to privacy, to heating up emotions, to reducing tolerance, and the like.

But the mosaic method permits far more complex and intricate growth. In the same paragraph he discusses radio as "that extension of the central nervous system that is matched only by human speech itself" (UM 302). Radio then "crosses" what are the two most intimate technologies, a hybrid which could not help but produce extraordinary phenomena, e.g. Hitler "the somnambulist" or Orson Welles' 1939 show on the Martian invasion of Earth which caused the great panic. In presenting the "crossing" of radio and speech as two human technologies, McLuhan does not demote speech to being merely the "content" of radio. The hybrid that results from the "crossing" of the two technologies generates an energy which produces these remarkable by-products.

If exasperation can be suspended, by overlooking how Hitler used film as he did in his propaganda, it is worth tracing some other components of the mosaic. Radio "neutralizes" nationalism, but "evokes tribal ghosts." This meeting of eye and ear, of explosion and implosion, then becomes linked to Joyce, whose *Finnegans Wake* is presumably about the "electric circuitry . . . Orientalizing the West": "The west shall shake the east awake . . . while ye have the night for morn . . ." (MM 145). In the context of his discussion of the radio, he cites a passage from the "waking" section of the *Wake*: "In that european end meets Ind" (UM 302, cf. FW 598). Perhaps Joyce does see in such quotes the end of European man through the opening of the ear (after all Joyce used the labyrinth of the ear as a kind of personal symbol). But McLuhan pushes this to the point that he has Joyce saying: "The opening of the European ear brought to an end the open society and re-introduced the Indic world of tribal man to West End woman" (UM 302). Leaving aside his considerably condensed "reading" of Joyce, this immediately relates the "radio" section to the themes of the orientalizing, and awakening, of the west as well as a multitude of other themes.

Presumably the audience is to weave back and forth discovering connections, much as he might in *Finnegans Wake* itself. As he does he builds up a McLuhanized image of radio—"image" being used here in the symbolist or Kenneth Boulding sense of the term—a cluster or node of associated elements. Now in that image radio will cut two ways—one because it is "hot" and another because it is "electric." Radio, which is electric, will emphasize participation:

> If we sit and talk in a dark room, words suddenly acquire new meanings and different textures. They become richer, even, than architecture, which Le Corbusier rightly says can best be felt at night. All those gestural qualities that the printed page strips from language come back in the dark, and on the radio. Given only the *sound* of a play, we have to fill in *all* of the senses, not just the

sight of the action. So much do-it-yourself, or completion and "closure" of action develops a kind of independent isolation in the youth that makes them remote and inaccessible. (UM 303)

For the reader familiar with *The Gutenberg Galaxy* this might create distracting "noise," for there McLuhan presents print as an individualizing medium which takes man out of social participation and puts him alone in his study. Since one of his themes about contemporaneity and youth stresses their urge for participation, the qualities of "remoteness and inaccessibility" as marks of youth appear rather paradoxical. But within the McLuhan mosaic such paradoxes are perhaps possible in states of dire conflict. In *The Gutenberg Galaxy* he had also referred to the battle between "eye" and "ear," pointing out:

> It has been said that the inevitable war is one whose causes have not been discerned. Since there can be no greater contradiction or clash in human cultures than that between those representing the eye and the ear, it is not strange that our metamorphosis into the eye mode of Western man should be only less agonizing than our present shift into the auditory mode of electronic man. But there is enough inner trauma in such change without the auditory cultures and the optical cultures flinging themselves at each other in outer manifestations of sadistic self-righteousness. (GG 68)

Thus the battle described in the "radio" section of *Understanding Media* radiates through McLuhan's work as a whole. Similarly, the agony attributed to it in *The Gutenberg Galaxy* becomes one of the main themes of *War and Peace*, where McLuhan discusses the fact that "perhaps it is, above all, the sense of pain that the modern artist has discovered" (WP 13). So naturally, "All new technologies bring on the cultural blues" (WP 16), carrying the McLuhan explorer back to the "Phonograph" in *Understanding Media*, back to the jazz age and to the ultimate influence of the phonograph on the radio. In other words, the method is endless because McLuhan feels that he is probing and rendering forth processes, not presenting completed points of view.

Interfaces can be productive even if they are incorrect or untrue, as far as McLuhan is concerned. Consequently, he can reply to critics that he is not interested in the validity of his probes. The mere act of juxtaposition creates the energy that begins to provide patterns in the vortex. Since moral judgement, by creating biases, inhibits the process of discovery, we must operate on the assumption that "values are irrelevant," according to McLuhan. This position is attractive in an era when there is an absence of meaningful definitions or discussions of value and a general turmoil about values: "The mere moralistic expression of approval or disapproval, preference or detestation is currently being used in our world as a substitute for observation and a substitute for study. . . . Anybody who spends his time screaming about values in our modern world is not a serious character" (M:HC 286–7). This is convenient as an underpinning for a role of detached, pseudo-scientific observer, assuming what McLuhan describes as the Gutenberg stance: "I employ the greatest boon of literate culture; the power to act without reaction—the sort of specialization by dissociation that has been the driving force behind Western civilization" (*Playboy* 158). Civilized detachment becomes the obvious antidote to moral compunction.

C. Wright Mills, who would have shared McLuhan's view of the role of the imagination in research into man and society, sharply criticizes those who use the jargon of the social sciences as a way of exercising a "curious passion for the mannerism of the uncommitted":

> Whether he wants it or not, or whether he is aware of it or not, anyone who spends his life studying society and publishing the results *is* acting morally and usually politically as well. The question is whether he faces this condition and makes up his own mind, or whether he conceals it from himself and from others and drifts morally. (*The Sociological Imagination* 79)

McLuhan is recommending moral drift in the name of a "suspended judgement." But even in deciding for the stance of the civilized, detached observer he is making a value decision with moral implications. The fact that he selects radio as the villain of the Hitler situation and does not mention documentary film such as *The Triumph of the Will*, or the effect of the newsreel, is another decision about values—an extremely complex one. It is not good enough to suggest that Eliot and others created a poetry where it was possible to suspend moral judgement. There are two problems: first, McLuhan's essays are not solely or exclusively poetic; and second, even a decision such as the one McLuhan describes Eliot making—that the creative process provides a retracing of the cognitive processes for the reader—is a moral decision. McLuhan questions the worth of Wyndham Lewis' having attacked the position Eliot assumes, yet this must mean that McLuhan values the Eliot position. Perhaps like Addison, McLuhan hopes to be a "Spectator," inculcating a new society through changing men's manners and consequently their morals surreptitiously.

McLuhan is a Catholic. Is it possible that there is no moral judgement or value judgement involved when he describes the pill as "mechanical," as out of keeping with the "electric" age which is organic? The point is that the pill can be interpreted either way, your interpretation rising out of your value system in part. Biochemical change is an organic process, but chemical processes are to a certain extent "mechanical." The commitment to calendar time in the daily taking of the pill can be regarded as linear, or its association with human rhythm and process, the menstrual cycle, as non-linear. To deny that a value judgement of some kind is involved is itself a very complex moral act. Yet there is an interesting way in which a Catholic feels himself involved in a universe where truth is revealing itself through history —and this may precisely colour McLuhan's assumptions about values.

How far can the commitment to Catholicism go in determining the choice of materials? Is the interest in St. Thomas' *Summa* and its exegetical techniques, the poetic vision of Dante, the "manifestatio" of stained glass in the Gothic Cathedral, and the interest in mediaeval universalism totally objective or is it coloured by the fact of McLuhan's personal history and commitment? While he specifically denies any theological intent in his interviews in *Playboy* and with Gerald Stearn in *McLuhan: Hot & Cool*, there are still some basic Catholic commitments involved—such as the association of the image of the Corpus Christi with modern theories of participation. McLuhan himself reminds us of his own deep suspicions of cultural and social change, of his basic conservatism. These, he claims, do not enter his work any more after the writing of *The Mechanical Bride*. He told the *Playboy* interviewer:

> I don't like to tell people what I think is good or bad about the social and psychic changes caused by new media, but if you insist on pinning me down about my own subjective reactions as I observe the reprimitivization of our culture, I would have to say that I view such upheavals with total personal dislike and dissatisfaction. I do see the prospect of a rich and creative retribalized society—free of the fragmentation and alienation of the mechanical age—emerging from this traumatic period of culture clash; but I have nothing but distaste for the *process* of change. As a man moulded within the literate Western tradition, I do not personally cheer the dissolution of that tradition through the electric involvement of all the senses. . . . I am not by temperament or conviction, a revolutionary; I would prefer a stable, changeless environment of modest services and human scale. (*Playboy* 158)

This statement could almost be associated with Wyndham Lewis' defence, in *Time and Western Man,* of the virtue to be found in the Catholicism of Bishop Fulton Sheen as a stabilizing, traditional protection against the "time philosophy" of Bergson and Whitehead.

The danger involved in adopting a value-free stance of "grasping the modes of operation" of the media without deriving any joy from it is that the inherently "cool" comprehension, which is "simultaneously involvement and detachment," may have its own built-in bias. There is the paradox in McLuhan's own work that such a stance is print oriented and therefore to some degree linear. Furthermore, the examination of non-linear phenomena with linear tools of analysis is supposed to result in a distortion of comprehension. In addition, it is quite possible that a number of biases do enter into the process, and that these biases ultimately link up with the initial abandonment of value-oriented questions.

Returning to the question of dialectic conflict and polarization, with these biases in mind, it is interesting to note that McLuhan locates them as essential to the process of "grasping" or "comprehending." In an interview with Gerald Stearn he comments on opposed pairs such as "hot" and "cool":

It's very difficult to have a structure of any sort without polarities, without tension. . . . this is Blake's whole notion of hateful contraries—without polarities, there is no progression, no structure. For a literary person who likes things to move along in one direction on one plane, polarities are distressing. (M:HC 297)

Not only Blake, but the Metaphysical poets and most modern critics associated with Richards or with the New Criticism, found the patterns resulting from polarities of interest. Coleridge's whole doctrine of the "imagination" is founded on such polarities as much as Pope's and Swift's conception of "wit." There are differences in the way they embrace these patterns, but polarities are still present, and important, and recognized as such. Literary involvement does not necessarily appear to exclude a sense of polarity at all.

In fact, McLuhan's remark is useful in revealing the static quality of his own historical polarities, in view of the fact that a positive attitude favouring a poetry of tension has appeared among poets at various times through the history of literature, just as has the attitude prompting poets to periodically make new demands for returning to an emphasis on the spoken language. Recognizing this immobility of McLuhan's historicity is not to deny the basic importance of his insights in *The Gutenberg Galaxy*, but to suggest that a lack of refinement such as his can result in lack of delicacy; and lack of delicacy can result in lack of comprehension of detail; and lack of comprehension of detail can result in total distortion. Besides, if there are polarities of this kind there are also scales of gradation. When McLuhan discovers the unconscious being born at a certain point in history, when print creates the Africa within, distortion occurs for two reasons:

1) the realization that the phenomenon of the unconscious seems to be discoverable in Greek art and ancient myth;

2) even if this is answerable, there are obviously degrees of consciousness and unconsciousness which are infinitely more interesting than the pure state. Following McLuhan's polarities leads us into the position of thinking that something like the visual sense is a singular object, when it is really a complex process. It also leads us to think that visual experiences are strongly biased towards their exclusively sight-oriented aspect even

though that bias may differ considerably even in visual experience of print or perspective, such as someone feeling himself walking down a Utrillo street as the eye interacts with sensory memories.

The creation of massive mosaics does not solve the problem either. No matter what rationalization can be worked out later, the mind can only grasp certain patterns without a tendency for "closure" to set in. McLuhan then has a responsibility with respect to his pattern, which is not exercised if, in order to get balance, it is necessary to read the entire canon of McLuhan. He also has the problem that the way a poem is to be read is not the same way that his own work should be read.

When Gerald Stearn asked him: "If you consider your prose an art form, then your books might be considered as extensions of McLuhan, poetical or artistic outbursts having nothing to do with media?" he replied:

> The "suggestion" is delightful and far too flattering, based, I think, on an almost ethereal whimsy. But it implies that I have used media analysis as a means of private self-expression. Of course when you talk back to the environment you begin to use it as a means of self-expression. However, I am anti-environment. (M:HC 293)

Here his view of conflict brings McLuhan to admit his own subjective involvement in the process, since the only way to be the "enemy"—adopt the anti-environment stance—is through the type of operations an artist carries on. But if the work is self-expression, it is no longer relevant to say the process is free of total involvement unless a severe intellectual schizophrenia is being developed. In *The Medium Is the Massage* he identifies the anti-environmental enemy figures as:

> The poet, the artist, the sleuth—whoever sharpens our perception tends to be antisocial; rarely "well-adjusted," he cannot go along with currents and trends. A strange bond often exists among antisocial types in their power to see environments as they really are. (MM 88)

Eventually, the role of the anti-environment in McLuhan will have to be examined in detail, since it is basic to his theory of revelation through conflict or interface. But it is important to see that he regards his own stance, insofar as he is an artist, as an anti-

47

social role. Such a role, according to his own statement, necessarily becomes a means of self-expression even if it is not art (though it certainly seems that McLuhan as poet manqué discovered the art of the essai concrète without knowing it).

Is it possible that there are assumptions that enter into the fabric of McLuhan's work and cut across his probes? McLuhan constantly rejects any concern with the implications of media such as advertising, in spite of what other analysts say. Yet it appears unavoidable to conclude with Raymond Williams on behalf of the May Day Manifesto group that:

> It is here, centrally, in the styles of advertising, that the view of life on which contemporary capitalism depends is persistently communicated. We may believe or disbelieve, be amused or annoyed by this or that particular advertisement. But what is present throughout is an offering of meaning and value in terms of the individual consumer. (*May Day Manifesto* 42)

What Williams' group is speaking about is part of the "form" of the advertisement *not* just content. McLuhan has tried to use the term media to refer specifically to the technical execution while evading the way the formal requirements of the technical execution and the formal involvements of the presentation interpenetrate. In doing this he seems to evade the economic and some of the social aspects of the ad as they manifest themselves in the form as form. If ads as ads "are the richest and most faithful daily reflections that any society ever made of its entire range of activities" (UM 232), then the approach of *The Mechanical Bride* is needed to supplement the approach of *Understanding Media*. But what happens to McLuhan in his later works is a flight into a philosophy of modernization, a secular theology.

Modernization (says Raymond Williams) is indeed the theology of a new capitalism. His description of the way in which modernization works invokes familiar echoes from McLuhan's discussion of the way that all phonetic alphabet oriented tradition is disappearing in the new electric age:

> Modernization is the ideology of the never ending present. The whole past belongs to traditional society, and modernization is a technical means for breaking with the past without creating a fu-

ture. All is now: restless, visionless, faithless: human society diminished to a passing technique. (*May Day Manifesto* 45)

Modernization works as a strategy to preserve the status quo in the areas where it could be most upset—the social and the economic. It says, "attitudes, habits, techniques, practices must change: the system of economic and social power . . . remains unchanged" (ibid.). Subconsciously, if not unconsciously, this might be an extremely attractive solution to anyone who fundamentally is not a revolutionary and prefers "a stable, changeless environment," since it would accept the inevitable changes but, by arguing that they cannot be controlled anyway, abandon responsibility in the economic and social spheres.

Critics who are trying to be pro-McLuhan, but who still wish to appear committed to more traditional literary values, choose the line of praising *The Mechanical Bride*, applauding the erudition and selected insights of *The Gutenberg Galaxy* as an academic study, and admitting *Understanding Media* must be important. McLuhan's response has been to reject the "moralism" of the earliest work, *The Mechanical Bride*, and to continue developing further in the direction of the later, *Understanding Media*.

5

How Dr. McLuhan Stopped Worrying and Learned to Love the Totems

Yet there are ways in which all of the three major works are interrelated. For example, McLuhan's development of the essai concrète following *Understanding Media* goes back to *The Mechanical Bride* with its medley of illustrations from ads, comic books, newspapers, witty questioning subheads, witty headline-like headings, and short essay-like verbal presentations. Many of the principles of analysis of the *Bride* are part of *The Gutenberg Galaxy* and *Understanding Media*. Poe's maelstrom and the vortex, which appear a number of times in the *Bride*, are important themes in *Understanding Media* and provide the closing sections of *The Medium Is the Massage*. In fact, in the *Bride* (148), he uses Poe to denounce an over-facile moralism; it is not, he says, of value to merely attack vulgarity and stupidity, for to-day too much of these qualities is intermixed with valuable articles.

In *Understanding Media*, he stresses the importance of games as media: "Games are popular art, collective, social reactions to the main drive or action of any culture" (UM 235). He points out that they are "dramatic models of our psychological lives providing release of particular tensions" (UM 237). Pursuing the general importance of games, a theme which comes to him partly from Piagetian psychology on the development of children and partly from the seminal study of games and culture, Huizinga's *Homo Ludens*, McLuhan points out that "art became a sort of civilized substitute for magical games and rituals [which is] the story of the detribalization which came with literacy" (UM 237). Here, in this crossing of Wyndham Lewis—"art is the civilized *substitute* for magic" (*Time and Western Man* 199, quoted by McLuhan in LC 83)—with his psychological and anthropological sources, McLuhan links games to art and to his own particular mode of analysis. Even when discussing as important a topic as Innis' mosaic methodology, McLuhan used the analogy of a game (introduction to *Bias of Communication* vii–x). But such an interest in games and their proximity to art as analytical mode is present in *The Mechanical Bride* where one of the witty subheads to a section entitled "Murder the Umpire" asks: "Modern business is a game just like philosophy or art, only more creative?" (MB 135).

McLuhan answers the question in *Understanding Media* where he says:

> What disqualifies war from being a true game is probably what also disqualifies the stock market and business—the rules are not fully known nor accepted by all the players. Furthermore, the audience is too fully participant in war and business, just as in a native society there is no true art because *everybody* is engaged in making art. (UM 240)

But he had observed in the *Bride* that:

> . . . competitive sport is a direct reflex of the various motives and inner dramas of a society . . . sport is a magical institution, celebrating by a precise ritual the impulses that seem most necessary to social functioning and survival in any given group. (MB 135)

The Bride, in fact, as a playful book, is an illustration of McLuhan's thesis that play means "interplay," a notion which is further developed in *War and Peace in the Global Village* (171–3):

> Huizinga in *Homo Ludens* explores the deeply essential role of play as involving our senses themselves in abrasive dialogue, using "play" in the sense in which we speak of the "play" in a wheel or the "play" of emotions or the "play" of expression. The absence of this kind of play and flexibility carries us straight from the world of enterprise to the world of bureaucracy.

And naturally he emphasizes the importance of play for Joyce in *Finnegans Wake*; not too surprising in view of the parallel between an Irish wake and the funeral games of epic literature.

This consistency not only exists between the *Bride* and *Understanding Media*, it is an intrinsic part of *The Gutenberg Galaxy* as well. The theme of *The Mechanical Bride* is revisited in one section of the *Galaxy*: " 'Woman,' wrote Meredith in 1859, 'is the last thing to be civilized by man.' By 1929 she had been homogenized by means of the movies and photo advertising" (GG 212). Woman, who had been "integral and whole in a fragmented and visualized flatland [became reduced] to uniformity and repeatability and specialism" (GG 212). The *Bride* shows how the images of ads and movies presented a "mechanized" image for woman. Although skirts were shortened, the woman of the thirties and forties pulled herself in with corsets, and up with bras; glamour photos were taken on tiptoe, emphasizing the rigidity of the mechanical pull on the leg; the individual piece of anatomy—a leg with a stocking, a bust with a bra—were illustrated as fragments or replaceable parts. Finally, in the forties, the drum majorette appeared—"An adolescent love novice, a junior chorus girl in cavalry officer attire . . . instructed in the art of symbolic flagellation" (MB 122). The "line" and the "sadism" both were linked closely to the specialist and the mechanical.

There are many themes and interests that could be traced between the *Bride* and the *Galaxy*: the sleuth as a figure, Holmes, "the split man of the head versus heart," being a forerunner of the analysis of mechanical man right down to the sleuth-figure's "multifarious but specialized learning" (MB 107 & 109); the symbolist poets as important guides; Joyce as the "man of true distinction" showing the way out of modern dilemma; the aesthetics of Poe; the advertisers as rhetoricians; and Bloom as an adman.

But such integral development would be expected in most writers. What is more important is the way that the villain remains the same, but different. In *The Mechanical Bride*, the problem is the transformation of man into machine by the reduction of his sense of discrimination as a result of the way the "mechanical" system tampers with his intellectual and sensory life—a process carried on by business, industry, the ad agencies. It is a force to which he is susceptible because of a lack of training in discrimination, in subtlety, in complexity. In *The Gutenberg Galaxy*, the villain becomes "Gutenberg Man"—or at least many of his features such as the homogeneity, the repeatability, and the fragmentation. What produces Gutenberg Man, though, is not the operation of a specific environment and milieu, but the introduction at one point in history of one technical device. McLuhan seems to have discovered that he was looking at the wrong aetiology in the *Bride*, for the true coming-to-be of man as a schizophrenic was implicit in his adoption of a phonetic alphabet and then fully realized in the conversion of that alphabet into an instrument of greater power through its mechanization in the act of printing.

The theme of the "mechanical" quite rightly joins the *Bride* and the *Galaxy*, but only in that peculiar dialectic way in which one can move through the topics of the *Galaxy* to their paradoxical appearance in *Understanding Media*, just as in a Joycean dream the characters appear to shift roles and place. The tracing of this process is what is most of interest in considering the McLuhan books themselves. The McLuhan of the *Bride* may have been moralistic and may not have been turned on to "technology" in the sense of actual technological creations as "extensions of man," but he had evolved a subtle and sociologically oriented base for the analysis of the products of popular culture over a specific portion of the contemporary period. He "read" each of the products of popular culture as if it were a work of art and, in so doing, seemed to be extending the type of analysis that Kenneth Burke and others felt should be carried on. He defended the activity in terms of a true understanding of evaluation. Discussing a statement by Stan Lee (long before "Marvel Comics" became a craze), he agreed with Lee that comic writers should take heed:

DON'T WRITE DOWN TO YOUR READERS! (MB 151)

McLuhan observed that "there is little to choose between 'Dare Devil Comics' and *Gone With the Wind*. . . . But the superiority of the pulps is in their absence of pretentiousness, and the readers of this form of entertainment are altogether undeceived by it" (MB 151–2). Interested in value, McLuhan was not a "moralistic" critic about popular culture. He realized that the Al Capp of the forties and early fifties (before his sell-out, or as McLuhan describes it in *Understanding Media* [165], "The biggest casualty of the TV impact") could be "aware of at least the

54

possibility of a world both adult and imaginative [and] function as a critically conscious individual" (MB 63). Capp as satirist, McLuhan pointed out, provided "criticism which is embedded in his highly parabolic entertainment, [and] therefore, has a complexity which is the mark of a wisdom" (MB 64).

In the context of remarks such as Stan Lee's, and strips like "Li'l Abner" as well as other products of popular culture—the folklore of industrial man—McLuhan could point out that he was an industrial folklorist, because he was interested in the intellect, in discrimination, and in values:

> The basic criterion for any kind of human excellence is simply how heavy a demand it makes on the intelligence. How inclusive a consciousness does it focus? By this standard there is very little fiction in a century, very little music, and very little poetry or painting which deserves attention for its own sake. One function of the critic is to keep the best work free from the surrounding clutter. But, in order to free the mind from the debilitating confusion, it is not enough to claim priority for excellence without considering the bulk which is inferior. To win more and more attention for the best work it is necessary to demonstrate what constitutes the inevitably second-rate, third-rate, and so on. And in the course of doing this one finds that the great work of a period has much in common with the poorest work. The air of unreality which has hovered over the little magazine coterie culture in general is due to their neglect of close interrelations between the good and the bad work of the same period. The result of this neglect is, finally, failure to see the goodness of the good work itself. The great artist necessarily has his roots very deep in his own time—roots which embrace the most vulgar and commonplace fantasies and aspirations. (MB 152)

This statement deserves being quoted at length, since it stands in strong antithesis to the McLuhan who in the *Playboy* interview (158) says, "I don't like to tell people what I think is good or bad about the social and psychic changes caused by the new media," and who also says that *The Mechanical Bride* is a work all of whose major points have been made irrelevant by television (*Playboy* 74)—irrelevant like his observations on games, or on the mechanization of women which he says in *The Gutenberg Galaxy* is the *Bride*'s theme?

Most of the major currents that run through McLuhan's work are in *The Mechanical Bride*. If a concern with space is a major aspect of the pictorial-poetic comparisons of his recent *Vanishing Point*, Wyndham Lewis' concern with space and Bergson's with time are present as early as *The Mechanical Bride*. Joyce provides much of the energy for the conclusion of *The Gutenberg Galaxy*, but again and again Joyce forms part of the fabric of *The Mechanical Bride*. There is a statement about Joyce's theme and the theme of the book that is interesting to keep in mind later:

> The key to Superman is Clark Kent the useless. Therefore the more we create and centralize physical power, the more we suppress our human nature; and then that human nature queues up all the more to support the big physical power that crushes it. Far from being a conscious conspiracy, this is a nightmare dream from which we would do well to awaken at once. Return again, Finnegan.
>
> There is actually emerging a large number of independent critical minds today. As the nightmare moves to its unwelcome dramatic peak, the sleeper stirs and writhes. It is nice to be enfolded in a collective dream as long as the comfort is greater than the pain. But we have nearly passed that critical point. Consciousness will come as a relief. (MB 128)

Here the awakening of Finnegan is seen as a return of individual consciousness counteracting the tendency that we have to become our environment—machines making us like robots. McLuhan's use of the image of the point at the centre of the vortex, which is part of *The Mechanical Bride* as of most other McLuhan books, indicates how we should achieve control through understanding—a theme that would appear from his statement in *Playboy* (74) he has not entirely abandoned even now: "the central purpose of all my work is to convey this message, that by understanding media as they extend man, we gain a measure of control over them." But the control sought for in *The Mechanical Bride* was said to be "active." In the *Bride* passivity is constantly queried as a detrimental quality conducive to the "nightmare dream."

What McLuhan attempted in *The Mechanical Bride* was a pioneering effort. The only near parallels are in the work of Wyndham Lewis in *Time and Western Man*, which he acknowledges, and that of Reuel Denney in *The Astonished Muse*, which he probably did not know about. Neither Denney nor Lewis illustrates his work with actual exhibits nor does either provide a unique format for his book as McLuhan does in the *Bride*. The *Bride* uses its analysis of exhibits to make manifest the latent currents that underlie our industrial folklore and to provide some scale of comparison and contrast between various popular arts products. Most centrally, it illustrates one of the most important things that McLuhan has to teach—the essential importance of sensory training, perceptual training, and education in discrimination through the arts. His point of view is one of a Jeffersonian individualism which is fostered by a freedom that can only come about through a genuine freedom of choice. Such genuine freedom of choice can only result from a full awareness of how the various products of advertising, comic books, popular novels, newspapers, magazines, radio, and movies are working on the individual. In the process, it shows some of the similarities and differences between the most successful achievements of the arts, and of industrial folklore and the second and third rate. The standards for arriving at the assessment are clear, with consciousness, complexity, and intellectual involvement being very high on McLuhan's scale.

Because of these factors, there is an implicit social criticism of industrial folklore as well as sociological analysis involved in *The Mechanical Bride*. Certain economic theories such as eighteenth century market theories; certain philosophical positions such as Descartes' mechanistic philosophy and Leibnitz's monadism; certain educational theories such as Hutchins' "Great Books" come in for sharper criticism and are identified as parts of the causal cluster that leads to the "mechanism" of the twentieth century. The real difficulty in the *Bride* is McLuhan's lack of basic sociological theory. There is no mention of Weber or Durkheim; no serious awareness of Marx; no reference to Simmel; no reference even to George Herbert Mead, whose *Mind, Self and Society* had such a profound influence on Kenneth Burke as well as on a generation of sociologists. This is not to tax McLuhan with failing to use the type of social scientist whom he obviously opposes in the *Bride*. Rather these individuals are social theorists whose concepts form the fabric of any contemporary forties' view of man and society.

Bibliography is not necessarily essential, if the theoretical framework is really present, but McLuhan's *Bride* seems to succeed more because of its literary qualities and because of the power of applying the techniques of literary criticism to popular culture than it does because of its theoretical awareness of the social structure of the society which it is analyzing. There are assumptions that are open to serious question: Is all North American society as homogeneous as McLuhan makes out? When he speaks of the rich and the poor, is there a real concept of the peculiar dilemmas of urban poverty? It is also interesting that the entire book is written without any attention to the role of the blacks in American society and the effect of the "mechanical" culture on that role. In fact, the whole ethnic problem is subsumed under a discussion of Maggie and Jiggs. Such a narrow treatment assumes a type of homogeneity that may be true of some immigrants, but not certainly of all groups.

The naïveté concerning social theory also leads McLuhan into disregarding the significance of economic factors in the questions that he is discussing. While he can say with relation to education in the *Bride* that "a power economy cannot tolerate power that cannot be centrally controlled. It will not tolerate the unpredictable actions and thoughts of individual men. That is plain from every gesture and intonation of current social and market research as well as from the curricula of our schools" (MB 128), he rather naïvely abandons the possibility of genuine poverty in the present cultural situation. Discussing what he calls the "poor rich" using an ad for Harry Winston, "rare jewels of the world," McLuhan comments that "it may very well be that the effect of mass production and consumption is really to bring about a practical rather than a theoretic communism" (MB 55). While such comments may reveal some of the weakness of people coming to view themselves as "replaceable parts" in an economy geared to "consumption of uniform products," it does conceal some basic differences that vitiate the social structure and its metaphysical assumptions. While most might see Joyce and writers of his kind as the only true "men of distinction," it seems over-facile to say that in America low, middle, and high are consumer ratings and nothing more, while at the same time to emphasize the distinctions of high, middle, and low brow in a society "where distinction and culture are a matter of consumption rather than of discriminating perception and judgement" (MB 59).

The essential bias of *The Mechanical Bride* can be discovered from the title of an earlier discussion of Henry Luce's empire, "The Psychopathology of *Time, Life* and *Fortune*." This article first appeared in *Neurotica* before the publication of the *Bride*, not in 1955 after the *Bride* as some critics have suggested. (Unfortunately the issue was seized by the authorities because of "Answers to an Ad," an article by G. Legman which printed responses that had been sent to an ad seeking a partner for sadomasochistic activities.) As the title suggests, and as his analysis of the drum majorette, for example, demonstrates, McLuhan approaches his cultural objects with a "psychoanalytic" bias. His method is "symbolic" and "psychological" in the formalistic sense, but he does not carefully correlate his analysis to the total person or to the society. It is as if Kenneth Burke had become fixated in an early stage of his development and had developed the psychoanalytic aspects of his work without the fuller sociological and psychological analyses of the culture. McLuhan's work in the *Bride* is excellent as a demonstration of some of the potentialities of an artistic approach to the study of culture, but it also seriously exhibits the weaknesses of such an approach without accompanying theoretical orientations.

Nevertheless, *The Mechanical Bride* is an important book, for little other analysis that has been done of popular culture or folklore shows such a range and subtlety in dealing with pattern, form, symbol, and motive. The problems that McLuhan has in combining a sophisticated practical literary criticism with a rather simple awareness about other matters find a parallel in two writers who influenced him—Wyndham Lewis and Ezra Pound. Lewis even describes Pound as a "revolutionary simpleton" in *Time and Western Man,* a quality which underlies some of his works such as *Guide to Kulchur.* Critics could easily overlook many of Pound's fine insights gained from using his artistically sensitized antennae, for he was presumably disqualified from serious regard because of a failure in successfully achieving an overall theory. In a different way Lewis, too, might be accused of the same fault, although unlike Pound's his "revolutionary" streak was "counter-revolutionary," stressing the need for a return to tradition. In spite of this, the two approaches are not altogether different, nor do they differ much from McLuhan's.

Like Pound, McLuhan in the *Bride* values a Jeffersonian individualism, "a self-regulating democracy based on a farmer-craftsman economy" (MB 134). Like Lewis, McLuhan is fundamentally for conservation of values. Recently too, he expressed major personal reservations about the coming of the electric age since he fears "the dissolution of that tradition" (*Playboy* 158). Lewis similarly sought after stability and emphasized tradition—in fact, criticized Pound for attempting to merge the instability of the Bergsonian philosophy of flux with an attempt to preserve tradition. In addition to sharing many of Pound's and Lewis' conservative views, McLuhan is also a Catholic who is committed to other conservative positions, such as the reservations concerning birth control pills that he presented in the *Dew Line* (vol. 1, no. 12, 17). Consequently his sharpest critics have often suggested that his general philosophy is totalitarian and there is, of course, an implicit danger of this in his commitment to the Jeffersonianism of Pound's or Lewis' conservative views in *The Art of Being Ruled*, for both Pound, in *Jefferson and/or Mussolini*, and Lewis, in *Hitler*, ended up praising totalitarian regimes. McLuhan's defence of both himself and these writers would be an assertion of an apolitical intent which is obviously sincere. But how consistent would this be with his own or Lewis' deep interest in Machiavelli's view of the state as a work of art? Such a view of the state can hardly be pursued without some political implications, even if they are those of the anarchist who certainly seems to be one-half of the split man that is *McLuhan politicus*. The trouble is that the other half of this split man is the logical complement—an uncritical Dadaist, one aspect of a possible totalitarian demos.

McLuhan, a paradoxical Janus of the Media world, seems to have two faces: one like Paul Goodman, and the other like Wyndham Lewis. The whole of the *Bride* is involved in such tensions. One pull is towards the society of the present—its businessmen, its ad agencies, its producers, and its PR men: the other is towards

60

the history of Western man in the past—in the philosophy of Descartes; in the theories of the eighteenth century economists; in the Puritan movement and its poets such as Milton; in the evolution of philosophies of work and hero-worship such as Carlyle's.

To recognize the complexity is naturally commendable and important, but in the *Bride* most of these are ultimately clustered about two poles: one, the Puritan sensibility; the other, a mechanistic philosophy. In very different ways, views of Max Weber and Norman Brown might coalesce with McLuhan's view of Puritanism. But in McLuhan, especially when joined with a critique of Descartes, these two poles provide attractive targets for a certain kind of dogmatic Catholic sensibility. They were characteristic targets for the Catholic critics and philosophers of the forties and fifties. So there emerges the paradox of a McLuhan who, while appealing to anarchist artists, or students of Norman Brown, might well contain an even stranger type of repression at the heart of his vision. Even in his more recent analyses, a strong commitment to the ultimate evolution of moral control exists:

> It's paradoxical that in the transition to a retribalized society, there is inevitably a great explosion of sexual energy and freedom; but when society is fully realized, moral values will be extremely tight. In an integrated tribal society, the young will have free rein to experiment, but marriage and family will become inviolate institutions, and infidelity and divorce will constitute serious violations of the social bond, not a private deviation, but a collective insult and loss of face to the entire tribe. (*Playboy* 65)

Though this is "rather harsh," McLuhan theorizes against Brown and Marcuse that under such tribalized conditions of extremely austere morality, "sexuality can take on new and richer dimensions of depth involvement" (*Playboy* 65). The attractiveness to a Catholic of the "austere morality," as well as its reassuring tone to the Puritan, makes this a comfortable kind of analysis, though it is precisely where the intriguing contradictions develop with respect to one side of the *Bride*, while seeming to support the conservative trends of another. In the *Bride*, McLuhan, discussing "Know-How" (an ad on "How to iron shirts without hating your husband!"), associates mechanization with tribalization by using a description of the tribe from Joseph Campbell's *Hero with a Thousand Faces:*

> It is precisely the same annihilation of the human ego that we are witnessing today. Only, whereas men in those ages of terror got into animal strait jackets, we are unconsciously doing the same *vis à vis* the machine. And our ads and entertainment provide insight into the totem images we are daily contriving in order to express this process. But technology is an abstract tyrant that carries its ravages into deeper recesses of the psyche than did the sabertooth tiger or the grizzly bear. (MB 33)

Did McLuhan become wooed by DDB&O so that he learned to stop worrying and love the totems? Does media, too, have a Dr. Strangelove who embraced technology when he realized it was shifting from the "mystery of time," which required "killing time," to a glorification of the mystery of space in the new electric age? The *Explorations* period and McLuhan's obvious explosion into *The Gutenberg Galaxy* and *Understanding Media* are marked by a growing interest in tribes, primitives, tribalization, and the coining of terms such as "lineal" and "non-lineal" taken from Dorothy Lee's discussion of the Trobriand language in *Explorations.* Therefore, the next stage of a look at McLuhan must be a recapitulation of his development and an examination of the Gemini-like volumes of the *Galaxy* and *Understanding Media.*

The clown and the professional fool have traditionally received a licence for what they do. The wisdom they uttered depended, in part, on the arrogant stance that they could adopt with respect to others. Lear's Fool is the only one who dares to utter the paradoxes that force Lear to confront the dilemmas of his human situation. Traditionally, the fool clothed himself in the robes of his office. Today part of the university's role as a social sanctuary for criticism allows him to come forth in academic robes. At least metaphorically, the robes are academic, for McLuhan dresses his paradoxes and develops the material of his intellectual "con game" out of a wide range of erudite sources which he uses in whatever way he sees fit and with a pose of superiority to those colleagues and thinkers with whom he does not agree.

6

The Gutenberg Galaxy

McLuhan himself tells us that in studying media "It's vital to adopt a posture of arrogant superiority." Amplifying this theme, he observes that "instead of scurrying into a corner and wailing about what media are doing to us, one should charge straight ahead and kick them in the electrodes" (*Playboy* 158). At some point this moves from a mere stance towards media to actual attacks on his critics and on thinkers with whom he disagrees. Characteristic of his transference of this "arrogant superiority" to the interpersonal is his attack in *McLuhan: Hot & Cool* (273) on the well-known anthropological linguist, Dell Hymes, who presumed to write a critical review of *The Gutenberg Galaxy*. McLuhan, assisted by his colleague and co-editor of *Explorations*, the anthropologist E. S. Carpenter, accuses Hymes of "importing, uncritically, literate assumptions into non-literate areas of study [a result of] using models of perception that have no relevance to their materials." Invoking aid from Carpenter as an expert, he quotes a letter of Carpenter's saying that "Hymes is bluffing. . . . The authorities he cites [chief of whom is Leonard Bloomfield, the famous American specialist who is generally recognized as the father of contemporary American linguistics—AUTHOR'S NOTE] make no contribution to this subject, nor do anthropologists or linguists generally." This is certainly a stance of "superior arrogance" with respect to a rather large body of people.

Hymes had incurred McLuhan's wrath for observing that in *The Gutenberg Galaxy* "The contrast between oral and typographic communication is carried to ludicrous extremes, as a vehicle of cultural criticism and historical explanation. It can no more stand against an adequate view of human history than any other single-minded exegesis known to us." He further suggests that the areas in which McLuhan is involved might profit more from the contributions of "serious and empirical sociolinguistic work [because they] offer us more as a basis for understanding and action [than the *Galaxy*, which is] a mixture of passionate concern for the quality of human life (admirable), and a two-term view of its entire content and evolution (deplorable)" (M:HC 173).

In replying to Hymes, McLuhan completely evades the fact that Hymes has cited articles, such as Bloomfield's analysis of "Literate and Non-literate Speech," which clearly demonstrate that it is possible to make a grammatical mistake in some primitive societies. If Hymes misunderstands McLuhan's hyperbole, McLuhan fails to have a respect for a sense of fact, such as Bloomfield's analysis of reports about "good" and "bad" speech in the Menomini tribe. McLuhan has said that it is impossible to make a grammatical mistake in a primitive society (GG 238), meaning apparently that "grammar" is only something that appears in grammar books. Bloomfield has shown that primitives do, however, have distinctions between levels of speech and do recognize differences between over-casual, correct, and over-pedantic speech just as English speakers do. McLuhan may be right in suggesting that the lack of books conditions a different attitude, but the insight need hardly by achieved at the expense of other people's equally valid work.

While this example may seem merely a way of looking at one of the less attractive aspects of McLuhan's stance as cultural clown or fool, it actually shows the way in which McLuhan's rhetoric becomes badly involuted and twisted in trying to pursue the particular path of wisdom through folly. McLuhan's analysis of primitivism became an important factor in what developed during the *Explorations* period—the transition from the *Bride* to the

Galaxy and *Understanding Media*. The *Bride* had looked on the tribal drum as one of the great threats to man's sense of discrimination and contemporary civilization. Tribalism, and consequently retribalization, had from that perspective seemed to require a society which was passive and static. During the *Explorations* period, McLuhan met and worked closely with Ted Carpenter, an anthropologist interested in language, culture, and personality and who was studying Eskimos. The association led to a growing interest on McLuhan's part in the dimensions of the primitive and to a reassessment of what this primitivism meant.

A fundamental distinction for him developed from his acquaintance with the writings of Dorothy Lee published in *Explorations* on "Lineal and Non-Lineal Codifications of Reality." Dorothy Lee, analyzing Trobriand Islander speech, had argued that the Trobrianders did not perceive lineal order as a value. They avoided seeing patterns as connected by lines, so that a circular city would become for them a series of humps in a pattern. Similarly, in describing personal relations, only negative and unsatisfactory relations were discussed in anything resembling a linear (cause-and-effect) type of language. Carpenter had, in *Explorations Two, Five,* and *Nine,* observed similar qualities about Aivilik Eskimo language and thought. From this McLuhan and Carpenter generalized that tribal cultures approach things in a non-linear way, perceiving patterns as gestalts (or later mosaics), while civilized men tended to the linear.

Now here is where McLuhan's metaphorical mind functions brilliantly. It is not a difficult step to move from Dorothy Lee's distinction to the fact that type (and phonetic writing) organizes itself in lines moving from one side of a page to another and that especially the process of mechanizing this so that it is repeatable (i.e. print) is bound to have an influence on the way people think and perceive. Consequently, Gutenberg Man—the lineal man— makes his entry into the McLuhan intellectual world. So far, as long as we are talking about some native cultures and some of the possible effects of print and not limiting human perception in an absolutist way, such probing is not only unobjectionable, but stimulating in raising a variety of questions. If this leads to further speculation, as it has done in the work of Walter Ong, concerning the influence of the presentation of charts and outlines on the schematization of knowledge and the preference for certain taxonomical systems, it is still more valuable. Even if the ethnographical facts prove to be erroneous or inadequate, the particular questions they have posed are not. The insights gained may still have application to the way that certain modes of organizing pages and formats and certain technological procedures develop from a form—the printed page and the book—which comes to dominate man's reflective activity. The whole area of speculation, in fact, leads to *The Gutenberg Galaxy,* which Raymond Williams has described as indispensable for those interested in communications theory today.

What does go wrong is that, as the area of generalization broadens and the connections made accelerate, something in the way of gross distortion enters. Unlike non-verbal systems such as logic, to which McLuhan seems hostile, the verbal systems can develop rapidly, thereby increasing cumulative distortions.

The distinction between lineal and non-lineal, as far as it calls attention to certain ways of organizing and perceiving reality, can be useful. To see what can happen you need only look again at Carpenter criticizing Hymes' supposed lack of knowledge about primitives; he argues that for McLuhan "lineal thinking alone is not capable of grasping or understanding our world in a global manner." Answering Hymes' charge that McLuhan's view of human history is "a single-minded exegesis," Carpenter replies that it is not McLuhan who is "single minded" and "over-simplified," but Hymes who fails to achieve "all-at-onceness" because of an "obsolete" approach which does not "open the way for multiple models simultaneously applied" (M:HC 268).

The contradictions involved in Carpenter's argument, which follows McLuhan's method, can only be tolerated by denying logic which itself is one way of immediately assuming a selective view of reality, since of necessity the whole principle of contradiction is excluded. Yet also, of course, it is not, for it is necessary to believe that the "exclusive" universe of non-linearity is also an inclusive universe. Like the strategy of modernization referred to earlier, this is a rhetoric which at an academic level is equivalent to the old query "Have you stopped beating your wife?" But the confusion can go further and reveal the real problems which can develop from McLuhan's sharply opposed distinctions.

If Hymes' models are "obsolete," Carpenter argues, it is because he did not understand and appreciate the models of Klee and others, while presumably McLuhan does. Yet turning to Klee it is simple to discover that Klee would never support McLuhan's distinction concerning lineal and non-lineal, since Klee's re-creation of a re-tribalized art depends on the very sense of "line" which is negated in the term non-linear or non-lineal. If the Trobriand Islanders actually reject line for pattern (which does not precisely seem to be what Dorothy Lee is saying), Klee sees his work as interrelating linear and gestalt, line and pattern. "I begin," says Klee in his workshop notes, *The Thinking Eye* (24), "where all pictorial form begins: with the point that sets itself in motion. The point (as agent) moves off, and the line comes into being— the first dimension." The answer to this by McLuhanists is that supposedly we are misreading Klee by not understanding his discussion of the point in motion, while actually Klee is truly primitive, participatory, tribal, and therefore flat—non-simultaneous analyses can only result in misunderstanding. Klee's very primitivism qualifies him *per se* for McLuhanity as being non-linear.

As regards primitivism, Siegfried Giedion, one of McLuhan's major sources and a world authority on primitive cave art, interestingly enough reveals an emphasis in the very opening of his *Eternal Present: The Beginnings of Art* (19–20) which informs the reader of the importance of "outline":

If there is a continuous tendency throughout prehistoric art, it is the ever-increasing mastery of the outline. . . .

The vast complex of prehistoric art must, we believe, be treated according to its own nature. . . . The comprehensive idea consists in the outline or the contour of the object. The determination of the outline concentrates all this striving to come to terms with the formal and psychic content of an animal or human figure.

The "line" or "outline" as a way of obtaining the pattern (the fact that mosaic itself works through linear compartmentalization) might suggest that the McLuhanites should confine their use of "linear" to their own language, if they must use it at all. The reply to the critic who argues so, naturally is that he approaches the linear writers through their own literate habits and misses the meaning of McLuhan.

As a technique for avoiding criticism and avoiding coming to terms with specialists, McLuhan's strategy is excellent. Yet obviously the point is that one can be just as arrogant as McLuhan and Carpenter merely by taking Klee and saying that their own model which they use against Hymes actually stresses lineality as the basis of art and that McLuhan is bluffing. Little is gained this way, for much of the richness of Klee, much of the insight of Hymes, and much of the value of McLuhan would be lost.

McLuhan's rhetoric, adopted from advertising and headlines, leads to this linguistic ambivalence and the shock of "superior arrogance." Setting aside or compensating for the three factors—that McLuhan popularizes rather than innovates; that he uses "superior arrogance" as a protection and a clown-like mask; and that he develops a new form, the essai concrète—some of the problems of the *Galaxy* and *Understanding Media* become clearer.

Much has been said about the originality of *The Gutenberg Galaxy*, but McLuhan's own modesty assigns the credit to writers like Mallarmé, Joyce, Lewis, and Innis. These writers developed McLuhan's sense of the importance of media. *Finnegans Wake*, an experiment in the limits of the phonetic alphabet and the structure of printed words as well as other media, dealt with the ABCED-minded man, calling McLuhan's attention to the critical importance of Gutenberg on literary communications. In "Joyce, Mallarmé and the Press," McLuhan explores the development of this insight which allows for the panoramic, historic contrast between the pre-Gutenberg, Gutenberg, and post-Gutenberg worlds of the *Galaxy* and *Understanding Media*. A crucial assumption of this essay is the media as art form:

> Plato . . . saw writing as a mainly destructive revolution. Since then we have been through enough revolutions to know that every medium of communication is a unique art form which gives salience to one set of human possibilities at the expense of another. (M:HC 123)

The proof of the view is documented from Lamartine, Čapek, and especially Mallarmé and Joyce: "The only book possible from today [1831]," says Lamartine, "is the newspaper." Mallarmé saw the press as "a prelude to an era, a competition for the foundation of the popular modern poem" (M:HC 130). Joyce turned the press into creative form (as Mallarmé had done before him). In the "Aeolus" section of *Ulysses* he created for English new possibilities for prose and poetry adopted from the press and the world and showing the close interrelation between popular culture and poetry. Art is banality, Mallarmé declared, and Flaubert illustrated in *Bouvard et Pécuchet*. According to Pound, Joyce elevated this into an encyclopaedic principle of composition in *Ulysses*. One aspect of McLuhan's aesthetic popularizes the aesthetics of Joyce, Mallarmé, and Pound which he and his associate Hugh Kenner examined together in the forties. Just as Carpenter's anthropological background strongly influenced McLuhan's tribalism, Kenner's commitment to contemporary literature intensified McLuhan's sense of the "revolutionary" in Pound and Joyce, Flaubert and Mallarmé.

This aesthetic applied to certain critical points in history naturally raises a problem: How does the introduction of means for achieving new technical forms of presentation and transmission influence the nature of the sensibility and the biases of men in their intellectual lives? The key periods according to the *Galaxy* are the shift from oral to written, the shift from script to print, and the shift from print to the "charge of the light brigade [TV]." In this sense, the *Galaxy* is not a history as much as a sampler, developing probe-like essays into various possible problems at the crucial points of shift. Its companion volume, *Understanding Media*, is a here and how treatment of the range of media and what they are doing to the present and the future, though still in the format of individual, probably detachable shorter pieces.

The *Galaxy* finds its beginning and end-point in the literary (opening with *King Lear* and closing with *The Dunciad*). *Understanding Media* avoids the same close connection to the literary. Both share a crucial interest in media, which McLuhan says are unique art forms. They only become misleading if the titles McLuhan gives to media are taken as the limiting categories and it is not realized that every individual shift within media creates new media. Yet if this were pushed far enough, and it should be, then each individual use of any media is itself a unique form and becomes another art form in which the message of the *Galaxy* and *Understanding Media* disappears. The formal nature of films, or TV programmes, or newspaper pages is once again returned to the interplay between the technical imperatives and the specific formal shaping of the individual presentation. At that instant meaning becomes important, which is, of course, the very position McLuhan denies. McLuhan, in this way, is one of the last Victorians, and as Richard Hoggart has analyzed the danger, McLuhan becomes an aesthete:

> . . . mass communications do not ignore imaginative art. They must feed upon it, since it is the source of much of their material and approaches; but they must also seek to *exploit* it. They tend to cut the nerve which gives it life—that questioning, with all the imaginative and intellectual resources an artist can muster, of the texture and meaning of his experience; but they find the body both interesting and useful. Towards art, therefore, the mass media are the purest aesthetes; they want its forms and styles but not its possible meanings and significance. ("Mass Communications in Britain" in *The Modern Age*, ed. Boris Ford 453)

McLuhan himself, as a popularizer, becomes mass media and discovers a form for using the form of the imaginative arts while simplifying the meaning through creating the essai concrète and achieving the status of a superb "ape of art." Such a mode has its limits, but knowing its limits releases its values for us.

Since McLuhan's theme constantly returns to the importance of the arts and the *Galaxy* actually uses Joyce as a "ground bass" (Ezra Pound, *Kulchur*), Shakespeare as a prelude, and Pope as a grand finale, one way to approach the *Galaxy* is through the handling of poetry and literature. To begin at the end and retrace what happens in a McLuhanesque (post-Poe, post-symbolist) manner, the proper starting point is *The Dunciad*. McLuhan presents Pope's poem as anti-printing press or anti-mass produced book. The difficulties that he encounters in maintaining this thesis might well be the crux of the difficulties in the whole of the *Galaxy*, if not in all of his work.

Pope's *Dunciad* is an extremely complex poem which has been the object of a lengthy study by Aubrey Williams (*Pope's* Dunciad), a work McLuhan cites with some approval. In an early issue of *Explorations*, I contrasted *The Dunciad* with *Finnegans Wake*, observing that in the *Wake* both Vico and Hegel, and Bruno, become part of the satire:

> None of them, however, completely escape the satiric focus of the dreamworld, for the *Wake* is the reverse of the *Dunciad*, exposing the nightworld of the introvert at work and ending with the break of day. In the new-day world, the artist, Shem, has become like Shaun, and the administrator, Shaun, has become like Shem. The structure of the work is such that Shem and Shaun appear on the surface and are 'reamalgamerged' into the total community of redemption. ("Here Comes Everybody," *Explorations Two* 71)

The technique of *The Dunciad* is an important aspect of painting the "soul's groupography," for, according to Joyce, what Pope did in *The Dunciad* was to combine "the stern poise for a swift pounce," working on the principle that the "same thing rivisible in nightim, may be involted into the zeroic couplet" (*Explorations Two* 68). As McLuhan suggests in the last sentence of his treatment of Pope in *The Gutenberg Galaxy*, *The Dunciad* describes the nightmare from which Finnegan is trying to awake—a nightmare of subjectivity and personal history.

What McLuhan does, though, is to reduce the richness of *The Dunciad* to his single-minded purpose. In the headlines introducing the first of the three chapters on the poem, he declares:

> Sheer visual quantity evokes the magical resonance of the tribal horde. The box office looms as a return to the echo chamber of bardic incantation. (GG 255)

The words refer to the hero of the later version of *The Dunciad*, Colly Cibber, the poet laureate who was a famous dramatist and theatrical producer. He had incurred Pope's wrath for, among other things, defending a box office philosophy of the mass arts and for having suggested that satire could be undone merely by our refusal to laugh. Apparently, McLuhan who views *The Dunciad* as the "epic of the printed word" sees such activities as consistent with the more general theme:

> . . . the explicit study of plunging of the human mind into the sludge of an unconscious engendered by the book. It has been ob-

scured to posterity, in keeping with the prophecy at the end of Book IV, just why literature should be charged with stupefying mankind, and mesmerically ushering the polite world back into primitivism, the Africa within, and above all, the unconscious. (GG 255)

Now apparently *The Dunciad* is tied up with the unconscious, but the unconscious is hardly tied as exclusively with the book and its introduction as McLuhan suggests. The particular satire of subjectivity that Pope engages in is directed in part against scholasticism, which considerably pre-dates printing, for even the title of Dunce is taken from the followers of Duns Scotus, the Scotists. *Dulness* is also a technical term for the mediaeval blurring of the senses resulting from an over-strong emphasis on the scholastic. The modes of subjectivity are certainly related in considerable part to literary activity, for the poem is about the uncreation of the word by the Dunces and their leader Cibber, who Pope describes as the anti-Christ of wit. But the activity goes far beyond the immediate problems in irresponsible publishing or even the new learning. "The gloomy clerk" described in Book IV as taking "the high priori road" is not merely a victim of printing culture, any more than the particular parody of the Eucharist that McLuhan quotes can be reduced to a mere commentary on the fragmentation of the senses by print.

McLuhan, by arguing that the entire Fourth Book, added in 1742, is concerned with the "translation or reduction of diverse modes into a single mode of homogenized things" (GG 261), immediately limits a whole series of complex intertwined levels of meaning within the poem. Certainly it is about print. In addition to what McLuhan mentions about the fact that parts one, two, and three are involved with authors, booksellers, publishers, and critics whose whole life activity is centred about print, it is also possible to point out that the whole book itself in the case of *The Dunciad Variorum* is part of an elaborate work of art, including the shape of pages, the indices, the title pages, and even as McLuhan points out, the image of Minerva's Owl as a frontispiece. It is specious to associate the presence of the owl in Pope with the later use of the owl by Innis, for the owl is fundamentally a symbol of the drift of civilization from one area to another, not just a reflection of the fact "that the entire operation of print in our lives is not only unconscious but that for this very reason it immeasurably enlarges the domain of the unconscious" (GG 260).

Pope is quite carefully associating a moral criticism of the activity of the bad artist, or the bad intellectual, with his criticism of bad techniques and bad intellectual systems. Therefore, he is not merely "offering a formal causality" devoid of any interest in individuals, any more than he merely develops such a simple theme as "the fogs of Dulness and new tribalism are fed by the printing press" (GG 259). The fogs of Dulness are a result of disturbed sensation, but what disturbs sensation is a question of inadequate intellectual and sensory concern on the part of the individual, not mere manipulation by some physical device such as the printing press.

McLuhan forces an either/or situation rather than permitting a both/and. Pope is interested in the effects of mass printing and a number of other potential perversions of human communications. This either/or way of looking at the poem dominates McLuhan's approach. For him, Pope's poem must be first of all anti-print; for Pope it is a question of balance. *The Dunciad* could not succeed in being a work of art without the mass print world that produced it. Its very operation in converting the dross of the banal world into the poetic vision of the poem actually works against the "uncreating of the word" by the Dunces, the priestess Dulness, and her son Cibber. As the various banalities are woven into a poetic vision, the way to provide an order to the activities of the Dunces unfolds itself. Even the parody of the Eucharist, which McLuhan regards as a symbol of the fragmentation of the senses, introduces a participational symbol that works against the very attempts of fragmentation of the Dunces. If the poem is examined in depth, it has a complex theory of grace in which the very activity of Dulness, through the operation of wit and intellect, becomes undone, suggesting that in the economy of the world the creative powers of man can undo the attempts of man to undo his world.

Pope's vision is one of a balance between the world of print and the world of sense, a balance between the intellectual and the moral, a balance between the interior and the exterior. It is the excess, rather than the presence of a particular thing, that Pope sees creating Dulness. Even the unconscious as an Africa within is undone, for properly ordered the unconscious produces the poem through the agency of the mother and son, the mythic figures whose world is *The Dunciad*. Such a poem is neither pro-print nor anti-print. McLuhan shows the important role of the book in it, but misses the humanistic emphasis on man rather than technology and on harmony rather than opposition. If the critique of the interiorized man is linked solely to the world of print and the resulting denudation of the senses, the integrity of Pope's vision evaporates and the complex levels of interpersonal interaction between the human (the fact Cibber and others are real and responsible), the social context within which the interaction occurs, and the philosophical can be lost in what is a justifiable technological concern.

This, though, leads to McLuhan's major weaknesses. Movement by way of hateful contraries can be productive if, like the "involting" of Pope's "zeroic couplet," a balance is achieved. But "hateful contraries" are unproductive if they generate a kind of either/or attitude in which individual details are lost in the insistence on the fact that eighteenth century man is print man and twentieth century man, electric, post-Gutenberg man. One of the difficulties of McLuhan's way of proceeding is that it does not really allow for the individual like Pope who, in some ways, may be standing outside of the particular deterministic tradition which McLuhan is using. In the process the complexities are lost, the details disappear, and what makes for the individuating dialectic of this thing and nothing else becomes a vacant possibility. More concretely, the closing lines of *The Dunciad* for McLuhan become reduced to the statement: "But the new mechanical instrument and its mesmerized and homogenized servants, the dunces, are irresistible" (GG 263). This is his observation on the lines:

> In vain, in vain,—the all-composing Hour
> Resistless falls: The Muse obeys the Pow'r.
> She comes! she comes! the sable Throne behold
> Of *Night* Primaeval, and of *Chaos* old!
> Before her, *Fancy's* gilded clouds decay,
> And all its varying Rain-bows die away.
> *Wit* shoots in vain its momentary fires,

The meteor drops, and in a flash expires.
As one by one, at dread Medea's strain,
The sick'ning stars fade off th' ethereal plain;
As Argus' eyes by Hermes' wand opprest,
Clos'd one by one to everlasting rest;
Thus at her felt approach, and secret might,
Art after *Art* goes out, and all is Night.
See skulking *Truth* to her old Cavern fled,
Mountains of Casuistry heap'd o'er her head!
Philosophy, that lean'd on Heav'n before,
Shrinks to her second cause, and is no more.
Physic of *Metaphysic* begs defence,
And *Metaphysic* calls for aid on *Sense*!
See *Mystery* to *Mathematics* fly!
In vain! they gaze, turn giddy, rave, and die.
Religion blushing veils her sacred fires,
And unawares *Morality* expires.
Nor *public* Flame, nor *private*, dares to shine;
Nor *human* Spark is left, nor Glimpse *divine*!
Lo! thy dread Empire, CHAOS! is restor'd;
Light dies before thy uncreating word:
Thy hand, great Anarch! lets the curtain fall;
And Universal Darkness buries All. (*Dunciad* ll. 627–56)

The very operation of the images provides a vision of uncreation, which is itself a creation. It picks up the image of Minerva's
owl and the Great Mother (Dulness) of the poem and subtly con-
verts them back to the mythical status of a Minerva, for as Mc-
Luhan observes, "Pope in making Dulness the goddess of the unconscious is contrasting her with Minerva, goddess of alert intellect
and wit. It is not Minerva but her obverse complement, the owl,
that the printed book has conferred on Western man" (GG 262).
But here again the reason the figure of Dulness has power in the
poem is because Pope can, through his wit, associate it with the
figure of Minerva, and the very wit involved undoes the operation
of the figure of Dulness involved, thus restoring Minerva. Pope
knows that *The Dunciad* is a self-transcending poem, whereas
McLuhan reduces it to a mere report on what happens to wit and
sense because of print. If the "Dunces are invested with unciviliz-
ing powers of epic proportions," the epic proportions of the poem

divest this power of any effectiveness and do it by the operation of print.

The difference is that Pope is following the way that Richard Hoggart, in "Mass Communications in Great Britain," says the artist works, while McLuhan is analyzing him the way mass media work. For McLuhan then, Pope's work becomes merely a utility and he has in his own formal operations seized the form— the formalistic pattern he keeps speaking of—but lost the meaning. To Pope this would be the operation of a scholastic dunce, an inhabitant of the literary badlands of *The Dunciad* world. But that conclusion is susceptible of generalization to the whole of the *Galaxy*, for the analysis of *The Dunciad* is the grand conclusion. The operations of print are manifold.

Depth analysis and a total approach should not result in formulae which equate a poem with a doctrine on print. The answer might be that Pope could not achieve depth and density and totality, but this is not what the *Galaxy* seems to say. In *The Dunciad* McLuhan never mentions the relation of the poem to Pope's analysis of bathos ("the art of the profound") in *Peri Bathos: or the Art of Sinking in Poetry*. Again, if he had, *The Dunciad* would merely reveal the disorientation through print, leading man into depths of unconsciousness. But the poem, which is made of bathos (of the profound), becomes the very stuff poetry is made of, so that the art of sinking ironically becomes the art of rising or, really, the art of finding a balance. The balance depends on the tensions McLuhan so loves, but the ones that in his own approach he seems to reduce to a nothingness.

If there are such severe difficulties in comprehending the complexities of Pope, there seems little awareness then that Joyce, the "ground bass" of the *Galaxy*, is really fundamentally carrying on quite a different kind of activity, too. If Pope in *The Dunciad* shows a vision of coming nightmare, which is redeemed only by the way it becomes vision, Joyce sees a way out of the nightmare through a printed book that depends instinctively on the nature of phonetic writing and print. Joyce steers for a balance like Pope:

Joyce continues the neo-classical tradition of wit in his attempt to portray the "soul's groupography" in a comic mode. The effect aimed at is the inclusion and participation of the individual in the work as a whole—an effect that Pope and Ben Jonson had attempted. Joyce has the advantage of a more complex language enriched by a greater variety of art forms, but his problem was common with theirs—to steer a mean between the extremes of romanticism (enthusiasm) and rationalism. It has hardly been noticed that he shares their interests in unity: his works confine themselves to moments of time and points of space; they deal with everyday occurrences and present a comic view of mental activity. When Joyce appears during the inquest of Yawn, he divulges the roots of his "communionistic" technique. It is the "handtouch" of "Bygmester Finnegan of the Stuttering Hand," for the stutter of HCE breaks the flow of ALP and begins the transference of information, just as the "zeroic couplet" broke the flow of Renaissance lyricism to "charge" language with meaning. Joyce's work shows an increased sensitivity to written language which has been partially reduced back to a flux. His techniques of arresting eye and ear are an attempt to push the dynamic model in the arts to a point where a more complete participation on the part of the producer-consumer-reader is possible. Though dealing with the magic lantern world, he is attempting the careful and precise analysis of vivisection. The movement of the *Wake* is towards day—"my coming forth from darkness," accomplished through the gift of language, "Be thy mouth given unto thee! For why do you lack a link of luck to poise a pont of perfect peace?" The satire implicit in the title is a key to the resolution of the work—for Joyce's favorite phrase was "Wait till Finnegan Wakes!" (*Explorations Two* 76–7)

The period from *The Mechanical Bride* through the writing of *Explorations* was a period of transition for McLuhan— a period during which his major works were to take shape. The transition culminated with his being commissioned by the United States Office of Education to carry out a study of the effects of media. That study, which achieved publication in a mimeographed form, became the first version of *Understanding Media.* In order to look at the modern media age, though, McLuhan was forced to relate it to his role of literary historian and critic, for it was from these historical and critical roots (similar to those of Raymond Williams) that McLuhan's vision had grown.

7
This Is the Stuff That Myth Is Made Of

The Gutenberg Galaxy is the product of that growth and if McLuhan's method of composition is to be understood, it is supposed to re-create that process in his readers. The *Galaxy*, therefore, was the intellectual cornerstone of what McLuhan was to come to be, even if *Understanding Media* actually conferred upon him popular notice and acclaim. Consequently, it is in the *Galaxy* where complex citations of a wide range of academic material are to be found and where, if McLuhan had had his way, the various headings of sections would have appeared as marginal glosses evoking the mediaeval tradition of which he frequently speaks and to which he seems to have deep commitments. The glosses would have been an equivalent of headline technique for academics, a strategy which McLuhan later combines with other devices in *War and Peace in the Global Village.*

The style of the *Galaxy* is therefore closer to a dense, technical academic prose than any of his later books. Its main appeal would seem directed toward the type of academic in rebellion against the semantically directed oversimplifications of New Criticism and also against the older, often oversimplified generalizations of the historian of ideas. For history of ideas, it substitutes an emphasis on the history of techniques and, especially, of the purely technologically determined aspects of techniques. For the semantic analysis of the mind carried on by New Critics and pursued by McLuhan in the *Bride*, it substitutes an even more abstract type of formalism—the emphasis on those aspects of form determined by the modes of transmission of information. By these strategies McLuhan manages to move the concerns of the book further away from areas which he would label content, whether it be content of a historical-ideological or of a synchronic-semantic analysis. Yet he manages to preserve the importance of a kind of history (history of techniques and technology) and a kind of formal analysis (the analysis of the form of transmission apart from the form of what is transmitted). In achieving this he fails to distinguish between two levels or kinds of form that writers on semiology, such as Roland Barthes in *Elements of Semiology*, have insisted must be made.

McLuhan's emphasis on the history of techniques and technology, and his analysis of the mode or form of transmission are important and admirable. Unfortunately, in developing these themes, he empties his account of any of the other aspects of reality, thus creating the distortion of a history of techniques without any content with which the techniques may interplay to produce a way of handling concrete artifacts. By abandoning any means of relating to meaning in the more traditional sense, he similarly empties the remaining reality of any semantic significance susceptible of semiological analysis. His taking such a step is basically a key repudiation of the techniques of the *Bride* which insisted upon the equivalent of a close reading of the text in the cultural analysis of ads, comics, and films. The total effect of such a repudiation, though, is to create a history that while apparently dynamic and progressive, is in actuality just a series of static states. Real history is a constant dialectical interplay, as Harold Innis' treatment of media in a historical complex makes clear. McLuhan's history must rather emphasize states or periods when, for no apparent reason other than some technological accident, techniques such as printing and the accompanying visual print, or telephone and television, gained ascendancy.

This account could be qualified if one carefully chose certain parts of McLuhan, just as the discussion of linear in the previous chapter could be altered if one selected McLuhan's remarks on the importance of Blake's "bounding line" (GG 265) in achieving tactility. Such verbal complexities are unavoidable in coping with McLuhan's way of operating, and it is possible only to discuss the major tendencies which manage to keep the work in progress to see if they sustain its development or not.

The Gutenberg Galaxy centres around a series of basic contrasts: the oral vs. the written; the visual vs. the auditory; the visual vs. the tactile; the linear vs. the mosaic (or non-linear); the individual and civilized vs. the tribal and participatory; phonetic vs. non-phonetic writing; script vs. print. From these basic pairs rises a wide variety of other relationships, but the major weight of the work quite obviously centres around an account of history in which the invention of the phonetic alphabet breaks up the illiterate situation of primitive man into an abstract, somewhat linear form. In so doing, it creates a specialized approach to experience which did not exist in the spoken language, but it does not go so far as to completely alienate man from his original state where he lived in a participatory, auditory-tactile universe.

The second revolution, though, the invention of movable type, does just that. It elevates (through mechanization) the effects of the phonetic alphabet to a point where they caused man to become removed from the tactile and auditory world, fragmented his sensory life, and created an intense bias towards the visual. The discovery of electricity led to the third revolution beginning with the telegraph and moving to the computer and the television set. This final revolution reverses the effect of the second, returning man again to a sense of the auditory and the tactile, reintegrating his experience, and removing the bias towards the visual. At the same time, the development of man which had, with the discovery of phonetic writing and then of print, moved more and more towards individualism, reverses itself in the direction of a neo-primitivism and tribal participation.

Stated in these terms it is clear that McLuhan has created a fiction, perhaps a myth, but certainly a far from adequate historical analysis. The mythic possibilities of McLuhan's account rise from the very points that he chooses to explore, for they focus on some of the major intellectual questions that arose in the latter part of the nineteenth and the earlier part of the twentieth century and have now become the preoccupation of the average educated man of the present. By choosing categories such as eye and ear, script and print, print and electronic media, McLuhan brings into dramatic focus some of the chief dilemmas of the contemporary communications explosion. Choosing terms like individualism and participation, civilization and tribal existence, fragmentation and organic unity, McLuhan taps the insecurities that have grown up as a result of awareness of ethnocentrism, of the need for abandoning self-centred individualism, and of the desire for a non-alienated existence in the modern world. Any harmonic medley of these terms is bound to have a far reaching effect in itself only if it ensnares the mind in a contemplation about their interplay.

This is the stuff that myth is made of. The only difficulty is that myth, unlike poetry, is a depoliticized logos that loses the intense detail of any real poetry or real history. But myths can be important and if at times their containers (like Addison's) are partly poetic or artistic they can be revealing and worth analyzing. The *Galaxy* is the starting point for achieving such importance in McLuhan's mythic world, for that is where the detailed intellectual justification, if any, for that world begins.

The *Galaxy* approaches its subject from an attempt to establish an inner correspondence to external phenomena. The theme occurs in the first section-heading following the opening analysis of *King Lear*:

> The interiorization of the technology of the phonetic alphabet translates man from the magical world of the ear to the neutral visual world. (GG 18)

The concept that McLuhan has in mind behind the statement, he attributes to Edward Hall's *The Silent Language* where Hall speaks of the fact that today "man has developed extensions for practically everything" (GG 4). This McLuhan sees as an "outering," so that clothes and houses which Hall describes as "extensions of man's biological temperature-control mechanisms" become, for McLuhan, a type of technology in which man projects outward ("outers" or "utters") his ability to control the temperature of his body. The phonetic alphabet, then, becomes a way in which man extends his ability to segmentalize language so that it too is "outered" or "uttered." For McLuhan these two processes are analogues and they both become, within his definition, "media" (a subject he amplifies in *Understanding Media*). The difficulty is that McLuhan does not make a distinction between print as a secondary or tertiary mode of transmission and housing as a primary construct, i.e. whereas print uses writing which uses speech which itself is an uttering in the most primary sense, the house and clothing occupy a very different relationship. Even if eventually houses or clothes become signs, they become signs in a very different sense from speech and its projections, as Roland Barthes' *Elements of Semiology* clearly shows.

McLuhan, however, chooses to use this concept of extension without asking questions about the differences between his kinds of extensions and the weapons, or furniture, or power tools that Hall discusses. Hall after all does say, "All man-made material things can be treated as extensions of what man once did with his body or some specialized part of his body" (GG 4). McLuhan links the notion of extension to the notion of "closure" or "completion" as found in psychology and discussed by J. Z. Young in *Doubt and Certainty in Science*. Presumably, the concept of closure, related to the concept of extension, indicates that each extension seeks a closure and that it attempts to suppress other extensions. What occurs to make such a translation purely speculative is that McLuhan mixes or, it might be said, intermingles, two different things: the internal sensory activity and a series of bodily extensions which are not necessarily extensions of the sensory system, but of the total productive systems of the body. "Closure" is a concept involving brain activity; "extension," a concept involving motor activity. McLuhan will tell us such a statement is linear and visual-oriented, but there is the small fact that if my foot is broken it does not have the same effect as the sensory system being deranged, in the higher mental processes, by schizophrenia. Nor does an appeal to the post-amputation "pain" that remains where a limb had been (an example he uses in *War and Peace in the Global Village*) assist in solving the dilemma. It may be that in some quasi-mystical, occult kind of way there some day might be a relation found between the senses and an extension such as a hammer or a car (perhaps the "vibrations" the young speak about), but even this is not the same as involvement in the central core of the nervous system, the brain, where the need for closure arises.

McLuhan's *Galaxy*, however, needs closure, since he is attempting to establish a bridge between the outer phenomena, the extensions, and the inner phenomena, the organization of the sensorium. By juxtaposing Hall and Young—an anthropologist against an anatomist specializing in the brain—without comment, his method asserts that the connection is made. By further juxtaposing Hall with a definition of language, from Leslie White's *The Science of Culture*, as "a tool which made it possible for man to accumulate experience and knowledge in a form that made easy transmission and maximum use possible" (GG 5), the three steps are complete: the linkage of sensory completion, extensions of man's body, and speech as a tool and extension. As a result, using the sanction of Hall and Young and White, it is possible to treat print and phonetic writing as extensions affecting sensory balance.

Unfortunately, McLuhan is trivializing an important method of discovery, for perhaps by examining together the whole of Hall, the whole of Young, and the whole of some reputable accounts of language, serious insight into the complexities of human semiology might emerge. But this would be a more complex process than McLuhan is carrying on. What he achieves is the suggestion that that is what he might be doing. What he is actually doing is allowing three bits and pieces to sit side by side as does the maker of a collage who is interested only in the arrangement of these bits and pieces. Unlike visual material, though, quotations have references, inhere in texts, and do not necessarily evoke the whole of the text by their mere citation. The result, in McLuhan, is to establish by assertion without actually manifesting the process: for example, Hall, Young, Leslie White, and vibrations equal speech as an extension of man's sensory system which, when it is extended in print, is changed by the effect of print on the sensory system.

For this is what McLuhan requires—a bridge between the visual sense and print, a bridge between the auditory sense and speech. His analysis insists on correspondences between external phenomena (chiefly technological—little is ever said about the social context of speech) and internal processes. To take the inner first, since "interiorization" seems to be McLuhan's own beginning point, the McLuhan doctrine of the senses in the *Galaxy* becomes a key. His concept, as modern as it may appear, is closely linked in McLuhan's mind with the doctrine of the *sensus communis* in mediaeval philosophy. According to his account, the *sensus communis* works through a ratio of the senses acting as the key to the cognitive processes by a means of translating and transforming the information of the various senses. McLuhan's tendency to speak of a five-sense (and usually in fact a three-sense) sensorium in his works is linked to that rather naïve psychology.

There are two problems here: first, McLuhan's treatment of individual sensory mechanisms; and second, his account of sensory interplay which is connected with the idea of a common sense that acts as a translator of sensory activity into cognitive processes. (See "Joyce, Aquinas and the Poetic Process," in Connolly, ed., *Joyce's Portrait: Criticisms and Critiques*; and Bernard Muller-Thyme, "The Common Sense, Perfection of the Order of Pure Sensitivity," in *The Thomist*, vol. 2, no. 3, 1940.) Since so much of the *Galaxy* depends on what is at stake in his use of visual, auditory, and tactile, it is essential to come to an understanding of what McLuhan means by these terms.

Superficially, McLuhan's use of "visual" seems completely erroneous. He discusses the present age as one that has a pronounced "visual" bias inherited from the pre-electric Gutenberg era way of regarding things. Yet specialists on visual art, such as Gyorgy Kepes (a theorist McLuhan frequently cites on the visual arts), make observations such as:

The appearances of things in our man-made world no longer reveal their character: images imitate forms; forms cheat functions; functions are robbed of their natural sources emanating from human needs. Our cities, our buildings (counterfeit inside and out), objects for use, the packaging of goods, posters, the advertising in our newspapers—even our clothes, our gestures, our physiognomies—are often without visual integrity. . . .

To give direction and order to this formlessness, we have to go back to our roots. We need to regain the health of our creative faculties, especially of our visual sensibilities. (*Education of Vision* i–ii)

This statement of Kepes' sounds more like the McLuhan of *The Mechanical Bride* than of the *Galaxy*. More important, it suggests, in terms of the sources McLuhan appears to credit, that the world is as impoverished visually as it is in tactile and auditory experience. John Fekete, commenting on the problem of McLuhan's treatment of vision, has pointed out that McLuhan fails to "recognize the existence of a unified and objective independent reality reflected, in its full movement in human consciousness, in such a way that different senses respond to different aspects of the same reality." Naturally such a failure, which results from McLuhan's basic involvement in the same kind of idealism as Northrop Frye's, can only trap one within an abstract circle of unrealities—which is, of course, precisely the problem with McLuhan's whole discussion of vision.

Terms in the *Galaxy*, such as "visual" and "tactile," have nothing to do with the range of meaning within which they are normally used. Taking McLuhan's term "visual," it is possible to criticize him (erroneously) as Wylie Sypher has done in *Literature and Technology* (74–126) for failing to recognize that there are different kinds of vision. Sypher distinguishes light and colour vision from geometric and stereometric vision. But, in fact, Mc-Luhan, too, does distinguish between them to the extent that he speaks of colour television as increasing tactility or of black and white television, which he analyzes as "light through" rather than "light on," as fundamentally tactile. Sypher is right with respect to the term, but not with respect to McLuhan's use of it, for Mc-Luhan uses "visual" normally with respect to stereometric or geometric vision and "tactile" with respect to light and colour vision. If this is so, it symbolically and metaphorically suggests that geometric vision emphasizes one sense, while colour vision is based on the interplay of the senses. Most theories of vision, however, would suggest there is substantial interplay involved in the learning of geometric vision, possibly to an even greater extent than in the problem of perceiving colour and light.

In the *Galaxy*, McLuhan associates the concept of "light through" (the basis of the mosaic mode of television and therefore of its tactility) with Gothic stained-glass windows, following Panofsky who, in *Scholasticism and Gothic Architecture*, discusses the windows with light coming through them as representative of the mediaeval technique of "manifestatio." This interest also shows a close link between McLuhan's theories of the visual as associated with "light on" rather than "light through" and Joyce's use of theories of vision and light in the closing sections of *Finnegans Wake*.

The *Wake* is a night book which discusses the process of dreaming as a coming-forth by day. Consequently, it comes to a conclusion (or at least a quasi-conclusion) with the rising of the sun. One of the concluding sections has the sun rise on a triptych stained-glass window in a chapel. The different parts of the triptych relate to the three colour receptors usually posited in a three-primary system of colour perception. Following this image, there is a debate between St. Patrick and the archdruid Balkelly (Berkeley) over the nature of vision—white light vs. colour—which ends with a reconciliation of the two theories as differing approximations to the same reality in spite of the archdruid's idealism and Patrick's realism.

McLuhan lifts the interplay of Joyce's imagery and the cognitive values of his analysis without comprehending the importance of recognizing that all of this information is a way of approximating the same realities. Patrick and the archdruid are both discussing waking up, but one in terms of light and the other of colour where the light that Patrick discusses has to do with a world of perspective, distance, depth, etc. But what McLuhan tries to do is to translate Joyce's discussion into a flat discussion of a pseudo-scientific nature. In the process, Joyce's richness and the richness of a scientific account of the senses are both lost, although superficially McLuhan's adaptation of Joyce's account to a general theory of sense interplay calls the average person's attention to complexities that are usually overlooked and that may be extremely sophisticated. While popularizing Joyce or popularizing the shifts within scientific thought as they impinge on human communications, McLuhan raises questions that are far too often overlooked by individuals working in these areas.

"Visual" then, as a McLuhanesque term, needs to be carefully watched each time it is used. The "play" with the word that he carries on is relevant because it is playing with the popular senses of the term and a multitude of specialized senses which the popular sense often overlooks. By bringing them into interplay, McLuhan reveals the disastrous weaknesses in popular knowledge about the whole mechanism of perception, sensation, and cognition and the way in which such weakness is therefore bound to vulgarize and cheapen popular life (even if this is not the moral that the McLuhan who is legitimating adman and media man admits drawing from it).

But if this is true, then what the term "visual" means in the *Galaxy* has to do with certain modes of perception developed out of a certain context of participation and *not* necessarily determining so radical a change in the sensorial system as McLuhan might make us think. To take a simple example: the lines indicating the tactility of experience to which a barefoot pilgrim is exposed, as rendered by a Renaissance painting, can be paralleled with reasonable ease to photographs of barefoot hippies or of barefoot Vietnamese. The point is that in each case the visual translations of the tactile, whether in a perspectival or post-Gutenberg perception, are in many ways similar. If there is to be any continuity to the most basic of languages, the body language, or to language itself, there must be a continuity as well as a change which McLuhan's radical accounts of unique technical revolutions attempt to overlook.

The treatment of the term visual in something like *The Gutenberg Galaxy* owes its impetus particularly to the importance that criticism after I. A. Richards again placed on metaphor. To McLuhan, using a term this way is a probe, and playing on translations of it is a way of discovery. This may be all right, if ultimately what is discovered can be reintegrated into the kind of total vision of man that McLuhan talks about—the kind of vision some critics might argue is in Joyce or Shakespeare or Walter Scott. Unfortunately, in McLuhan it seems not to turn out this way. The reason is that the particular range of "visual" always must be reduced back to a pseudo-academic argument about the nature of print and the effect of a print-oriented attitude on the way things develop. This immediately ties the relationship of clusters of terms too tightly together for them to be successfully separated by the occasional contradiction or paradox.

"Visual" then, in the *Galaxy*, becomes not only tied to geometric vision, perspective, and print-orientation, but also to mechanism, to puritanism, to schizophrenic-type alienated behaviour, to individualism. Yet if vision and print produced individualism, is it not during that period that one of the major modes of rebellious individualism was to be tactile, to enjoy the other senses, to run naked? The modern reversal in values that McLuhan posits was always present to the individual sensate person, as he knows. What he is actually talking about are public values, for to act thus in Salem would have led to exposure as a witch, and elsewhere to being an eccentric (that is, except in areas so impoverished that this type of life was enforced—in such areas Dickens develops many of his most intense multi-sensory effects).

When McLuhan talks about Dickens' rebellion against mechanism in *Hard Times*, he is speaking about Dickens' view of the way that the rich attempted to impose a way of life on the poor. In the scenes of poverty in *Hard Times* and *Bleak House*, odour, touch, even taste, play major roles in assaulting the reader's sensorium with the horrors of impoverished urban life. To associate Dickens with a primarily eye-oriented age is difficult. Even if one of Dickens' techniques—the masterful description—is visually oriented, it is much more complex, as Sergei Eisenstein's discussion of Dickens and the cinematic suggests. Again, it would be oversimplifying to say that McLuhan does not realize this, but it is important to be aware that his distinctions cannot ultimately handle this kind of relationship. McLuhan's mosaic reduces far too much of the emphasis in Eisenstein to a discussion of montage as a specific example of juxtaposition or collage rather than treating the full complexity of film form.

Early in *The Gutenberg Galaxy* (26), McLuhan draws his distinction between "eye" and "ear," the "auditory" and the "visual": "Civilization gives the barbarian or tribal man an eye for an ear and is now at odds with the electronic world" says the gloss on the section. Arguing the centrality of the "phonetic alphabet" (as a new extension of man) in Greek society, McLuhan stresses the "utter discrepancy" between the phonetic alphabet and other kinds of writing: "Only the phonetic alphabet makes a break between eye and ear, between semantic meaning and visual code" (GG 27). Apart from the fact that these are two different statements and that the first one would make Gutenberg man dyslexic and unable to read, the first statement is false and the second true only within a limited sphere of reference.

Writing, naturally, does involve a break between semantic meaning and visual code, but even non-phonetic forms of writing such as Chinese gradually evolve into syllabaries and therefore also result in a break between semantic meaning and visual code. But phonetic writing, rather than initially dividing eye and ear, in fact depends on the working together of eye and ear, for it depends on the ability of the eye to assign different signs to different phones which the ear perceives. Now this is a kind of fragmentation, but as an abstraction it more or less closely approximates the very kind of fragmentation on which speech itself depends. Before ever placing a voiced or unvoiced bilabial stop [b] or [p] into a system of letters, it is necessary to know that "bit" and "pit" can be distinguished because the difference of voiced from the voiceless is significant.

Yet while making all these mistakes, McLuhan reminds the reader that the dynamics involved in script and print are important and must be carefully considered. He realizes, as the totality of the *Galaxy* shows, that what really makes his point important are facts about what changes because of script or print. The repeatability of print makes the visual reproduction of diagrams, drawings, art works, and visual prints possible and opens up for the first time vast quantitative increases in visual information that is identical from one reproduction to another. This is bound to change both the sensibility and the intellectual development of man. With respect to a point such as the one under discussion, the fact that makes it important is that by the nineteenth century most readers had tended to become heavily eye-oriented, suppressing the kind of slower, contemplative reading on which much earlier poetry depended.

Yeats and others could discuss Morris' poetry and many novels as shaped around the printing press, where scanning and skimming came to be encouraged, as well as the possibility of extending a single tone over a vast extent of work. McLuhan's sensitivity to print came from his literary training and especially his study of rhetoric, of Mallarmé, and of Joyce. Joyce, especially in *Finnegans Wake*, re-created a language in which the reader had to integrate eye and ear by having to bring into simultaneous interplay an oral reading and a visual reading, an activity which also had the effect of slowing down the reader and making him contemplate puns and other linguistic effects.

The *Galaxy*, in its technique of distinguishing phonetic writing from print by insisting on the increasing tendency to accept fragmentation, as a matter of course fails to see that a complex kind of fragmentation is required both in Joyce's work and in many of its earlier models. The mosaic is an assemblage of fragments, bits and pieces. Just as speech and writing, its very mode calls attention to the way it is a result of a multitude of elements. The particular strategy McLuhan is discussing is the way that such assemblages then become totalities transcending the parts. But surely this is not unique to the twentieth century and is a fact implicit in virtually any form of intellectual or artistic existence. The *Galaxy*, and to a much greater extent McLuhan's later books, tries to sweep away this type of recognition of the essential nature of the bits and pieces by using concepts, such as totality, integrated whole, and the like. But this is precisely where McLuhan's mixed form, which is neither art nor intellectual, philosophical prose, comes to such disaster.

George Lukacs, discussing the drama and epic, very succinctly sums up the need for totality in major art forms:

> Tragedy and great epic thus both lay claim to portraying the totality of the life-process. It is obvious in both cases that this can only be a result of artistic structure, of formal concentration in the artistic reflection of the most important features of objective reality. For obviously the real, substantial, infinite and extensive totality of life can only be reproduced mentally in a relative form.
>
> This relativity, however, acquires a peculiar form in the artistic reflection of reality. For to become art, it must never appear to be relative. A purely intellectual reflection of facts or laws of objective reality may openly admit this relativity and must in fact do so, for if any form of knowledge pretends to be absolute, ignoring the

dialectical character of the merely relative, i.e. incomplete, reproduction of the infinity of objective reality, it is inevitably falsified and distorts the picture. (*The Historical Novel* 104)

McLuhan, as the title *War and Peace in the Global Village* betrays, is trying to write academic epic. But the particular mixing of genre as he carries it out is not that of the Menippean satirists whom he loves and who excelled in this mode (though ironically enough *The Gutenberg Galaxy* refers again and again to those individuals—Rabelais, Erasmus, Pope, Swift, and Joyce). What their visions were that McLuhan's are not, are satiric visions of the intellectual world of their time. If McLuhan writes satire, he deliberately conceals it behind a façade for the purpose of making it commercially viable and he conceals it so well that few of his critics have accused him of writing it at all.

Even if, however, the treatment of the senses and of the linguistic phenomena are more suggestive than useful or correct, the most impressive thing about the *Galaxy* is its humanistic erudition. Therefore, as a way of seeing the transition from the *Galaxy* to *Understanding Media*, it is useful to explore that erudition in terms of seeing McLuhan as the new Renaissance humanist receiving support from and paying court to the Executive Suite rather than the Throne Room.

The Gutenberg Galaxy is fundamentally centred around the history of the Renaissance. The works, individuals, themes, attitudes, and analyses all relate to the development and meaning of Renaissance history in Western culture. That age, the era of transition from mediaeval to modern, must be a key for any examination that attempts to understand both the originality and the eclecticism of McLuhan's insights. So many of the witticisms and so much of the theory stem from it—his attitudes towards the arts and the artists; his way of seeing nature (and the "nature" created by man) as art forms; his view of technologists and scientists as contemporary schoolmen or *moderni*. Even McLuhan's own posture as a new humanist discussed in the last chapter relates to traditions that are transmitted through the Renaissance from the earlier heritage of humanism and scholasticism.

8

Humanist Manqué and Pseudo-Clown

In the *Galaxy*, McLuhan very rapidly adopts a safe position with respect to the corporate power of the contemporary world. Part of this is hidden by the mask of the learned fool; part of it is a result of his relation to the powers of the managerial world. His intensely Catholic and mediaeval sense of the corporate may even have made the executive suite as attractive a base of operations for him as the throne room had been for the early humanists. In any case, it is perfectly consonant with the way that he, and others whom he endorses, analyzes the role of the corporation in contemporary society.

There is an interesting rapprochement here to be examined between McLuhan and individuals from the management consultant world. A good example would be Peter Drucker who sees the Catholic Church as a corporation, even more efficient than General Motors. Many, as has Drucker in his latest book *The Age of Discontinuity*, have shifted from influencing McLuhan to being influenced by him. Just as the adman may be seen as a rhetorician with his roots in the Renaissance revival of the Roman conception of the orator, so, if our interpretation of McLuhan's stance is correct, it would appear that the joker in the executive suite has his roots in the jester in the king's court.

The Gutenberg Galaxy opens with King Lear and closes with the Dunciad, both humanistic works that are deeply involved in problems of folly and wisdom. McLuhan himself loves to play with puns and witticisms, to clown, and to joke. In fact, the essence of his method is a way of allowing his mind to play freely with the language and the images of contemporary society. So it is not surprising that works in which the play of wit is important seem more central to the Galaxy than might be expected—works such as Rabelais' Gargantua or Swift's Gulliver's Travels or Joyce's Finnegans Wake.

The key to all of this and how it is related to McLuhan's professional role as an educator and his self-imposed role as corporate clown may well emerge by looking back at the Renaissance, not only as McLuhan sees it but also as it is treated in works he uses as references.

One such source is Josef Huizinga, a Dutch intellectual historian noted for The Waning of the Middle Ages, his work on the transition from the Middle Ages to the Renaissance. Huizinga also wrote Homo Ludens: A Study of the Play Element in Culture. This book is a point of reference for McLuhan in both Understanding Media and War and Peace in the Global Village where he discusses the significance of games as a medium of communication. Huizinga demonstrates in his discussion of the "ludic" or play element of culture how it is related to other humanist themes such as comedy, folly, and drama. The fact that Huizinga wrote The Waning of the Middle Ages is not divorced from his interest in the play element of culture, just as McLuhan's interest in Huizinga and the complex of ideas which distinguish yet relate comedy, folly, wisdom, games, and play is not separate from the fact that McLuhan originally began his scholarly career as a Renaissance specialist. People like Huizinga and Panofsky (the art historian who was also interested in the Middle Ages and the Renaissance) provided important guides for McLuhan's media study, as may be seen in his doctoral thesis "Thomas Nashe and His Place in the Learning of His Time" (shortly to be published by McGraw-Hill).

94

In the various issues of *Explorations*, McLuhan wrote, on a number of occasions, about the importance of the sixteenth century in the history of media as well as about the importance of the shift from manuscript to moveable type in the Renaissance. With the publication of *The Gutenberg Galaxy*, these ideas became the foundation stone for his historical theories of media and technology. Yet the interest here is hardly separable from his more general interest in the Renaissance and its significance, something which considerably pre-dates his involvement with media and pop kulch. The Renaissance weaves together many of the issues to which McLuhan constantly returns in his work: educational theory; a theory and use of wit and comedy; the development of paradox as a literary and artistic method; the birth of the essay style; the transformation of mediaeval universalism into individualism; and a view of culture in which there is an intimate relationship of an intellectual élite to the power of the state or to the power of the Church as a superstate. Each of these themes has apparent significance throughout the McLuhan canon, but each of them is implicitly involved in *The Gutenberg Galaxy* as an introduction to the first general enunciation of his media theories in *Understanding Media*.

The way to begin an understanding of *The Gutenberg Galaxy*, then, is to find what McLuhan found important in his study of Nashe. Among other concerns, the Nashe thesis dealt with two central themes of McLuhan's early criticism:

1) The development of a theory of style which contrasted the Senecan and Ciceronian approaches to rhetoric and rhetorical theory (which also forms a part of McLuhan's article, "An Ancient Quarrel in Modern America" [LC 223–34]);

2) The interplay in the history of the trivium (the studies of grammar, logic, and rhetoric) between the Ancient and Modern, the humanist and the scholastic, the logician and the grammarian, the learned orator and the analytical dialectician as producing contrasting approaches to the nature and relevance of education.

These two themes that he found to be part of the background of learning in Nashe's time were, for McLuhan, interrelated. He suggests that there are affinities between the broad aims of Senecanism and the scholastic movement, just as there are affinities between the broad aims of Ciceronianism and the philosophy of Augustine or the theories of the humanists. He recognized that these affinities shifted and appeared in different mixtures in different individuals, so that in the Renaissance a humanist might be interested in the Senecan, or a Puritan in the Ciceronian.

If such academic or historical concerns seem a digression from media and modern life, McLuhan insists as early as the *Bride* and as late as *Counterblast* (1969) that both are essential to understanding the scholastic-Puritan roots of the modern technologist. In addition, they are necessary to understanding the "liberal college programmes" attempt (such as Hutchins') to develop theories restoring an educational aim derived from a desire to produce the learned and prudent orator of the humanist tradition. Besides, the analysis which sees the history of the trivium as involved in modes of communication and modes of education, and which sees this basic set of studies of the trivium as a way of teaching the art of expression, leads rather directly to McLuhan's interest in the media as new languages of expression requiring a new equivalent to the trivium. It may well be that, in the applications of the analysis, McLuhan fails to adequately investigate all of the components and has oversimplified grossly the contemporary need: nevertheless much might be learned by our judicious return to the interests from which his own perspective developed and the use of them as a way of establishing a genuinely contemporary equivalent. Perhaps studies such as Roland Barthes' *Elements of Semiology* or Margaret Mead's "semiotics" (study of the total communication process, as she defines the term) are a step in that direction.

Basically, McLuhan views the history of the trivium—which provided much of the base for elementary education from the classical period to the eighteenth century—as vitiated by a quarrel between the two styles (let us call them for convenience the Ciceronian and the Senecan). His approach to these two styles, and the two different points of view inherent in them, suggests a very early interest in the technique of "hateful contraries," perhaps going back to his study of idealistic philosophy at the University of Manitoba and his interest, after his conversion to Catholicism, in the "paradoxical" technique of G. K. Chesterton. The Ciceronian point of view wished to train students to become the learned encyclopaedist, the *doctus orator*, who was also skilled in the arts of persuasion and who committed himself to the study of grammar (exegesis as well as structure of language) and rhetoric. The idea of the *doctus orator* was not only an Augustinian ideal, but provided the image of the humanist and the ideal of the Renaissance courtier. The Senecan point of view wished to train logicians or dialecticians and in the mediaeval period gave birth to scholasticism with its emphasis on the primacy of logic and dialectics. Its style was not continuous and eventually this, McLuhan seems to suggest, led to the development of the *pro et contra* (or *sic et non*) technique of logic characteristic of mediaeval disputation and going back in one form to Platonic dialogue. Renaissance humanism was born out of the conflict between the *scholastics* for whom logic and dialectic had become primary (incidentally using a method of oral disputation or dialogue) and the *humanists* who wished to return to the primacy of grammar and rhetoric.

Such a brief history of the problem is fully fair neither to McLuhan nor to the immense complexity of the whole dispute, though it is an area of which many enthusiasts and critics of McLuhan are too little aware. Given his "allusive" and suggestive style, it is implied in much of his work. His theory of style develops from writers such as Morris Croll, George Williamson, and many of the early twentieth century students of Renaissance prose style and classical rhetoric; his theories of education come from similar studies of the trivium and of rhetoric, from the studies of H. I. Marrou on classical education, and from the writings of Etienne Gilson and other mediaeval scholars on the conflict between the scholastics and the humanists.

It is from these points of reference that it was possible for him to produce the kind of analysis that calls Francis Bacon "the PR man of the Renaissance." In Bacon's writings, especially *The Advancement of Learning*, there is a discussion of the role of the two general kinds of style: first there is the short, aphoristic (and in Bacon's own practice, balanced) style which provides a way of presenting knowledge concocted for use, by following the contours of the mind (the basis of Bacon's *Essays*)—the "painting of the thoughts" as Pascal later suggested; second is the magistral style, a style concocted to persuade by delivering knowledge that had already been thought out in a manner calculated to "move" people (which Bacon uses in *The Advancement of Learning*). Though again this is only a sketchy presentation, we have seen that the basis for McLuhan's own method lies in part in Bacon's aphoristic style, and it is possible to see a way in which McLuhan might conceive of himself as a counter-Bacon (using Bacon as a counter-environment), taking traditional humanism and synthesizing it with the scholasticism of contemporary technology by abandoning the continuous (semi-magistral) style of the nineteenth century for a new, aphoristic style of the twentieth. Fundamentally, McLuhan may have seen this strategy as a defence of humanism as he had experienced it in the universities, and just as possibly a way of defending the Leavis type of humanism and reconciling it with the mediaeval humanism of St. Thomas Aquinas. In spite of this it may not have been what was needed in order to preserve the real values of the classical tradition or of Erasmus' humanism.

Throughout his early work McLuhan uses this historical knowledge of the Renaissance and its background as an analytical tool. In an essay on the Southern Agrarian movement, which appeared in 1945 in the *Sewanee Review*, McLuhan analyzed the conflict between North and South in similar terms. He argued that the South continued the tradition of the Ciceronian *doctus orator* in its educational system, producing a gentleman interested in politics, law, and the arts of expression, while the North produced technologists and financiers dedicated to specialism. The North through its Puritan institutions had inherited the tradition of the dialecticians, the schoolmen, and the *moderni*, who in their time had argued against the model of the Sophist or *doctus orator* in favour of an education based on dialectics. So for McLuhan, the history of the North and South was merely another stage in the educational conflict between humanist and scholastic, ancient and modern. In the process he also develops his method so that it can be extended to more general manifestations of cultural phenomena and national history (although the method also has all of the implicit dangers that are found in any approach to a culture or to history that merely pursues leading ideas and formal patterns without examining their specific manifestations). Not only does McLuhan's analysis of the background of the world of learning in Nashe's time illuminate the conflict between North and South, it also reveals the role that Edgar Allan Poe played in American literary history, and explains why Poe attracted the attention of the European continent, especially France.

Since Poe provides important images for McLuhan, and since he is a link with the South, it is important to realize that in another essay McLuhan links Poe's European reputation to his Southern educational training and its roots in the same classical humanism that also produced Jeffersonian democracy, a politic he praised in *The Mechanical Bride*, possibly following Pound's lead in *Jefferson and/or Mussolini*. McLuhan's analysis of agrarianism may very well stress the more authoritarian aspects of humanism as they were transmitted into the South, and thus fail to see the way the philosophies of Nicholas of Cusa or Erasmus might be rediscovered in the new humanism emerging among East European Marxists such as Kolakowski or Svitak. This pattern is not only evident in Southern agrarianism, for McLuhan also discovers it in other contemporary American controversies of the forties. In "An Ancient Quarrel in Modern America" he argues that the humanist-scholastic controversy, the ideal of the *doctus orator* as opposed to the dialectician, lies behind the controversy between Hutchins and his great books programme, and liberal educators like Dewey. Dewey, in McLuhan's historical script, plays the role of the *moderni* and Hutchins, the humanist (and possibly just as an additional corroboration it is amusing to note that Hutchins comes from Kentucky, south of the Mason-Dixon line). Although McLuhan may have rejected the stance of his early period up to *The Mechanical Bride*, it is interesting to note that Dewey re-emerges in this role in *The Gutenberg Galaxy* as well as some later works. The ancient quarrel is really generalized to a view of the basic tension between the two cultures running through the whole American tradition, a perspective that might have emanated even more forcefully from a Canadian accustomed to thinking in terms of biculturalism.

Yet it is not only this particular example that McLuhan is interested in, for the history of humanistic educational conflicts has a crucial importance to McLuhan in explaining the causes of a variety of historical phenomena. Some of his insights from this period, particularly as they were developed in his thesis on Nashe, were taken up by writers like Walter Ong in his writings on Ramus; W. K. Wimsatt and Cleanth Brooks in some parts of their *Literary Criticism: A Short History*; Aubrey Williams in his work on Pope's *Dunciad*; and Hugh Kenner in his criticism of Pound, Joyce, Beckett, and others.

Ong's work on Ramus, the Renaissance dialectician and rhetorician, has important bearings on McLuhan's own treatment of the role of printing and moveable type in developing a certain kind of sensibility and certain educational biases in individuals like Commenius. Ramus figures, in *The Gutenberg Galaxy*, as an evidence of the visual bias of print culture, since his particular dialectical method with its tendency to organize knowledge in tables develops not only out of the scholastic logical mind with its anti-humanist predilection, but does so under the influence of print technology with its bias in favour of methods of presenting learning in terms of schemata and outlines. What this earlier work of McLuhan on the Renaissance does, as well as the work of Ong which can be paralleled to it, is to raise serious doubts about the oversimplification that occurs in McLuhan's thesis about print—a limitation which in some ways grows out of a modernist (scholastic) sensibility seeking to attribute cultural change to a certain mode of operation, as much as it determines the mode of operation.

It should be apparent that McLuhan's involvement with the Renaissance is extensive and that the role of Bacon, Montaigne, Erasmus, and others in his thinking is highly significant. Much of his way of approaching Renaissance style, in fact, corresponds to Bacon's own discussion of style in *The Advancement of Learning* which, as has been indicated earlier, probably lies behind McLuhan's own form of writing. Bacon speaks of the *Essays* as style concocted for use (built up on a *pro et contra* logic and employing a modified development of the Senecan style) and of his other writings, such as *The Advancement of Learning* itself, as being presented in a magistral style designed to persuade (built up on the modification of a continuous Ciceronian style).

In their purer Renaissance forms, Bacon naturally attacks both styles as extremes. Bacon adopts the use of grammatical techniques of exegesis in order to apply them to the "reading" of the Book of Nature. He sees the mind as basically functioning in a *pro et contra* technique of dialectic in delivering such thought for use in the *Novum Organum* or the *Essays*. Similar analysis lies behind McLuhan's statement in the *Galaxy* that: "It is complete acceptance of the Book of Nature that makes Bacon so very mediaeval and so very modern. But the gap is this. The mediaeval Book of Nature was for *contemplatio* like the Bible. The Renaissance Book of Nature was for *applicatio* and use like movable type. A closer look at Francis Bacon will resolve this problem and elucidate the transition from mediaeval to the modern world" (GG 185). Earlier it was observed that McLuhan in *Understanding Media* resembled his own description of Bacon as PR man for the *moderni*. Just as Bacon joins the grammatical and the dialectical, the humanist and the scholastic, so McLuhan can appear to marry the scholastic-technological with the humanist tradition.

To see the sixteenth and early seventeenth centuries as producing bridge builders between script-oriented and print-oriented cultures is a natural outgrowth of McLuhan's thesis with its strong emphasis on the key importance of the discovery of moveable type. Even without following McLuhan's analysis of the primacy of that discovery, the shift of relation between the elements of the trivium (grammar, logic, rhetoric), and its use as a mode of communication and a mode of education, is one apparent phenomenon creating extensive shifts in communication, culture, and education during those centuries. Shifts in one set of attitudes and relations would obviously effect the other, so that the themes of the age which Bacon seems to summarize are prevalent throughout the age as McLuhan points out: "Another view of the book as bridge between the mediaeval and the modern is given by Erasmus. His new Latin version of the New Testament in 1516 was entitled *Novum Organum* in 1620. Erasmus directed the new print technology to the traditional uses of *grammatica* and rhetoric and to tidying up the sacred page. Bacon used the new technology for an attempt to tidy up the text of Nature" (GG 185).

Erasmus, deeply involved in education as well as theology, is a key figure in the processes outlined from *The Gutenberg*

Galaxy to *Counterblast* (1969). Such writers as Huizinga held him to be one of the key figures of the humanist transition from mediaeval to Renaissance. As a figure he provides some contrast with Bacon, and could hardly be described as a PR man in quite the same way. Possibly the whole process of trying to understand McLuhan as a humanist manqué is to understand where he tries to join the Erasmian, the Baconian, and other sixteenth and seventeenth century models in an adapted form to his own vision of the twentieth century.

There are various Renaissance life styles for intellectuals. At one extreme there is that of Aretino, at the other, Thomas More. Naturally these are extremes, but the Aretino style, according to McLuhan in the *Galaxy*, is one based on using the new intellectual tools to gain power and patronage as far as possible. Quoting Samuel Putnam's introduction to his translation of Aretino's works, McLuhan points out: "If Aretino, at this time, was probably the most powerful man in Italy, perhaps in the world, the reason is to be found in the new force which he had discovered, that force which we today would call 'the power of the press'" (GG 194–5). Aretino's hypocrisy and dishonesty vitiate his sense of "the gigantism that is latent in the uniformity and repeatability of the printed word" (GG 194). But this is after all only one extreme of the currents that created Bacon as a PR man of a different kind and which made other humanists powerful servants of various princes—the desire to use their knowledge for power, especially presented with improved means of dissemination and transmission. The life of Thomas More, who eventually relinquished his power as a statesman rather than relinquish his principles, appears involved with his commitment to dialogue as a mode of expression as well as to his traditional religious commitments to a mediaeval sense of communion and community. More's writings polemically engaged the opponents of his theological position or played with satiric visions of the City of Man against the standards of the City of God and a City of the Future.

Between More and Aretino is a vast scale of subtle differences which somehow seems to disappear in McLuhan's analysis of the power of the new medium over the ways of seeing, sensing, and acting. Yet even in More, as in Erasmus, there is an association with power and a strategy to attempt to develop their individual Lucianic and skeptical intellectual poses within the power complex of the Renaissance. More and Erasmus—readily able to cast each other in the roles of learned fools, as Erasmus' title *Encomium Moriae* (Praise of Folly) with its obvious pun on his friend's name suggests—used techniques of irony and comedy to pursue their own works and they stressed the importance of witty learning, the jesting tale, and the jest book. Satire, comedy, wit, and humour became strategies for preserving the humanist ideal in a real world that strove against it. McLuhan appears to translate some of this into the twentieth century, but so far he has not produced full satiric fictions like More's *Utopia* or Erasmus' *Folly*, preferring rather to temper his wit within the essai concrète, a less ambitious and comprehensive form.

Erasmus, as one of the leading figures in education and the arts of communication in the Renaissance, has strong affinities with the way that McLuhan sees himself in his own time. McLuhan likes to combine erudition and wit and he sees himself as providing guiding power to the educational system as well as deriving power from association with the world of the corporation. As recently as *Counterblast* (1969) McLuhan has linked Erasmus, "the first to act on awareness that the new revolution would be felt in the classroom," with the fact that "the same situation confronts us" (132). Such statements should make the role of *The Gutenberg Galaxy* and *Understanding Media* as part of an educational programme abundantly clear. The Harvey-Nashe controversy analyzed in the thesis led to contemporary poetry and contemporary advertising; the Gutenberg phenomena added to this should lead to comprehending modern media and communications—so, at least by implication, reasons McLuhan.

What we have been seeing is the way that an analysis of the age of transition in the Renaissance is transformed into an analysis of the contemporary world as a similar age of transition. In the process, McLuhan chooses not Erasmus alone as model but something like a composite of Erasmus, Bacon, More, and a few others. Furthermore, just as he feels that they seem to have taken their guidance from the arts, he adopts Joyce, Pound, and Lewis as his guides.

This means, as ahistorical as McLuhan may seem to be, that the history of humanism and educational theory are central to his thought. The Renaissance development of perspective ("point of view" and "vanishing point"), as described by Panofsky, becomes one of these central themes of the shift from mediaeval to Renaissance to modern. The interest in this process culminates in a collection of verbi-visual essays (essais concrètes) which juxtapose illustration, poetry, pensées, and text—*Through the Vanishing Point*. The interest in exegesis as a way of understanding becomes another central theme rising out of the activity of Bacon and his mediaeval roots and relating it to the way that the school of New Criticism to which McLuhan had allegiance in the forties, reflected a modern attentiveness to the word as object of exegesis. Even the role of learned advisor (or sometimes "con man"), which fascinates McLuhan in practice as well as theory, becomes part of the Renaissance view of the philosopher-statesman and of the modern relevance of Aretino, Machiavelli, More, and Erasmus. These are the figures of *The Gutenberg Galaxy*, but they are also in metamorphosed fashion guiding figures in the process of working out a way to come to terms with the electric age, a pattern particularly evident in Canadian politics where one of McLuhan's princes, Pierre Elliott Trudeau, embraced Machiavelli as having contemporary significance.

McLuhan brings to his contemporary analysis all this weight of erudition derived from an extensive study of the Renaissance. If he were right and the contemporary moment were in some ways an electric age Renaissance, the temptation to apply his study for the purposes of futuristic prediction would indeed be great. And this is just what he himself seems to have done. Without for the moment questioning whether history can be treated this way, it is useful to ask whether McLuhan's own analysis is adequate.

Here it seems necessary to return to Erasmus and suggest that it is not. In the first place, McLuhan lacks the fundamental skeptical traits of most of the Renaissance and especially of Montaigne. Besides, his analysis seems to lead to problems like this: the Renaissance thinkers were deeply involved in asserting the primacy of the individual, and in the nature of morality and moral decisions; the new age is, according to McLuhan, becoming more corporate and tribal and consequently the individual moral decision must give way to the determination of the group by external factors such as technology. If this simple reversal were right, then perhaps a reversal of the analysis of the Renaissance might also be right. But it certainly is not, and by its very nature denies some of the relevant insights of both the newer Marxism of Eastern Europe and the new movements of youth and others in North America. Even the Renaissance was not unaware of the dilemma of individual and corporate, for More could use the currents of past history to create a Utopia which had an ongoing relationship to the history of the future, while still realizing that the personal interventions of his "hero," Raphael Hythloday, into the world of Utopia could have an influence on its history and on Raphael's own moral being.

The significance of the role of the intellectual as jester takes on considerable meaning in terms of handling such ambiguities. This is a constant humanist theme whether in Petronius or Lucian, More or Erasmus, Swift or Pope. Today it has become an important image to Eastern European philosophers, such as Leszek Kolakowski whose essay "The Priest and the Jester" defends a philosophy of jest and inconsistency, which is summarized in another Erasmus-like essay "In Praise of Inconsistency." McLuhan as an intellectual jester certainly fails to achieve those qualities that Kolakowski, whose position is closer to Erasmus, invokes in defending the philosophy of the jester as crucial in the contemporary world—the qualities of distrust of stabilized systems, rejection of the absolute, and the constant effort to consider all the reasons for the co-presence of contradictory ideas. In fact, Kolakowski could be describing Erasmus or More's position when he says: "Thus we opt for a vision of the world that offers the burden of reconciling in our social behaviour those opposites that are the most difficult to combine: goodness without universal toleration; courage without fanaticism; intelligence without discouragement; hope without blindness. All other fruits of philosophical thinking are unimportant" ("In Praise of Inconsistency" 36–7).

Erasmus, as a philosopher of jest, combined morality with a playfulness that allowed him to toy with the relative and the contradictory in a manner that McLuhan does not begin to approach in depth. This is because Erasmus focuses on the person in inter-action with the world, not on a summation or multiplication of mechanical elements and processes. Erasmus focuses on the erotic in man; McLuhan on a mechanical bride or bridegroom. The dialectic of McLuhan plays along the surface, while that of Eras-mus or Joyce involves greater depth and complexity.

Joyce is the cornerstone of the McLuhan vision according to McLuhan's own version of it. Joyce as jester has natural affinities with Erasmus as he has with the other writers in the humanist tradition that McLuhan frequently links with him—Rabelais, Cervantes, and Pope. One of the fundamental attractions of Joyce, as we have seen, was his use of the pun. In fact, an entire Mc-Luhan article develops out of one of Joyce's quips to a critic of his puns: "Yes, some of them are trivial and some of them are quad-rivial" (LC 23). The pun, instrument of the fool, the clown, or the jester, is a basic technique for Joyce and McLuhan.

Recently, in the *Dew Line* (vol. 1, no. 10, April 1969), Mc-Luhan investigates humour beginning with the pun as an example of "breakdown as breakthrough." The qualities that attracted him to Joyce must have been closely wrapped up in the way in which the language of Joyce "draws attention to the nature of language itself as multi-levelled," for this theme appears in those two ar-ticles as far apart as the fifties and the early seventies. But Joyce's remark and McLuhan's fascination with it also link three diverse areas of McLuhan's interest: the figure of the clown and the phi-losophy of folly; the importance of appreciating the nature of natural language; and the relevance to the contemporary world of the traditional arts of communication as reflected in classical education.

McLuhan's Joyce (for it is different from Joyce) may well pro-vide a way of getting at what McLuhan the erudite scholar and literary critic is trying to do in his essay style. After all, McLuhan has said of Joyce:

> We need new perceptions to cope. Our technologies are generations ahead of our thinking. If you even begin to think about these new technologies you appear as a poet because you are dealing with the present as the future. Most people look back for security. Much greater perceptions and energies are needed than simply mine in the

world in which we exist. Better talents are needed. James Joyce had these talents in a much more refined state. Joyce had a complete ecology of the man made environments which these critics should have read and studied long ago. (M:HC 301–2)

A phrase like "Where flash becomes word and silents selfloud" (FW 267) is precisely the kind that attracts McLuhan. It suggests relations between media and language even though in its context these may be somewhat less than central. McLuhan takes it and juxtaposes it with a discussion of Pavlov and Dewey and Dewey's supposedly inept educational strategies faced with a new modern world (WP 68). Since the source in Joyce is the school room or "triv and quad" section there is an appropriateness in the juxtaposition, for Joyce is discussing symbol as an element in human education. What happens in the transposition though is crucial. Joyce's world is one with a social action occurring among a group of persons in terms of interaction among them. The children are studying in a schoolroom atmosphere. McLuhan removes this to a discussion of the way Pavlovian and Deweyesque theories about the robotization of man just do not work in the electric world.

A favourite phrase used in a number of McLuhan books for explaining the relevance of Joyce is:

> The West shall shake the east awake . . .
> while ye have night for morn.

Now for McLuhan, this is fundamental to everything because it is about the orientalization of the West by electric technology and the meeting of East and West. Nathan Halpert in *McLuhan: Pro and Con* has pedantically queried McLuhan's misquoting of the phrase, which as it appears on page 473 of *Finnegans Wake* is "Walk while ye have the night for morn." Yet the pedantry has a point, for McLuhan's rendition eliminates the directive to a human person and the interest in a basic human action, whether or not he or Halpert happens to be right about Joyce's basic intents. Joyce's phrases always seem transposed into a somewhat sterile world when they move from the *Wake* to McLuhanese, for their two ways of viewing language (and everything else) are really rather different.

Joyce's brother Stanislaus wrote to him about his artistic vision being involved with "the relation or at least an analogy between the imagination in the intellect and the sexual instinct in the body [which] is worked out with a fantastic horror. . . . It is undoubtedly Catholic in temperament" (Ellman, *James Joyce* 590). No one can worry about McLuhan being charged with such activity. His writing tends to be free from the extremely basic awareness of the whole range of bodily experience, from the most public to the most intimate, that embarrassed Joyce's brother and his early reading audience. Yet Joyce, like Rabelais, Cervantes, and Pope, deeply involved his literary vision with the sensual, the sexual, the cloacal, and the erotic. The whole of *Finnegans Wake* (even if it is an index to media and many other things) is about what happens in one night in one bedroom in and out of one man's dream. For that matter *Ulysses* also ends in a bedroom. Joyce's work is intimately personal; in McLuhan the person qua person never appears.

From this base, it is also interesting to note the nature of the humour of Rabelais, Cervantes, Pope's *Dunciad*, and Joyce's *Wake* which McLuhan describes as the "four massive myths of the Gutenberg transformation of society" (GG 147). They all use a humour that is as immediately related to the world of Norman O. Brown's *Life Against Death* as to *The Gutenberg Galaxy* or *Understanding Media*. Even though McLuhan has mentioned Brown's views ("The Future of Sex," *Look*, 25 July 1967), unlike Joyce or even Brown he does not make the erotic central except through his rather interesting insistence on "tactility" as the mark of the more integral, that is, the more sensual.

Though Joyce does pursue the analogy between the imagination in the intellect and the sexual instinct in the body as a crucial part of his vision, it does not mean that he fails to see man as closely tied to the new technology. His hero, HCE, is described as a "paradigmatic ear" and a "patternmind" both of which suggest analogies with the technological, and HCE is also associated with highly technological modes of transmission:

> their tolvtubular high fidelity daildialler, as modern as tomorrow afternoon and in appearance up to the minute, (hearing that anybody in that ruad duchy of Wollinstown schemed to halve the

wrong type of data) equipped with supershielded umbrella antennas for distance getting and connected by the magnetic links of a Bellini-Tosti coupling system with a vitaltone speaker, capable of capturing skybuddies, harbour craft emittences, key clickings, vaticum cleaners, due to woman formed mobile or man made static and bawling the whowle hamshack and wobble down in an eliminium sounds pound so as to serve him up a melegoturny marygoraumd, eclectrically filtered for allirish earths and ohmes. (FW 309–10)

But this side of HCE is never separated from the more basic erotic and sexual aspects of his activity which, for Joyce, generate everything. In some way this relates Joyce to a complex tradition of writers which includes the "massive myths of the Gutenberg transformation" that McLuhan cites, as well as Swift, Sterne, Erasmus, and others. McLuhan is attracted to this tradition and yet he seems rather different from a Joyce or a Sterne or a Rabelais in his public sensibility.

The tradition involved lies, in one way, at the heart of *The Gutenberg Galaxy*. It is a learned tradition—all of the writers are erudite and witty; it is a bawdy tradition—all of the writers have been accused of vulgarity and irreverence; it is a tradition focusing on heroic figures (Rabelais' Gargantua, Cervantes' Don Quixote, Pope's Dulness, and Joyce's Ulysses and Finnegan) who are also related to the world of man:

> In the work of Rabelais, obscenity is used to attack pride because such pride keeps men and women apart. Rabelais actually spiritualizes lust into moments of profound social communion. His men and women do not "surrender" to each other, but they *play* together. Love lies in laughter and pleasure, not agony and death. The difference between men and women becomes a principle of joy and life. His courtiers delight in their difference because they look forward to overcoming it. (Duncan, *Communication and Social Order* 306)

They are all works involved with human folly, and all play with systemizations of human folly. It is this last link, i.e. systematized human folly (which McLuhan seems not to have made explicit in *The Gutenberg Galaxy*), that makes them attractive to what McLuhan is about. Technology is a system; the electrical age and its computers impose systems. McLuhan is interested in what the system of printing did to man and naturally finds himself attracted to the whole range and type of systems that entered European history in the latter part of the Middle Ages and the early Renaissance.

But Joyce and the others bring the systems into conflict with the real relations that occur between individuals. The juxtaposition of system against system and of systems against the human has an intrinsically comic and satiric dimension. Unfortunately, Joyce's wit does not transplant well into McLuhan's garden, because the juxtaposition of the human as creator and generator of system against the systems he generates or creates just does not occur. Fundamentally, this may be because McLuhan is anti-creative by his own admission, having a "distaste for the *process* of change" and "not by temperament or conviction, a revolutionary." He prefers "a stable, changeless environment of modest services on human scale" and dislikes the way that electric media are "unraveling the entire fabric of our society" (*Playboy* 158).

Yet McLuhan seems to take over not only the intellectual interest of these writers, but something of their stance and attitude. In different ways, all of them participate in pursuing a philosophy of folly based on such traditions as Cusa's "learned ignorance" or Erasmus' Folly. Such involvement creates some alliance with figures of fools, jesters, and clowns (figures that are tied to the kind of wit used in their works). McLuhan follows them in this fascination, for he relates the clown with the integral view of the coming world—"the medieval clown dominates the role of the writer until the Addison-Steele discovery of mass-production flow of equitone" (CB 25). The reason for this fascination he explains:

> When the whole man moves into a specialist area he is a clown. Hence the appeal of the comics. Clowns are integral. Every society has an acrobatic area for specialists. The clown in any society is what is left over, unused, from this acrobatic high-wire act. His act is to attempt the high-wire or specialty, using human wholeness. (CB 28)

Here McLuhan seems to relate the clown to the pose that he adopts as author in *Counterblast*—the attack of the generalist against the specialist by using a technique of opposition. This strategy of "blasting" McLuhan learned from Wyndham Lewis, who argued that all great art is satire and the artist is the enemy. *Counterblast* might be taken as a blast from the opposite point of view from Lewis, except that McLuhan, who reassures us that it is in Lewis' spirit, always seems closer to Lewis who throughout his work shared McLuhan's distaste for process and change, attacking works he felt were based on a philosophy of process such as Joyce's *Ulysses*. *Counterblast,* which in presentation is a celebration of print and its potentialities, ends up by once again recognizing the uniqueness of print to achieve certain ends. It makes extensive use of coloured ink, distorted letters, various typefaces, and unusual layouts. One section (CB 98), which is printed in large capital letters, makes the following seemingly casual comment:

> It would be a mistake to suppose that the trend of culture toward the oral and acoustic means that the book is becoming obsolete.

The word *obsolete* is set lengthwise on the page, below and to the right of the above statement, and marks off an explanatory paragraph which is printed in smaller, regular sans serif type:

> It means rather that the book, as it loses its monopoly as a cultural form, will acquire new roles. Nobody seems to know much about why the paper-back flopped in the 30's and succeeded in the 50's. But it is a fact which probably has some relation to TV, on one hand, and to LP, on the other.

Perhaps the appearance of this statement is more significant than may at first be evident. *Counterblast* is, after all, a book written by a man who has for a long time allowed himself to be associated with the death of the book. Its emergence here confirms the idea that its voice—the tone with which it speaks—is not the Addisonion equitone discussed earlier. It is, much differently, the voice of a "learned clown" enmeshing readers in his paradoxes and wit. Yet, if this is so, there is an essential difference between the McLuhanesque pose as clown and that of the humanist, or between Lewis and Joyce for that matter. The McLuhanesque clown allows a perpetual ambiguity about whether he is writing "straight" or working in a "multi-levelled" tradition of "wit." The Folly of Erasmus or the persona of Martinus Scriblerus (Pope's editor of *The Dunciad*) or even the dream of Joyce's dreamer are elaborated in a fictive comic tradition. The McLuhanesque clown (like Wyndham Lewis) tends to work in terms of "hateful contraries," the essence of the "blast" technique; the Joycean or the humanist intermingles and intermixes in a much more complex way, though still using naturally a dialectic or paradoxical movement within this more complex structure.

At the moment though, these concerns show that there are issues involved in *The Gutenberg Galaxy* about which McLuhan is either unaware or unwilling to communicate. They also show that McLuhan's pose as clown is conscious, but unlike that of some clowns, used for exploitation by being pseudo-serious. "What if he is right?" cries Tom Wolfe, unable to extricate folly from life style and life style from vision, as most of the rest of us also find difficult. What *The Gutenberg Galaxy* does is to reveal how closely imbedded in these traditions McLuhan's way of approaching the world around him is. If specialist technologists are the modern scholastics, then it becomes easy to turn the satiric strategies of humanism against them because Swift and a large number of science fiction writers, especially Kornbluth and Pohl, have already explored this particular mode. Yet *The Gutenberg Galaxy*, like *Understanding Media*, suggests the way in which McLuhan is unsure, lacking in total commitment to the comic mode and the clown-like role.

Now if our age serves as a bridge between Gutenberg and electronic technology as the sixteenth-seventeenth century did between script and print, then Joyce is the master bridge builder as McLuhan uses him. His work provides the means by which McLuhan relates tradition to modernity, or closer to his view of Eliot, sees the past as an immediate part of the here and now. Yet McLuhan's clown-like pose is essentially different from that of the more deeply committed humanists. A metaphysics of folly, such as Erasmus' *Encomium* presents, is a profoundly philosophical position, in the Renaissance as well as in the contemporary world. As we have seen, Kolakowski has argued for precisely just such a philosophy of the jester as the basis for humanism, deriving his argument from a metamorphosis of the theological tradition. McLuhan's view, though he obviously is acquainted with that tradition, is quite different from Kolakowski's account of the jester and much closer to Kolakowski's account of the priest as the upholder of the Establishment, the believer (like Wyndham Lewis) in the quest for the philosophical absolute. "The priest is the guardian of the absolute," Kolakowski tells us (*Towards a Marxist Humanism* 33), and McLuhan, whose eschatological view of media holds out an optimistic Utopian vision, ultimately is "a guardian of the absolute." McLuhan appears admittedly ambiguously clownlike, for like a Joycean Jesuit he is a priest-joker; but this is distinct from the follower of folly, the philosopher of jest, whose philosophy "In every era . . . exposes as doubtful what seems most unshakable, reveals the contradictions in what appears obvious and incontrovertible, derides common sense and reads sense into the absurd" (ibid. 34).

McLuhan, in articles like "The Psychopathology of *Time, Life* and *Fortune*" and in books like *The Mechanical Bride,* may have started with a jester's way of regarding problems, but as Kolakowski points out:

> Priests and jesters cannot be reconciled unless one of them is transformed into the other, as sometimes happens. . . . In every cra the jester's philosophy exposes as doubtful what seems most unshakable, reveals the contradictions in what appears obvious and incontrovertible, derides common sense and reads sense into the absurd. In short, it undertakes the daily chores of the jester's profession together with the inevitable risk of appearing ridiculous. Depending on time and place, the jester's thinking can range through all the extremes of thought, for what is sacred today was paradoxical yesterday, and absolutes on the equator are often blasphemies at the poles. The jester's constant effort is to consider all the possible reasons for contradictory ideas. It is thus dialectical by nature— simply the attempt to change what is because it is. He is motivated not by a desire to be perverse but by distrust of a stabilized system. In a world where apparently everything has already happened, he represents an active imagination defined by the opposition it must overcome. (*Towards a Marxist Humanism* 34)

If *The Gutenberg Galaxy* does not begin McLuhan's movement into the role of being a priest in jester's clothing, then certainly *Understanding Media* does so. Such activities as the *Dew Line*, particularly issues like "Agnew Agonistes," confirm the extent to which this priestly role has become fully confirmed. Yet Kolakowski in his way is just as limited as McLuhan, for the true jester must certainly attempt to balance the extremes of chaos and the extremes of order, to marry something of tradition with something of the Revolution. The point is that McLuhan, who appears to be like an Erasmus or a Pope or a Joyce, does not demonstrate this balance, any more than Kolakowski argues for it.

The role of jester or of gamesman is a traditional one. Huizinga in *Homo Ludens* points out that "what we have said of the playfulness of the Renaissance will be found to hold good of Humanism as well" (181). Erasmus especially represents this spirit since "his whole being seems to radiate the play spirit. It shines forth not only in the *Colloquies* and the *Encomium Moriae* (*The Praise of Folly*) but in the *Adagia,* that astonishing collection of aphorisms from Greek and Latin literature commented on with light irony and admirable jocosity" (ibid. 181). Yet Huizinga, who also comments on Erasmus' spirit in his *Men and Ideas,* emphasized its contemporary relevance as a way of restoring peace and sanity to a world which does not know how to handle its new powers. This comic spirit of Erasmus, as intensified by Rabelais and Cervantes and Pope, is what Joyce brings to bear on the contemporary situation, for he is the humanist adopting the dialectic of his countryman Scotus Erigena to the contemporary world through the focus of a dream using the vehicle of the philosophies of Cusa and Bruno.

But the way of Erasmus and the humanist vision does not mean just a stance of moderate and witty skepticism employing a dialectical and paradoxical approach to a subject, it also means a commitment to a marriage of a scholastic education with a humanistic one. It means, as McLuhan appears to keep asserting, a re-evaluation of what the basic arts of communications mean in the contemporary world—how one duplicates the Erasmian feat today. To complete the re-evaluation, though, would mean balancing the various basic approaches to symbolic study and expressive languages that are available. Following T. S. Eliot, for example, it would mean introducing the best basic work from linguistics and logic, and this would appear at the moment to mean a recognition of Chomsky and of the anthropologists and psycho-linguists (writers McLuhan apparently rejects) as well as embracing the logical knowledge of Russell and Whitehead and Wittgenstein about which he seems entirely innocent.

But it means more than this because it also means understanding some of the attempts at synthesis, such as Roland Barthes' *Elements of Semiology* or Pike's *Language in Relation to a Unified Theory of Human Behavior,* and some insight into structuralism and dialectical artistic theory, such as in Levi-Strauss and Lucien Goldmann respectively. Besides this it means being aware of these movements in relation to basic theories about psychology and sociology and anthropology, all areas where McLuhan seems to be fairly naïve. If he were not, certainly he would have devoted some attention to the views of individuals like Kenneth Burke and Hugh Duncan or Lucien Goldmann who have in different ways bridged psychology, sociology, and literary criticism even if not always in the most satisfactory way possible. Such knowledge would be equivalent to the ways that More and Erasmus, Pope and Swift had their antennae tuned to their own periods. McLuhan, rather than attempting such a general synthesis, picks and chooses without ever relating what he picks or chooses to some kind of discussion of theoretical orientation. Goffman and Hall may be valuable in sociology; Piaget's study on children and their concept of space may be useful (though why not also his study of the "intelligence" except that it is embarrassingly involved with structure and logic); so may Riesman on inner-directed and other-directed types. Yet all of these are random eclectic choices unless it is made clear how they relate to or conflict with one another.

Any "curious universal scholar," as the humanist poet Spenser described Chaucer, would certainly range over such diverse areas of interest, if his intent were really to achieve some synthesis of the contemporary world situation. But McLuhan does not operate in this way, because it places constrictions on his particular vision and limits the range of his discussion. Such "superior arrogance" if fully informed might be justified, but presented as a way of achieving easy visions or quick results, the justification is open to question, especially when it argues for a value-free method of handling basic social problems and presents potential future Utopias while eliminating the opportunity to discuss whether the eschatology involved is ultimately rigidly determined.

Behind all of this, like Erasmus or More, Swift or Pope, McLuhan is deeply interested in how to educate people and sees his activity as intimately involved with that education. As we have seen in articles like "An Ancient Quarrel in Modern America," his work on the Ford Seminar in Culture and Communications reported in *Explorations*, and the first run for *Understanding Media*, he showed a consistent awareness of the place that various ways and means of transmitting communications should have in an effective contemporary education. Essentially, as his article "James Joyce: Trivial and Quadrivial" makes clear, he was at that time seeking a reintegrated educational system.

In this earlier stage of his career he seems to have seen the possibility for evolving such a system in some kind of rebirth of the trivium, and his examination of communications under Ford auspices was a natural development of his studies concerning this. He seems to have reasoned that if grammar, logic, and rhetoric were the basic subjects and were involved with the arts of expression, then the humanities must be ultimately concerned with the contemporary equivalent of such a programme. If so, is not this to be found in the study of other media of communication including the gestural system of the human body about which we have become so self-conscious? Can it not be pursued further in the study of other media of communication which supplement human gesture and the human voice—photography, film, the phonograph, or television?

The relations between this type of quest and the *Bride* have already been discussed in part, and the central importance of the *Galaxy* as a continuation of the search becomes apparent as soon as it is pointed out. It could be argued that Bacon and Erasmus were vitally interested in up-dating the arts of communication. Bacon's constant concern with different types of style might suggest so, and Erasmus' whole educational programme from the *Colloquies* to his rhetorical writings does suggest it. Following that thread, if the book in the Renaissance influenced Erasmus and Bacon more than anything else, the film and television or similar media must influence the educational and artistic revolutions of today. Yet it is also necessary to realize that McLuhan limits to one perspective what was many-sided and avoids all of the changes in social relations and their concomitant effect on thought that might have influenced an Erasmus and a More or a Bacon.

The difficulty in demanding such a comprehensive appreciation is that it is almost impossibly complex. First of all, it would be necessary to re-examine the whole role of human language and its relation to other types of expression, as suggested above. Eliot has pointed out that the contemporary humanist, critic, or poet should study his linguistics, his logic, and his sociology and this would mean his Chomsky and Quine and the *Principia* and the theories of sociology involved with symbolic expression and its relation to society. If this were done, one would know logic and grammar in humanistic terms as few of us in literary studies do. If one were to follow this programme, it might be discovered that a new study of language as a mode of expression could develop and that ultimately, as Roland Barthes seems to be attempting, it might be related to a wide variety of modes of expression, whether games or housing or clothing or the structure of films. Yet even if this comes to be, the basic knowledge about language and speech could hardly be confused with other kinds of activity, nor would its distinctness be lost as Steiner seems to fear in *Language and Silence*. *Understanding Media* may reflect an extreme confusion of which Steiner takes serious note, but this may be only a temporary lapse rather than a clear assessment of the total insight potentially available if people were to integrate the contributions of Ferdinand de Saussures, Chomsky, and others.

McLuhan did see the trivium as reborn in Valéry and Joyce, this rebirth being part of his theme in "James Joyce: Trivial and Quadrivial" and the most productive outgrowth of his Nashe studies. He believed the study of symbolists and post-symbolists would lead to a recognition of the new substitutions or equivalents for the trivium, and as he more and more fully intuited a new

117

rhetoric in modern media he could even conceive of this new education as occurring in a classroom without walls. As a foundation for this conception he proposed a theory of language as gesture, closely allied to man's apparent drive to develop liturgies, so that learning could really occur in the process of things happening rather than in some kind of discursive manner. What he evades, however, is the synthesis of linguistic and poetic, logic and rhetoric that would have to come about if rationality and irrationality were to be placed back in proper balance within man.

Erasmus and Pope believed in that balance; McLuhan, at least apparently, does not. Yet if the structuralists and transformationalists are to be rejected for using lineal logics or bypassed for their irrelevance, they are significant enough to come to terms with. Joyce, it would really seem, can combine the highly structured and the intuitive in a way which McLuhan seems at one point to embrace and at another to reject. But it is significant that when McLuhan uses Joyce rather than exegeting Joyce (*War and Peace* rather than the article in the *Literary Criticism*) the richness of Joyce rapidly disappears and the jests lose their complexity.

The *Galaxy* is an excellent example of the way that positivistic activity in the sciences influences cultural analysis and criticism. Its eclecticism, its uncritical pragmatism, its scientism, and its insistence on objective, value-free orientations virtually disqualify it from real status as a prolegomena to a philosophy of man and communications. Yet it would be absolutist folly to reject the partial wisdom of McLuhan's insight, and perhaps it is necessary for a pioneer in such areas to have a certain audacity and a certain blindness. To bring together at all the vast proliferation of information in these areas, to attempt some kind of integration, almost ensures a certain amount of error, a certain danger of charlatanship that must be risked for human sanity as well as for the advancement of speculation. But in the act, is it really necessary to dilute the sources of one's power without making apparent the reasons for the dilution?

M cLuhan's world-wide reputation comes from *Understanding Media,* and it is to this book that we must turn to further consider McLuhan the humanist and educator.

Few people remember that the first version of *Understanding Media* was that mimeographed report reproduced for the National Association of Educational Broadcasters under an NDEA contract "to provide an approach to media and a syllabus for teaching the nature and effects of media in secondary schools." In pursuing this earlier project, McLuhan tried to follow procedures from art criticism. In the "Report on Project in Understanding Media" (III 1), he claims his approach was confirmed by Heinrich Woelfflin who held the belief that *"the effect is the thing that counts, not the sensuous facts"* (McLuhan's italics). Woelfflin does say this about the difference between Michelangelo's and Bernini's sculpture, in his *Principles of Art History* (62), but McLuhan elevates a specific difference to a general principle. What began as a curriculum designed to show how to present an understanding of media effects through a type of artistic analysis as part of an educational programme became one of the major books of the sixties. The result firmly fixes McLuhan in the role of a modern-day humanist.

Nothing would seem to confirm more the fact that McLuhan sees himself as an Erasmus of the media world than his analysis of Erasmus in *Counterblast:*

> It was very hard at first for the contemporaries of Erasmus to grasp that the printed book meant that the main channel of information and discipline was no longer the spoken word or the single language. Erasmus was the first to act on the awareness that part of the new revolution would be felt in the classroom. He put the old oral scholasticism into his *Adagia* and *Similia.* The same situation confronts us. (CB 132)

To follow *The Gutenberg Galaxy* with a project of curriculum design for educators strongly suggests that McLuhan tried to put

9

To see the World in a Single Phone

the old literary humanism into the guidebooks for the "new revolution" (now the old media revolution) in the classrooms of the sixties. What appears to be at its root is a transference of the historical knowledge of language and literary studies and the methodological knowledge of aesthetics and art criticism to a new kind of media analysis, an analysis of the effects rather than the sensuous facts. It is intriguing to see, along with McLuhan's shift in approach, the transference of the major prejudice of I. A. Richards, the founder of the New Criticism in literature, from literary criticism to media analysis, for in *The Principles of Literary Criticism* Richards argues in favour of a criticism based on effects rather than structure or intention.

As the report for the educational broadcasters became transformed into the book which declared "The medium is the message," it retained its close alliance with the arts. Media, in fact, became, according to McLuhan, symbolic translators, an idea which he associated with the Latin term *translatio* (metaphor). "All media are active metaphors" (UM 57). Consequently, the way to approach media is similar to the way one approaches metaphor, as an art form. Any technology could be treated in this way for McLuhan, because technologies metamorphosize or translate nature into human art. Consequently, in approaching the problems of *Understanding Media* an artist's perspective is important, for only the arts can handle the world of contemporary media. "Our conventional response to all media," as McLuhan asserts, "namely that it is how they are used that counts, is the numb stance of the 'technological idiot' " (UM 18). Therefore, only those interested in form as form and the nature of effects—the serious artists—are "able to encounter technology with impunity" (UM 18).

The role of the artist goes even further than that, for McLuhan follows Wyndham Lewis in arguing that "The Artist is always engaged in writing a detailed history of the future because he is the only person aware of the nature of the present" (UM 65). Now McLuhan broadens the definition of the artist in ways which follow a lengthy tradition and especially suggests a similarity to Renaissance attitudes such as Puttenham's or Sidney's, pointing out that the artist is "the man in any field, scientific or humanistic, who grasps the implications of his actions and of new knowledge in his own time" (UM 65). Art, therefore, becomes somewhat synonymous with "integral awareness." But it also becomes a protective device against the process of change, for he also claims that art provides "exact information of how to rearrange one's psyche in order to anticipate the next blow from our own extended faculties" (UM 66). This still reflects some interesting overtones of I. A. Richards' view that a poem rearranges and reharmonizes the nervous system in preparation for action, though McLuhan's emphasis appears to be defensive rather than neutral as Richards' appears to be.

Obviously after such statements, McLuhan must, in pursuing *Understanding Media,* assume the primacy of art as a mode of understanding. His education theory, like that of the Renaissance, seems to join the arts and the basic educative processes. The artist, after all, is an educator in such a perspective, "teaching delightfully" as Sidney put it, and that view is quite consistent with McLuhan's earlier analyses of Joyce's educative role in "James Joyce: Trivial and Quadrivial." It is with this in mind that the principle "The medium is the message" must be approached and the whole of the analyses of media placed. Raymond Williams and Kenneth Burke can find value in McLuhan precisely because of this close affiliation with the arts and the awareness of the aesthetic component as a vital factor in contemporary society.

"The medium is the message," then, becomes quite comprehensible as a way of approaching the problem of form in media. Art is first of all involved in what Focillon and Read call the *life of forms,* and *Understanding Media* explores the forms of life. To reinforce his artistic approach with more apparently "scientific" or "disciplinary" approaches, he uses the work of Kenneth Boulding in *The Image* where it is suggested that "The meaning of a message is the change which it produces in the image" (UM 26), which is essentially a way of treating meaning in terms of change of form. Yet McLuhan seems to go further than this and to be lured by his own devices—to allow the formula to come to mean that the medium is everything and the message is irrelevant as a way of approaching the meaning. In his earlier report he had said:

. . . any and all curricula are obsolete with regard to subject-matter. All that remains to study are the media themselves, *as forms*, as modes ever creating new assumptions and hence new objectives. (Report IV 1)

Now with such a view it becomes important whether or not form and media are synonymous or whether only media themselves are metaphors. But in effect the term "media" itself is also a metaphor for thinking about form in some special ways.

What does McLuhan choose to treat as "media"? His first and now very famous example is the electric light, the "medium without a message." The electric light, he argues, is pure information, and this demonstrates clearly that the content of one medium is always another. Seeing that McLuhan is interested in the arts, there is certainly an intriguing mythic reason for beginning with "light," and with man-made light, for it is the original translation of nature into art at the most basic of levels—"Let there be light." Somewhere the pseudo-poetry of *Understanding Media* surely carries this emotive overtone. But what does it have to do with the concept of media itself? It really stretches the analogical use of the term medium to the utmost and allows the reader to instantly become aware that the wide range of "mediums" participate in that class of things called media in an analogical, and a rather broadly analogical, way.

A glance at the chapter titles of *Understanding Media* Part II confirms this impression, for the list of media includes: The Spoken Word; The Written Word; Roads; Number; Clothing; Housing; Money; Clocks; The Print; Comics; The Printed Word; Wheel, Bicycle and Airplane [all gathered together as one]; The Photograph; Press; Motorcar; Ads; Games; Telegraph; The Typewriter; The Telephone; The Phonograph; Movies; Radio; Television; Weapons; Automation. The list is interesting, for it links things that exist as expressive forms in very different ways. Each of the classes might be regrouped, but what McLuhan does, using his analogy, is insist that we recognize the analogies between them as cultural expressions even at the risk of some considerable confusion about the fact that Speech, Clocks, Motorcars, Ads, The Telephone, and Automation all express cultural messages in rather different ways with rather different intents.

In the earlier study, he linked this quite openly to what it really is—the study of cultural objects:

> We are obliged today to learn the language of objects, and especially those objects that are media. For they can pull the rug out from under your world or pop a new one under you while you are unawares. (Report III 13)

But it is also interesting that in the earlier report he did not include anything that would not normally be described as a medium except possibly the telephone and telegraph, which are still forms of telecommunications. Using the concept media, in a rather broad way, rather than using the concept of cultural objects, forces attention on the latent expressive import possibly implicit in cultural objects. But when it is linked to a principle like "The medium is the message," it leads to some rather complex and possibly confused developments. To relate together media in all the different connotations involved, McLuhan must adopt the theory that technologies are extensions of ourselves and attribute this character to all of the media. This is so important it forms the subtitle of *Understanding Media:* "The Extensions of Man."

Now each of these media, according to McLuhan, can be considered as "extensions," for speech is a kind of outering of the self, and the motorcar, an extension of the foot. Again, of course, the technique depends on the use of a rather extended metaphor or analogy; but granted that, the analogy is comprehensible and can stimulate thought. Yet it is interesting to see how McLuhan actually develops this idea of extension. He relates it to the Narcissus myth. Narcissus' image mirrored in the pool becomes "an extension of himself" which "numbed his perceptions until he became the servomechanism of his own extended or repeated image" (UM 41). The poetic attractiveness of the Narcissus figure is that somehow it implies alienation while seeming to make the same implication about media and extensions. The result is that this figure of the benumbed, alienated personality adrift in a technological world that McLuhan has vaguely invoked becomes related to a solipsist ensnared by his own beauty, the prototype of any man confronted with the discovery of a new medium. Yet McLuhan naturally stresses that Narcissus falls in love with an extension of himself, not himself. Possibly in the sixties Narcissus would have worn a black jacket and ridden a motorcycle?

The point to the parable (and the use of such parables is incidentally closely modelled on Bacon's use of allegory in his study of *The Antique Gods*) is that we are servomechanisms of our technologies (UM 46). To use an extension is to accept it into ourselves, upon which it drastically alters our perceptions. But McLuhan is prepared to push the matter much further and to suggest:

> Physiologically, man in the normal use of technology (or his variously extended body) is perpetually modified by it and in turn finds ever new ways of modifying his technology. Man becomes, as it were, the sex organs of the machine world, as the bee of the plant world, enabling it to fecundate and to evolve ever new forms. (UM 46)

The concept of "extensions" has led us from Narcissus, who lost his sexual identity in the replication of his image, to a new Narcissus who fecundates his image, the technology that he has generated and that is changing him. Providing one allows McLuhan's first formula to lead him on this path, the end is fairly certain, for McLuhan is merely limiting an account of "the life of forms" in the arts or in the biological world to man's artifacts viewed as forms. Even the image of the bee which he allows to enter comes from the traditional classical image of the poet creating new forms by sampling the older flowers of rhetoric and poetic. Now as a pedagogical device for bringing a man involved in a machine world to a comprehension of the life of forms, the process might have some value, especially if it were to go on to relate forms to society, and art to industry as Herbert Read has done. But here the intent and direction is rather different and the danger might well be in coming to believe that the mental embrace of the machines drained all sexual energy, leaving none for other organic activities.

Since each extension is taken by McLuhan to be an extension of the nervous system or the sensory system, each technology affects the general ratio between the senses. This is a natural enough development of his view in the *Galaxy*. We have seen its relation to the mediaeval doctrine of the *sensus communis* and its involvement with what McLuhan comes to describe as "tactility." In this respect again, the electric light is used as a crucial example:

If the student of media will but meditate on the power of this medium of electric light to transform every structure of time and space and work and society that it penetrates or contacts, he will have the key to the form of the power that is in all media to re-shape any lives that they touch. (UM 52)

In a similar way, "the press opened up the 'human interest' key-board after the telegraph had restructured the press medium [and] the movie took over the novel and the newspaper and the stage all at once [so that the phenomenon is really one where] media as extensions of our senses institute new ratios, not only among our private senses, but among themselves, when they interact among themselves" (UM 52–3). Now what really seems to be going on here is that McLuhan is speaking about a social phenomenon as if it were an interior phenomenon. He is studiously avoiding the analysis of social change, while attempting to account for it in terms of media effect on sensory and nervous structures in individuals as well as in some hypothetically extended world of media.

If we sweep aside the pseudo-objectivity of McLuhan's quasi-positivistic pose—his desire to account for effects by formal changes within given structures of physical or physiological or-ganization—and proceed to realize that his artistic mind can simul-taneously see these descriptions as analogues of what is happening in society, then his vision is much more tolerable. It may be that his own approach biases him so that, after giving us an account of how a cultural object like an electric light can change social rela-tions and aesthetic perceptions, he fails to be able to relate instru-ments such as the telephone or television to such questions as what they do to the total social structure.

To digress for a moment, let us examine McLuhan's treatment of the telephone. In his treatment of the concept of "extension" and ratio of the senses he co-opts a Joyce phrase, TELEVISION KILLS TELEPHONY IN BROTHERS BROIL (FW 52), and he suggests that since the telephone extends the ear and voice while television extends touch and sense interplay, this creates a media conflict (UM 265). Apart from the fact that Joyce applies his phrase (which he does not headline or capitalize) to a story-telling situation with a shift towards an evocatively descriptive style, the phrase suggests an emphasis of eye over ear. Yet surely Joyce's application is to formal considerations different from those which McLuhan invokes in "The Telephone," and telephony contains the pun "phony" to which McLuhan himself calls attention.

But McLuhan goes on from this to build up a mosaic of what the telephone is and how it affects us. Among other effects he suggests: the brothel disappears and the callgirl who is a generalist not a specialist appears; visible speech was a bad name for the phone, since it is impossible to visualize on the phone (according to Mc-Luhan). In fact, he argues that the phone by reducing visualizing (which the TV set paradoxically does as well) increasingly prepares us for the contemporary world and thus it is possible to suggest that the Bell Telephone research departments do not really understand the instrument. From this point he can lead on to questioning the fundamental research of Bell Lab workers:

> As already mentioned, the Shanner and Weaver hypothesis about Information Theory, like the Morgenstern Game Theory, tends to ignore the function of the form as form. Thus both Information Theory and Game Theory have bogged down into sterile banalities, but the psychic and social changes resulting from these forms have altered the whole of our lives. (UM 267)

The telephone properly understood then demands complete participation because of its very low definition (technical impreciseness in reproducing the signal), which McLuhan claims forces us to supply more of the completion, thus involving us more, and through such a demand could, if we understood it as a way of teaching math, reform our information theory. "Doodling" while on the phone is a function of this participatory nature of the phone, since "we strengthen and complete it by the use of all the other senses" (UM 267-8). Throughout other parts of the discussion of the phone there are suggestions about the phone and privacy and the phone as creating a situation where "only the authority of knowledge will work" (UM 272). The structure of the phone presumably favours pluralism of centres and decentralization and re-creates the need to play roles rather than occupy delegated jobs (UM 273). In this total analysis of the phone, there are many insights worth thinking about, but in the manner in which they are presented they appear as little more than that "superior arrogance" that McLuhan so often tells us is necessary when we approach media.

If McLuhan's analysis of the electric light is correct, then the patterns that the phone has created, both in the service industries like the phone company itself and in service industries functioning largely by phone, are an important feature of the way that the phone transforms social relations for some of these affected by it. *The New York Review of Books* (March 1970) recently showed some of the implications of this transformation: the mechanization of individuals; the subtle invasion of privacy and the like. It showed how the organizing of the phone company's service representatives into groups of ten with detailed manuals of instruction depersonalizes their activity. They are also subject to potential monitoring from a number of external and higher managerial level sources. This does not become part of McLuhan's image of the phone, though he does suggest that the phone brought down the walls and eliminated privacy in stock-brokerage firms, and he does hint that the phone is all right because the phone company does not understand it and therefore things will change for the better in spite of the phone company's rigidity.

But this optimism is based on assumptions about the magic of the phone and about its aesthetic nature, which may be only partial truths because viewed only in a partial perspective. It is the cumulative detail of McLuhan's vision that is frightening. The individual aphorisms are often enticing and exciting—suggestive, whether right or wrong—because of the problems they raise. But, in total, if it is assumed that the sensory mechanisms do not work the way McLuhan suggests they do (because in fact the phone as an extension is not really an extension of the sensory system except in a metaphorical way), then there is real danger that the phone does not automatically result in higher participation and decentralization. It may well be that that is how phones should be used for the best ends of man, but it does not necessarily mean that is the way they will eventually be used. Four and one-half centuries of book culture did not necessarily produce all of the optimal uses of the book that its Renaissance praisers might have expected.

But the point of absurdity is definitely reached when McLuhan rejects Information Theory and Morgenstern Game Theory because they ignore "the function of form as form." Here, as he points out earlier, he is really concerned with the inability of the theorists to understand the complexity of variables in the actual structure of a human social or psychological situation, which is not quite the same thing as understanding the function of form as form. In any case, the telephone by presumably favouring theoretical physics of a European variety (though Europeans were far less phone oriented) is not going to automatically change the situation merely by providing a new context for the teaching of mathematics. The fecundity of the McLuhanite imagination is excellent as a source of invention, but the total view of man's creative activity surpasses invention.

McLuhan discussing the phone omits many of the most vital aspects, although we may read them into his account by pursuing its suggestivity to the maximum. When he tells us to think about and study phones as cultural objects, he is doing a major service (though he is not a pioneer in doing it, as he himself would admit citing Mumford and Giedion), but when he will allow us to become hypnotized by features of the phone and its relation to the human person that are possibly accidental or incidental, it seems to me that he is dangerous if taken seriously and foolish if not.

Although he may seem to develop the telephone theme in later writings, the same essential prejudices are part of the way he considers the problem. In the January 1970 *Dew Line* entitled "Agnew Agonistes" he still finds himself involved with the phone and phone networks, for his theme is that the wire service is transforming news into a non-private activity like photography: "You cannot commit photography alone" (DL 3). So, according to McLuhan, the telephone and telegraph become devices for destroying government bureaucracies and business. He cites the example of the total erosion of the Postal System. Satellites, in fact, have carried the process to a point where it is occurring at a "self-liquidating speed." In fact, the whole Agnew phenomenon can be seen in one aspect as drawing attention to the fact that the phone's effect on human life has never been examined "except by the ad agencies—'Phone Grandma Today'" (DL 15). The conclusion is that:

> The telephone networks, as shapers of work and decision-making processes, far outweigh the messages conveyed on the wires. It is purest paradox that millions of commuters go to town just to use the phone. The abolition of old time—and space—values in every level of the social and political processes that accompanies the mere existence of the telephone, is merely an instance of the unstudied and unrecognized factors in the current crumbling of all existing bureaucracies of the world. (DL 16)

Now this both says and does not say what we have been discussing above, for while it suggests some knowledge of the nature and extent of what the phone does, it certainly avoids worrying about the bureaucratizing implications by suggesting that they are self-undoing. But is the matter that simple? Anything may affect us psychologically, but the effect is never necessarily analyzable in simple, single-minded directions. And besides, more than time-and-space values are involved in the changes that the value system undergoes. McLuhan makes us aware of the "cultural object," the phone, the possibility it might have "effects" on a massive scale, but he builds an automatic optimism into his mystique of what the phone can do. To see the world in a single phone is an act of creative imagination. In *Understanding Media*, McLuhan has plundered the possibilities and produced a Book of Commonplaces which might be used for exfoliating visions of the world out of a single phone.

But such visions necessarily need to be ordered visions, for even post-Gutenberg Man (Computer Man) has a rage for order (though an awareness that order is not equatable with the rigidities of narrowly conceived laws, moral rigidities, or police states). That order could move out from the formal contingencies of the phone as an instrument: out from the nature of phone conversations; the posture of teenagers and adults on phones; the demands on time that phones impose; the demands on performance that phones impose; the ways that phones accelerate activity; the effect of different modes of phone networks within an organization; the modes of organization that having phones impose on a person, on a household, on an office, or within the organization of the telephone system itself. From this to the type of business that phones make necessary, the way phones influence other information transfer, and the way that phones change views of privacy and provide threats to privacy and reduce our sensitivity to openness—all might be issues within some massive yet-to-be-written "Phonyad," or some brilliant sociological study of the phone. McLuhan cannot be condemned for suggesting this possibility, but he can hardly be praised for the random generation of a few creative thoughts as notes for a prolegomena to the phone as a cultural object.

If this lengthy digression suggests what McLuhan does with one medium in *Understanding Media*, it is possible to generalize the pattern to each of the media on his list. It is exciting to be reminded that television changes our whole life style by having it described as tactile, meaning the interplay of the senses; but again the important interaction between man and set, at home and in production, disappears in McLuhan's magic media land. What disappoints one is that a socially alert, psychologically tutored, philosophically disciplined use of the art would have provided so much more. The difficulties are further intensified when the level of abstraction of the social object under consideration in relation to the concept of media is not made clear.

A dress is not a phone, and fashion as an industry is not Bell Telephone. From McLuhan's point of view they may both share the disadvantage of not knowing their own business, but their relationships with people are very different. After what Carlyle has managed with clothing in the *Sartor Resartus*, McLuhan is disappointing in restricting his analysis of clothing so radically, and interestingly enough he does not mention Carlyle's philosophy, even though it plays an important role in *Finnegans Wake*.

McLuhan's theme favours a sensuousity which is more totally involving and naturally tactile as against the purely visual modes that he satirized in *The Mechanical Bride*. He suggests that American dress is moving to a more revealing inclusive mode—toreador pants, beehive hairdos (which date *Understanding Media*) and later examples such as minis, net stockings and cut-outs and see-throughs—suggesting that "To a person using the whole sensorium, nudity is the richest possible expression of structural form" (UM 122). With this no one can disagree, for it is at the root of the art of the nude and the erotic dance of the body.

Yet clothing is surely involved with a dialectic play between concealment and revelation which has as much to do with the erotic as has sculptured nudity. The real interest comes from appearing with bare breasts one day and in maxi skirts and long sleeves the next. Some genuine trends towards freedom are possibly present, but this is more likely to be found in the persistence of the bikini or the continuing increase of abandoning undergarments or the Brigitte Bardot inspired and Jackie Kennedy approved fashion of going bare-foot. One imagines McLuhan losing himself in his contrast between Europe and America which suggests the transplantation of the mechanical bride from America to Europe just as the freer sensuosity of Europe moves to America. Perhaps so, but where did minis and bralessness and net stockings and bare feet begin as contemporary styles? Certainly partly in America, but certainly partly in France, Italy, and England.

Kroeber and other anthropologists have made fashion a serious index of national states of mind. McLuhan has appropriated part of this insight, but he merely teases the reader by stripping a few American girls to their bikinis rather than examining the whole range of uniforms, alternative styles of dress at different ages, and the like. But just as teenage patterns and postures and manners do not become an intrinsic part of the phone, so too there is no real eroticism in McLuhan's discussion of the erotic revolution in American dress.

What is wrong with specifically discussing the effects on people themselves of textures which are more sensuous; of styles that demand more openness; of exposed skin which receives more sensation of heat and light and dust; and of the way in which the greater variety that this permits refocuses attention on the human image—its eyes and face and neck and breasts and navel and midriff and bikini-triangled pubic area and the legs and the feet? When McLuhan's "Mechanical Bride" shed her high-heeled shoes and took off her corset and her bra, the revolution of which he is prophet had in part occurred. Is not the proper human symbol of his so-called electric age then a sinuously moving, sculptured body with the freedom of a modern dancer undulating across the grass, feeling under her feet the ground at a be-in in a public park, as she moves to the rock rhythms of a pop group? Somehow McLuhan never wanders in these areas, for he manages to abstract the sensuousity and the person from their flesh in the process of analysis.

If clothes and phones are radically different objects of analysis, certainly films and television are even more so, and still more complex are the problems of speech and games. Ironically enough, in some ways McLuhan is best when speaking of speech and games. In part, it is because the first of these is a type of social structure, and the second is so intimately bound up with the social structure that McLuhan cannot avoid this relationship. But it may go deeper than that for the theme of *Homo Ludens* as set forth by Huizinga and the centrality of human speech are two great inheritances from McLuhan's humanistic tradition and could well be argued to be at the root of generating most of the other things (cultural objects) about which McLuhan speaks.

McLuhan, in *Understanding Media*, has an almost Blakean vision of speech as a fragmenting result of the Fall, a Baudelairian "Flower of Evil." He uses Bergson to establish that speech is a human technology, a fragmentation of consciousness, which it would seem likely any Chomskyite today would rather question. According to McLuhan, however, "language does for intelligence what the wheel does for the feet and the body" (UM 79). Speech acts to separate man from a cosmic unconscious, suggests McLuhan, asserting a Romantic view towards the division of consciousness and unconsciousness. Yet this split is only relative, for McLuhan also sees speech as integral and involving all the senses: "As an extension or uttering (outering) of all our senses at once, language has always been held to be man's richest art form, that which distinguishes him from the animal creation" (UM 80). But this is only an approach to integration, for McLuhan sees that there should be an electric technology arising which will make words unnecessary. He relates this to a way of overcoming the Tower of Babel, the division of consciousness that language causes. Fundamentally, he does believe in a mystical power in electricity itself to transcend the outering of man's intelligence and perhaps, Narcissus-like, return it within.

Possibly there are some critical points to be made. First, as a possible beginning point from which to look at human communications, there is no longer any concept of an expressive, erotic person who does not have a sharply divided personality. Rather than, as Freud, attributing this phenomenon to socialization in general, McLuhan relates it to the art of symbolizing in speech—and possibly if properly followed to its conclusion, the act of symbolizing in general. Such a view requires us to reject the possibility of internal psychological processes that are a natural development which the human being uses in producing speech symbolization. Most linguists would not reject those processes for they are, in fact, in some ways involved in most of those visions of the "poetic" as the first of languages—visions that presumably Joyce, and Vico and Renaissance criticism all set forth. For this reason, McLuhan's treatment of speech as an extension of the intelligence could well be suspect. Certainly the treatment is limited and uninteresting compared to what he said in his earlier works.

For his most interesting observations, therefore, it is necessary to turn from speech to game where he can forget a medium that may be assigned a specific technological role and must speak about broader systems and structures. As soon as he shifts into this area he can speak of the integral person, pointing out that humour is the "mark of sanity [and that] in fun and play we recover the integral person" (UM 235). Games are closely related to humour and to art. They are popular art, collective social reaction to the main drive or action of any culture (UM 235). Consequently, in games there is a dramatic use of the human person, for they are "dramatic models of our psychological lives providing release of particular tensions" (UM 237). Even here a note of romanticism comes in, for art is a specialized game which "became a sort of civilized substitute for magical games and rituals [and] is the story of the detribalization which came with literacy" (UM 237). This view of the fall from grace comes from McLuhan's commitment to Lewis' aesthetic that art is a civilized substitute for magic.

The real problem in all of this is whether there really is a fall from grace which results in a fragmentation of consciousness through technologies, or whether there is not an emergence of more consciousness through an increasing richness of expressive possibilities. Since McLuhan's game theory comes from Huizinga and anthropologists and poets, it has a strong element of implication that game and art as civilizing functions are also positive gains rather than poor reflections of magic and ritual. For games, even in the popular cultural sense, can be creations of Utopian visions which allow us to "interpret and complete the meaning of our daily lives" (UM 238). "The form of any game is of first importance," McLuhan points out, and he also says that art, games, pop art, and media of communication are alike. Any game, therefore, is a translator of experience, and any media is like a game or a work of art which, McLuhan says, is "rigged to produce an effect" (UM 244).

Homo Ludens is the concealed heart of *Understanding Media*. Unfortunately, it is something McLuhan strives to keep from becoming apparent, even though his greatest strength as a media analyst comes when he indulges in gamesmanship and allows his mind to play. But games reflect the way people are organized, their social structure, and their personal relations and personal view of self. If media are actually embedded in such relationships, and art works are embedded in such relationships, McLuhan's formula dissipates and he may more than wish that it had originally been *The Medium Is the Massage* rather than the *Message*, though even here there is some reason to believe the formula is far from adequate.

What *Understanding Media* lacks is a sense of drama, a sense of person, and a sense of the intimacy of personal speech. No matter how alienated our technological world, these are still basic. The speech act, as McLuhan has made out elsewhere, can use the whole body, not just words and the voice. In this act there is a basis for beginning to discuss man's expressive relationship to cultural objects.

If this rather long look at *Understanding Media* avoids the more dramatic modern media and the more startling elements of the galaxy or cluster that McLuhan calls the electric age, it is only because the real roots of McLuhan's dilemma about those areas rise from his whole way of seeing the history of man as a fall from grace—a Blakean fragmentation ever-intensifying through the evolution of speech, writing, social structures, print, and the like until finally forcing an apocalyptic contemporary *recorso*. Mischievously, one imagines McLuhan dreaming about the device Shepherd Mead invented in *The Big Ball of Wax*, a story in which someone is strapped to a chair and communicated with through electrodes, and the activity becomes the basis for an entire new religion. McLuhan the pedagogue and humanist knew enough to call our attention to the study of cultural objects and media of communication, to ask some interesting questions, and to pose some interesting paradoxes; but the vision that goes with it of an apocalyptic launching into a radically new future is too cynical about man himself. The progress of man's history must be considered more than the last throes of an Augustinian theocratic vision of what Paradise might have been.

A lengthy discussion of *Understanding Media* which does not talk about the press, the radio, television, advertising, computers, or even terms like hot, cool, and rear-view mirror may seem a curious sort of a *tour de force*. But that is the only way to begin to see precisely what McLuhan is doing. Even though television and film and computers and a trend towards the "cool" is the only way to get to "where it's at," according to Mc-Luhan, in order to see what is really involved in his analysis, it is necessary to focus on the arts and on form; on the sensory system; on the intimate concepts of personal expression and the fundamental modes of social expression. McLuhan of the *Media* is "with" television and telephone and an oral culture as the way to a cool, participatory return to the tribal global village. How does McLuhan bridge this essentially artistically based approach of *Understanding Media* and the broader vision of the new world which man is entering?

10
McLuhan as Electric Man: Intellectual Illumination by Short Circuit

This "brave new world" is a Utopian realization—an achieving of what the arts prophesied in the early twentieth century. Fundamentally, both the approach and the vision of *Understanding Media* are applied Eliot-Joyce-Picasso-Klee (at least as McLuhan sees these artists). Take his concept of "hot" and "cool," and the preference for the "cool" and participatory and its association with the retribalization of man.

Such an interest in "participation" plays a central role in Eliot's aesthetic theory. The *Four Quartets* can be read as a poetic celebration of a certain view of participation which was associated with the revival of interest in the liturgical and the ritualistic (elements McLuhan is always calling to our attention). In fact, the criticism of the forties and fifties, including some of McLuhan's, spoke of a participatory, ritualistic development in Eliot's work which manifested itself in dramas like *Murder in the Cathedral*. The same artistic concerns linked this interest in ritual, to some extent, with self-involvement in the creative process of the

137

poem. One strategy for achieving this sense of participation was the technique of discontinuity—especially juxtaposition and montage—recommended by people like T. E. Hulme and Ezra Pound. These techniques, which McLuhan has frequently discussed, create a need for participation by supplying juxtaposed images without stating the connections. Early examples of this strategy were such often quoted poems as Pound's "In a Station of the Metro":

> The apparition of the faces in the crowd
> Petals on a wet, black bough

and Eliot's rather metaphysical-like comparison from the "Love Song of J. Alfred Prufrock":

> When the evening is spread out against the sky
> Like a patient etherized upon a table.

There were parallel techniques in the visual arts, especially in the art of collage or in the collage-like still lifes of Picasso. The activity of involvement to complete the effect in such ideographic structures (as they were called, alluding to the Chinese ideogram) stressed participation as a value. Such an approach is close to the way that McLuhan treats television and other cool media as technological devices. T. E. Hulme, as prophet of this movement, had even linked the activity to the reversal of continuity favoured in the nineteenth century and, therefore, as favouring a return to Byzantine modes of artistic expression. Yeats explored the point in some of his poetry, and it is the point from which McLuhan's view of the mosaic as a series of assembled elements may very well arise. That such aesthetic insights could be related as well to visual artists like Klee, with his technique of "magic squares," allowed for not only more general principles to be grasped but some kind of growing sense of an orchestration among the arts, a concept that flowered in the Bauhaus as well as elsewhere.

Strategy after strategy of *Understanding Media* appears to come from such sources. A phrase like "rear-view mirror," borrowed from some insight into the modern world, is related to a way of seeing the present through the past. The interplay of past and present, apart from its affinities with Eliot's theory of history in "Tradition and the Individual Talent," also depends on the way that literary forms were developing. For example, if we look at Prufrock's dilemma through the rear-view mirror of Browning's dramatic monologue (in which the technique of juxtaposition radically alters the form of the dramatic monologue), the earlier form becomes in a way the content of Eliot's much more radically subjective treatment. Actually, in *Understanding Media*, McLuhan is dealing with a much broader aesthetic principle in which old forms generally, to the extent that they become part of the code of a new form, also become part of the new form itself. Put in a grossly oversimplified way this means that the form of some previous manifestation becomes the content of the next; paralleling the old medium becoming the content of the new. But this analysis of Eliot is oversimplified merely to suggest the way in which McLuhan's equally oversimplified use of the approach might have come about from his interest in contemporary arts.

Now McLuhan has never concealed this method of "popularizing" aesthetic sources. On the other hand, he has never suggested that he might have been led into thinking it works because of the old *history of ideas* tradition in literary criticism, at one time employed to suggest that an idea filtered down into the popular world after a period of time. Such a theory might regard the aesthetic insights of early twentieth century artists as having filtered into the media world after the turn of the century. The fact that as late as *Counterblast* (1969) and the *Dew Line* on "Agnew Agonistes," he uses a contrast between Addison's time and our own, would seem to suggest the way that this type of popularization obsessed his thought.

Even the key by which all of this gets linked to script and print may have started in earlier poetic thought. Pound coupled his technique of discontinuity to the Chinese ideogram as Eisenstein did with his film theory of montage as juxtaposition. The account of the ideogram founded on Fenollossa's study of the Chinese written character suggested a link between graphic strategies and more general techniques. This would have been confirmed in a different sphere by the graphic devices of a Mallarmé (which McLuhan analyzed in his article on "Joyce, Mallarmé and the Press") or the early beginnings of concrete poetry in e. e. cummings or Apollinaire. Such strategies obviously affect McLuhan's way of viewing the press as early as *The Mechanical Bride*, where we have seen that the layout was treated as if it were a symbolist poem or some kind of verbal adaptation of the principle of collage.

It is important to stress here that the newspaper's following a technique like a symbolist interior landscape does not result from the insights of the poets. Many of those insights, as McLuhan rightly observed, come from the press to the poets, rather than the other way around. What is derived from the poets is the particular way of looking at the press that McLuhan adopts. In *Understanding Media* he points out this relation between the poet and the press:

> The format of the press—that is, its structural characteristics— were quite naturally taken over by the poets after Baudelaire in order to evoke an inclusive awareness. Our ordinary newspaper page today is not only symbolist and surrealist in an *avant-garde way*, but it was the earlier inspiration of symbolism and surrealism in art and poetry, as anybody can discover by reading Flaubert or Rimbaud. Approached as newspaper form, any part of Joyce's *Ulysses* or any poem of T. S. Eliot's before the *Quartets* is more readily enjoyed. (UM 216)

Earlier in his discussion, before revealing this alliance, McLuhan had discussed the press as "a mosaic successor to the book-form" (UM 211), tying this to the way mosaic is "the mode of the corporate or collective image and commands deep participation . . . inclusive rather than exclusive" (UM 211). This view of the "collective" follows the general poetic tradition, for Pound is apparently "telling the tale of the tribe," and Eliot bases his *Waste Land* on collective tribal rituals.

Now it might seem inconsistent that McLuhan describes the press as a "hot" medium, but this is not so, for the press in its technique of organization blends ads which are "good news" with "bad news" in a collage that "cools" it down and produces reader involvement (UM 210). Such examples are interesting for they naturally raise basic problems about McLuhan's media as categories. If the press can include ads at the same time as ads themselves can be discussed as a medium, it is necessary to see that the press is mixed media in some ways and that media is a convenient metaphor, not a categorical classification as McLuhan might suggest. McLuhan is following Wyndham Lewis in realizing how relevant poetics (as discussed or implied in productions by other artists) become for the cultural analyst.

What happens to the press in this example of his approach is characteristic of what happens in the approach in general. McLuhan tries to separate techniques of handling artistic problems from the complex value system in which they are embedded and to which they are related. Consequently, his analysis of the press falls far below that of Joyce to which he refers again and again, for Joyce in *Ulysses* and the *Wake* finds ways of linking the problems which McLuhan separates. Joyce's treatment of the newspaper is involved with people in interaction and in examining the specific modes of fragmentation involved in the whole process of journalism. The "Aeolus" section of *Ulysses* ironically questions the power of the press, demonstrates its social commitments, and exposes the tension between press and literature; the "scientific method" of Joyce would be closer to Marx and Weber than to McLuhan.

In McLuhan's own terminology (borrowed from Lewis) the temptation is to say:

BLESS McLuhan
for demonstrating the centrality
of the arts in the world man faces

BLAST McLuhan
for transforming the artist into
a mere ape of god aping technologist
and scientist in pseudo-objectivity

In part, McLuhan has trapped himself into making all artists "apes of god" in the same way that Pierpoint and Zagreus appear in Wyndham Lewis' *Apes of God*.

It is impossible to attempt in a limited space the task of showing how artists are essential to understanding two basic questions: Where is social and psychological theory going? What should be the reasonable limits of positivism within the human sciences? The development of the sociology of knowledge and its related interests has important ramifications in view of the impact McLuhan has had as an intellectual wooer of many of our artists and intellectuals. The problem is that McLuhan builds into his aesthetics difficulties that are not inherent, making his own vision rather more accessible, but less useful.

In *Understanding Media* the key to all this is television, which for the purposes of that book becomes the sine qua non for seeing where the "new world" is going. In most ways TV becomes the symbol for the culmination of the process that the electric world has created—TV, within its effects as McLuhan outlines them, defines the general trends and nature of that new society. Consequently, the TV medium is dealt with by McLuhan in terms of its relevance to the world of the arts.

Since at the point of time of his analysis, the social effects of TV and film differed considerably, it became necessary for McLuhan to attribute technological and technique-oriented reasons for that relevance rather than ones involving sociological or socio-economic considerations. In contrasting film and television in *Understanding Media*, McLuhan argues that TV is a mosaic form which demands social completion and dialogue as opposed to film which is "hot" and a "supreme expression of mechanism," offering as product—"dreams":

> The mode of the TV image has nothing in common with film or photo, except that it offers also a nonverbal *gestalt* or posture of forms. With TV, the viewer is the screen. He is bombarded with light impulses that James Joyce called the "Charge of the Light Brigade" that imbues his "soulskin with sobconscious inklings." The TV image is visually low in data. The TV image is not a *still* shot. . . . The resulting plastic contour appears by light *through*, not light *on*, and the image so formed has the quality of sculpture and icon, rather than of picture. (UM 312–13)

Here McLuhan brings together two major artistic visions, but combines them with technical inaccuracies and weaknesses of technical knowledge concerning the nature of television. The attractiveness of this synthesis to many people is that the writer becomes a kind of Renaissance man (a view not dissociated from some of the cruder doctrines of the Bauhaus). This Renaissance man-type approach at least gives a sense that there is a human control of what is going on. Yet a certain amount of that could be achieved quite successfully without the pseudo-technical approach of McLuhan, providing his audience recognized the authority of the artistic mode of analysis and of speculation. But since they do not, especially academic society in virtually all fields, the temptation to act as a quasi-magus becomes almost a necessary strategy of humanistic survival in a hostile environment. Therefore, McLuhan possibly hopes his audience will read this kind of thing on a number of levels and arrive at a view a friend once did—that in McLuhan the technical inaccuracies do not really matter. The difficulty is that unless the whole strategy becomes more complex, and therefore less immediately available to the reader, further oversimplifications occur which do lead to serious confusion.

Examining the passage quoted above, we see that McLuhan invokes the important distinction made by the art historian Panofsky concerning the difference between stained glass and painting. In *Gothic Art and Scholasticism*, Panofsky shows that when *light* shines *through* stained glass an effect occurs which is a visual realization of a scholastic *manifestatio*. This is sharply differentiated from *light on* which creates a different kind of effect in painting. Now this light through, according to McLuhan, produces the effect of sculpture or icon and creates the same contrasts as between the TV picture and the photograph, a difference he attributes to the scanning mechanism in TV. With further metaphorical play and witty puns on language, he makes the viewer the screen in the television experience, rather than simply a member of the audience watching the screen as in movies. By some further legerdemain, which is not involved at this specific point in *Understanding Media*, he also differentiates TV (as electric and mosaic) from perspectival painting which depends on light on and which is associated with film. In the process he presumably also associates the story line he finds in film with print.

The problem a critic has is that McLuhan invokes important concepts and ideas about *manifestatio,* icon, perspective, and photography but then leaves them in an impossible cluster where they will eventually have to be rejected even if in some more intellectually articulated way they could be made relevant. Element after element builds into this web, for surely McLuhan's interest in "stained glass" and *manifestatio* is tied up with the conclusion of *Finnegans Wake* (his commonplace book) which comes as the light breaks through the stained-glass windows of a "chapel" (an anagram of the two sets of initials of the husband and wife—HCE plus ALP). Yet Joyce's analysis of light and its effects contrasts sharply with McLuhan's.

In fact, by McLuhanesque association, Joyce becomes equal to Panofsky as a major artistic source of reference in the passage. But even the quotations from Joyce are used with some rather great freedom; for example the first one, "the charge of the light brigade," does not actually appear as such in the passage on television where Joyce uses "the charge of a light barricade." In the *Wake* passage, the conversion of electronic images into impulses and back is being played on in an interesting way.

> In the heliotropical noughttime following a fade of transformed Tuff and, pending its viseversion, a metenergic reglow of beaming Batt, the bairdboard bombardment screen, if tastefully taut guranium satin, tends to teleframe and step up to the charge of a light barricade. Down the photoslope in syncopanc pulses, with bitts bugtwug their teffs, the missledhropes, glitteraglatteraglutt, borne by their carnier walve. (FW 349)

Joyce ties together interpersonal encounter with technological transmission in a passage which, if anything, suggests a highly analytical interplay with the medium. "The charge of a light barricade" has many more interesting innuendoes than McLuhan's reinterpretation even for McLuhan's subject, since to some extent Joyce is fusing technical language with human vision and respecting the analytical force as well as the social implications inherent in a medium which had not realized itself in any mass, public sense.

The other Joyce reference comes from later in the same section or chapter where the actual phrase is "How our mysterbilder has fullen aslip. And who will wager but he'll Shonny Bhoy be, the fleshlumpfleeter from Poshtapengha and all he bares sobconscious inklings shadowed on soulskin" (FW 377). There would seem some doubt, however, as to whether the specific reference in this latter quote has primarily or even secondarily to do with the specific technical structure of the television image, for light in a dreambook has a great deal larger role to play in the process of waking up. If the image of TV is low on data, so is McLuhan in his way of adapting Joyce and the arts, which possibly causes some of the reader involvement that teases his audience into admiration and debate.

McLuhan's justification here is the certainty that the vision of the modern arts is unqualifiedly his vision—that Joyce, in fact, is his particular poet much in the way that other English scholars think of themselves as Milton men or Shakespeare men—and that Joyce is the basis of the modern arts. Without restricting some of the major importance of Joyce, this has some limitations as a theoretical position. But even allowing the total centrality of Joyce, it matters whether Joyce is better than McLuhan makes him or not. Obviously Joyce is interested in complex interplays in a way McLuhan is not, and especially in an interplay between the analytical and the poetic. This is even apparent in the play with television where the breaking down and building up of images becomes part of the wit. Joyce is very interested in the process of "the decomposition of elements for the verypetpurpose of subsequent recombination" in a way McLuhan is not, for this is precisely the type of structuralism as opposed to interest in structure that disturbs McLuhan as linear and logical.

But what kinds of questions are *not* being raised about television by McLuhan? Set size, ambient light, social relationships, social contexts, economic factors are all swept aside in his concentration on a technical explanation related to the analysis and history of artistic techniques. McLuhan does raise such issues as what kind of personality appears best on TV, what TV does do to certain kinds of events, or even what kinds of activity should most appropriately be carried on by TV. It is characteristic enough for him to tell us that the "electronic magazine" type of show is superior to drama on TV, although he may attribute the reason for this to the mosaic structure of the image in the set. In this kind of question he is legitimately asking if certain ways of structuring artistic experience favour an approach that deals with some kinds of events and not others, a matter which led Kenneth Burke to suggest that McLuhan might have profited by reading Lessing's *Laocoön* more carefully (M:PC 173–4). For McLuhan cannot get around his purely technological bias to pursue thoroughly such questions even if they become relevant.

But then, as Burke also pointed out, McLuhan is part of a tradition of writers who are apocalyptic and not political (M:PC 174) —a generation one assumes partly produced by phenomena like the New Criticism which insisted on objectivity and therefore made it difficult to discuss a political perspective. Television is the symbol of contemporary apocalypse, paralleled only by the computer which, in *Understanding Media,* forms in some ways an incidental afterthought. Its apocalypse is foreshadowed by Eliot and by such works as Austin Farrer's *Rebirth of Images,* but also by such theologizing as Teilhard de Chardin's *Phenomenon of Man.* Consequently, it is an attitude, as well as a content, that is an outgrowth of a considerable ideological and artistic turmoil in the earlier twentieth century. But, in McLuhan, it is always close to a certain marriage of the technological future with the Catholic vision of an apocalyptic age of participation. This led to McLuhan often being right for the wrong reason.

The miniskirt, for example, as he suggests in the *Dew Line,* may have little to do with sex and more to with the search for tribal costumes. The analysis is based on a concept that youth wants to play roles not occupy jobs. But then there is the problem of still newer and newer and more and more varied styles—minis, maxis, midis, pant suits, culottes, and costumes that vary from ancient slave to ancient queen, harem pants to empire gown. Variety is not normally the essence of the tribal and the adoption of variety is not unqualifiedly the rejection of the individual, even if it is remembered that a fashion industry is producing most but not all of this variety of costume. There is a difference between role playing in a small tribe with a limited number of roles and the self-dramatizing role playing of our own society which, as Fellini's *Sa-*

tyricon suggests, might be closer to Nero's Rome than tribal Africa.

But, for McLuhan, the miniskirt, as tribal and role playing, meshes with television as part of a new tactile world of a multi-sensory nature. It leads to curious contrasts, but contrasts based on McLuhan's reading of his literary background. TV is a shift from film, because "Film . . . as a form [is] the final fulfillment of the great potential of typographic fragmentation" (UM 294), in which Chaplin naturally became central, for the "clown reminds us of our fragmented state by tackling acrobatic or special jobs in the spirit of the whole or integral man" (UM 290). Interestingly enough the clown as a figure (replacement in part for the fool discussed in Chapter 8) is a preoccupation of Mallarmé and the symbolists, as Wallace Fowlie indicated in *The Clown's Grail*. (McLuhan carries this so far that he compares Joyce's Bloom to Chaplin, which influenced the writing of a whole study built around Bloom as Chaplin.) TV then marks the critical shift by a mass medium into an utterly new mode independent of print. Therefore, it is intimately related to McLuhan's reading of where the aesthetics and philosophies on which he bases his work, following the artists, are going.

Involvement is one of the key words, and it is a word which links McLuhan with the youth, even though temperamentally they are profoundly opposed. In McLuhan's theory, involvement occurs by the forcing of closure, a concept he takes from Gestalt psychology and criticism which suggests that audiences seek to close patterns in intelligible ways:

> The TV image requires each instant that we "close" the spaces in the mesh by a convulsive sensuous participation that is profoundly kinetic and tactile, because tactility is the interplay of the senses, rather than the isolated contact of skin and object. (UM 314)

Now this corresponds, as far as value judgements are concerned, to an aesthetics of discontinuity and to the idea that there is psychological explanation for both the effect of discontinuous forms and their erotic overtones. But to limit that aesthetics to TV becomes rather suspicious when one realizes that all art involves such closure and that Leonard Meyer has analyzed music from periods of intensely linear, print-oriented cultures that way. Even Gombrich, who McLuhan so frequently cites as an artistic authority, uses the concept of closure for realistic as well as impressionistic painting. McLuhan is trying to read psychological import into the revolution in the arts of the first quarter of the nineteenth century revolution here and now by creating parallels with popular culture, e.g. mesh stockings which he says are TV- and tactile-oriented.

"Tactility" used this way, as a term meaning an interplay of the senses, a phenomenon which is intensified by discontinuity, has close relationships to the way that McLuhan uses the technological revolution as a means of convincing us that symbolist aesthetics are now transforming society. Interplay, according to *Understanding Media*, produces a curious effect:

> Synaesthesia, or unified sense and imaginative life, . . . had long seemed an unattainable dream to Western poets, painters and artists in general. They had looked with sorrow and dismay on the fragmented and impoverished imaginative life of Western literate man, in the eighteenth century and later. Such was the message of Blake and Pater, Yeats and D. H. Lawrence, and a host of other great figures. They were not prepared to have their dreams realized in everyday life by the esthetic action of radio and television. (UM 315)

But is this charge that "they were not prepared" valid? For not only Blake or Yeats, or even Oscar Wilde who held that nature imitates art, would certainly not have been surprised to see their poetic visions transforming reality. McLuhan's own account of new "synaesthesia" is an imitation of the integrated view of such mythic artists, though like theirs it is not the only vision possible, no matter what McLuhan may try to suggest, nor does his account have the poetic intensity of Blake's or Yeats'. Once adopted as a position and pursued with his dedication and comparative over-simplification, such an aesthetics of integration has the amazing effect of creating a picture of the world where Walt Kelly's *Pogo* can occupy the same relation to the book as film to TV, partly because "the comic strip is close to the pre-print woodcut and manuscript form of expression" and *Pogo* "looks very much indeed like a Gothic page" (UM 318). The richness of the suggestions generated can hardly be questioned, but then they come to be judged not as fact as McLuhan advances them, but as interpretation translated into metaphor for artistic presentation.

TV then changes everything. The "mosaic mesh" does not favour perspective in art, it encourages the disappearance of many things we take for granted—the assembly line; line structures in management; the consumer package in entertainment and commerce; the sex goddess like Marilyn Monroe—and it promotes the appearance of new media like the paperback book. The paperback book, the book in a "cool" version (presumably because it is less perfect in its printing and less well finished) appears along with the small car, which is like a skin and which Brigitte Bardot drives barefoot to feel the "maximal vibrations." Television has its own clothing and styles, which have gone "so tactile and sculptural that they present a sort of exaggerated evidence of the new qualities of the TV mosaic" (UM 328). His view of such shattering change is even expressed in an apocalyptic imagery of a new union of art and life, a fusion which employs the concept of an implosion, a moving inward—as opposed to the technological explosion of the industrial age:

> All this adds up to the compressional implosion—the return to nonspecialized forms of clothes and spaces, the seeking of multiuses for rooms and things and objects, in a single word—the iconic. In music and poetry and painting, the tactile implosion means the insistence on qualities that are close to casual speech. (UM 328)

This is the vision of an age of unity expressed by the persistent development of metaphorical and analogical devices. It is a necessarily exclusive focusing on what the world in question will do to the unity of the individual sensibility within it as that sensibility is reintegrated with others. Its imaginative way of seeing relationships with which to play and its intense integrative method of bringing these into its own mosaic provide a kind of artistic validity. McLuhan may well be thinking of older discussions of poetry and applying them today, so that the poet in our age becomes in part a sociologist and psychologist teaching delightfully, just as the Renaissance felt the poet to be both philosopher and historian (though naturally these previous roles are included as well as the present ones).

Understanding Media tries to present, in an artistic way, a theory of art about the total range of contemporary human expressions. But one of its difficulties is that its mode of vision tends to be exclusive rather than inclusive. McLuhan is a poet manqué and a popularizer, two roles which explain both his strength and his weakness. To have been more would have produced a major creative writer rather than an essayist who is a poet manqué.

Probably the aesthetic import of McLuhan's vision, as he sees it, is summed up by the way that he describes TV as a symbol, as an epiphany for the artistic movement from Cézanne:

> It is not hard to explain this sensuous revolution to painters and sculptors, for they have been striving, ever since Cézanne abandoned perspective illusion in favor of structure in painting, to bring about the very change that TV has now effected on a fantastic scale. TV is the Bauhaus programme of design and living, or the Montessori educational strategy, given total technological extension and commercial sponsorship. (UM 322)

The Bauhaus, whatever its weaknesses in thinking about technology or sciences, did not abandon linear modes of thought or teaching, though it obviously very strongly favoured "the sensuous revolution." Sensory experience and intuition hardly require the disappearance of thought, and dancing has even been compared to "thinking with the body." Klee's *Pedagogical Sketchbook* and his notes in *The Thinking Eye* are characteristic of a mind that mediates the worlds that McLuhan opposes. Whatever the value of aspects of his poetic vision, McLuhan fails to integrate but rather dissipates. For him man lives in a dialectic between fragmentation and integration. Joyce seems closer to the Bauhaus with his phrases like "feelful thinkamelinks" (one which incidentally McLuhan does not seem to use) than to McLuhan.

Discussion of the more conventional arts as media only appears by accident in *Understanding Media*, even though they supply so much of the take-off point for the insights. This sketchy treatment produces one of the deep problems in the book, for it means that, while dealing with human expressiveness and communications, McLuhan never involves drama, seldom poetics, and virtually never gesture and dance. There may be incidental suggestions such as saying the TV mosaic may "be seen as dancing can, but is not structured visually" (UM 334). But even suggestions like this one are revealing with respect to the prospect of the arts: Is dancing structured merely visually, or is it not one of the most tactile of the arts involving kinesthesia in McLuhan's terms and utilizing music for sound and rhythm?

Kenneth Burke, along with other critics, concurs in discussing this area of McLuhan's thoughts, pointing out that McLuhan only refers briefly to a dramatistic theory of human expression in the discussion of games and in the very skimpy discussion on language. Yet to understand even McLuhan's method, these sections are crucial, for they reveal what he does accept of the human dramatic involvement in the media process. Burke observes quite properly that McLuhan later tries to extricate himself from one difficulty in *Understanding Media* by shifting in his next book to *The Medium Is the Massage*, though Burke is fundamentally thinking only of McLuhan's getting out of the formal trap of medium and message. Burke has perhaps unconsciously also suggested one important dramatic inadequacy in that the new approach only allows the media to affect you. Perhaps McLuhan had read Burke's playful suggestion that if he were to rewrite *Understanding Media* with "massage" rather than "message" as a central concept, it would produce something that people would read. In fact, such a rewriting did create a good deal of bawdy and erotic and humorous (conscious and unconscious) interplay.

Some of the problems of McLuhan's failure to encompass a theory of drama in his media approach become more acute as he moves into his later works where the presentation and the vision are fused into a new form. The other great failure of *Understanding Media* goes along with it—the approach, inherited from *The Gutenberg Galaxy* and attributed to Innis, which involves the treatment of the history of media as a history of the way technology determined man's development. This vitiates the whole basis of *Understanding Media*, even though it is not a historical book in the same way as the *Galaxy*, for *Understanding Media* still depends on analyzing a historical turning point.

Tom Wolfe asks "What if McLuhan is right?" But what if in his theory of history (partly because he lacks a sense of drama and the complexity of conflict at any given moment) he has gotten things at least partially the wrong way round?

In *Understanding Media*, McLuhan tries to tell us that when television replaces (or in our terms appears to replace) radio we move more radically from "hot" to "cool," from the "mechanical bride" to the wild body. But is it not just as likely that the accumulation of media experience in all forms and its interaction with other social phenomena does this? Multi-image and multi-screen film began in the twenties, not at Expo 67. The skirt first shortened dramatically and began a move towards liberation in the twenties and not in the sixties. Isadora Duncan in loose-fitting garb and bare feet explored the joining of inner and outer tactility in the early twentieth century dance. Nudity occurs in early films around 1920 and the sexual revolution builds up through the ads and the photo magazines and the films.

The history that McLuhan is trying to write is the right history, but it is tied to a misleading and mechanistic framework unworthy of his insight and the artistic practitioners and theorists that he is popularizing. If thinking about extensions creates images in which men become the sex organs of machines, the resultant analysis is perhaps only too predictable—the schizophrenic split of the McLuhanesque universe.

By the time *Understanding Media* was finished, McLuhan
had sold his artistic approach to North American business
and, as Tom Wolfe has described, become essential to
all sorts of business activities. Advisor to *Life* and
Look, to advertisers and publishers, management
consultant of the new society, McLuhan became the figure of the humanist advisor to
corporations Drucker had outlined in his
books. McLuhan theoretically felt this
was right, for like some Renaissance
humanists who had found the throne
room more urbane than the monastery,
McLuhan found the executive suite more
"in" than the small college campus classroom.
Perhaps he would feel differently now, for most of
this occurred before the youth revolution began to
demand everyone's attention and attract McLuhan's.

11
The Essai
Concrète

McLuhan not only impressed the executives and the
managers, he became of vital importance to the newer
artists. John Cage, the composer, and Stan VanderBeek, the
film-maker, were among those deeply impressed by McLuhan
because they responded to the creative power of his method as
much as to any of his specific theories. Besides, with the close
proximity of avant-garde art to revolution, McLuhan's criticism
of bureaucracy, schools, universities, and similar institutions spoke
a message the artists immediately understood. After all, what Mc-
Luhan attacked needed to be attacked and still does. When he
points out, in a *Dew Line* on Communism, that our investment in
educational hardware is seriously open to question, whatever his
reasons, the query is legitimate and will appeal to the active creator who knows that it is. Possibly, even more centrally, Mc-
Luhan's interest in discontinuous methods of dealing with material
as a way of manifesting the human sensual involvement in a complex society appealed to Cage and others. Their art had its roots in
the same artistic revolutions of Dada, surrealism, serialism, cinema,
and the Bauhaus as McLuhan's and they could read into his
juxtapositions and his aphorisms aspects that possibly even he
himself had not grasped.

Yet the artists also saw what McLuhan so clearly did not see himself—the phenomenon that had dated McLuhan's use of media as a metaphor. For, in McLuhanese, by 1960, *the medium was the rear view mirror*. To think in media terms is to see the present through the intellectual categories of the past; when it becomes clear that the present is already involved with mixed media or multi-media which are the "breakthroughs through breakdown" one realizes the inadequacy of media as a way of thinking about the arts. But then that is the message the world of the arts has leapt ahead to deliver while McLuhan is still primarily speaking about other mass activities of the present that are using the insights of an immediate past.

McLuhan himself has had to respond to this rapidly changing world, especially after he has made part of it more visible to more people by his own pronouncements about its nature. Possibly he always wanted to work in a creative form, to be some type of poet. An early work called *Counterblast* (not the recent *Counterblast* 1969), imitating Wyndham Lewis' *Blast*, might suggest this. But after *Understanding Media*, there was nowhere left to go except to produce television, write computer programmes, or find some other "cool," tribal mode of expression. This may have been his wish as early as *Explorations*, which some of his playing with type and layout suggests, and he may have felt he could do so only after the theoretical justification provided by the *Galaxy* (with its minor intrusion into headline techniques) and *Understanding Media*. But after the publication of the *Galaxy* and *Understanding Media*, with even critics as sympathetic as Raymond Williams pointing out the limitations of the book as a form for someone who felt that the book was either being left behind or transformed, the traditional book form was inadequate for McLuhan's later work.

McLuhan tried television, records, and other media, but he did not seem to succeed as well when working that far away from the literate tradition in which he developed. His next major move was to develop further what we have called the essai concrète. The first of these appeared in *The Medium Is the Massage*, in which McLuhan employed the format in a way which he considers "cool" and involving. The essays mixed media—photographs, ads, cartoons, newspaper-style layouts, design, straight text—in a variety of layouts and arrangements. They became presentations rather than dissertations, allowing for illustration rather than mere verbal comment. The first two attempts in the form (*The Medium Is the Massage* and *War and Peace in the Global Village*) are more diversified in the range of imagery, though less rich in the actual use of typography and layout than a more recent one—the new form of *Counterblast* (1969)—but then it had different purposes.

The Medium Is the Massage and *War and Peace in the Global Village* are aesthetic realizations of the theories of *Understanding Media*, but so is a different type of McLuhan production, his *Dew Line*. Each issue comes out in a different format and, like *Aspen*, the multi-media magazine, has included from time to time, kits of slides, recordings, playing cards, and other items as well as posters, news sheets, and various kinds of lithographed and printed material. McLuhan's ideas in these later works are mainly extensions of those in *Explorations* and *Understanding Media*, although they do show some essential development—especially with respect to his views on technology as extensions of man and his development of the technique of "hateful contraries" which he links to a theory of environments and anti-environments. Except for *Counterblast* (1969), they do not indicate major changes in direction (apart from his uneasiness about the concept "media"), although this most recent work, even if it is in a hard-cover format, uses multicoloured type and does suggest some subtle changes of emphasis.

These later works, though, are corporate art, for McLuhan has collaborated with a designer, Quentin Fiore, in the *Massage* and *War and Peace* and with a visual artist, Harley Parker, in *Counterblast* (as well as in *Through the Vanishing Point*). The collaboration with Parker seems more successful than that with Fiore, possibly because Parker has worked closely with McLuhan for years and shares the same interests in Joyce, in various contemporary movements, in the visual arts, and in cinema.

The fact that *The Medium Is the Massage* appeared in black and white rather than colour (whether because of publishing limitations or not) would seem to have a number of interesting implications. Putting aside McLuhan's own preference for Joyce and Klee and Picasso and his apparent feeling that the world of colour is still more involving and tactile, the use of black and white underlines the very sharp polarization in most of McLuhan's approach. With the *Massage*, an increasing emphasis on the destructiveness and violence of change begins to play a more predominant role. Take, for example, the spectacular double spread on pages six and seven. The entire two pages are a solid black, broken only by four lines of white type. Running across the top, in lower case letters almost two inches high, is the exclamation "and how!" The fact that the letters run into each other and, furthermore, are not set evenly adds to the jarring effect. The violence of this typography is reinforced by a quotation from Alfred North Whitehead, which appears in smaller letters along the bottom of the spread and upon which the "and how!" is commenting: "The major advances in civilization are processes that all but wreck the societies in which they occur." This sort of juxtaposition and play with typography is very powerful, and it is difficult to imagine it being any more effective in colour.

We shall see other similar examples as we continue discussion of *The Medium Is the Massage*, but despite the cleverness and effectiveness of the presentations a number of difficulties do arise. In his analysis McLuhan already has begun to realize the weakness of the concept of media, because he now tries to make electric technology itself a medium:

> The medium, or process, of our time—electric technology—is reshaping and restructuring patterns of social interdependence and every aspect of our personal life. (MM 8)

Primarily, this merely simplifies the presentation of the closing vision of *Understanding Media* and makes it easier to relate to the computer and the view of information transfer that McLuhan had developed there. If drama as a medium seemed to be muted in *Understanding Media*, McLuhan, perhaps responding to criticism, speaks now of the present environment as "the electric drama" (MM 9). His style for dealing with this "electric drama" becomes more compressed and more telegraphic, being arranged in short aphoristic-like paragraphs. A typical arrangement will link a bold face quotation from someone with a number of aphorisms ranging over such subjects as probing, education by humour, the book itself as a "collide-oscope," and the necessity of approaching society through means or process, rather than substance, as the only way of grasping rapid change. Next to layouts such as on page ten, images are juxtaposed—in this particular case a blown-up finger-print. The aphoristic style of the pensée that develops out of the essay tradition is joined with the use of type and layout and photograph at the same time as the poets, in a parallel technique, are probing the effects of typographical play in concrete poetry.

Yet in such an arrangement McLuhan is examining ways of responding or feeling. The Whitehead quote heading the page opposite the finger-print questions the insistence on "hard-headed clarity in the study of ideas." The first of McLuhan's aphorisms below the quote uses the concept of "probe" to justify the effects created through the opposition of "seemingly disparate elements"— the juxtaposition technique outlined in *Understanding Media* which, for McLuhan, goes back to the aesthetics of Pound and Hulme. The next aphorism picks up the theme of the joke as a mode of linking two disparates and hence as a mode of learning— a view which stems from Freud's *Wit and the Unconscious* and Arthur Koestler's writings on creativity (though they are not mentioned). The third aphorism adapts a pun from Joyce to suggest the "collide" technique of the *Massage*—the "hateful contraries" which, in their "interfaced situations" (as McLuhan now calls them, borrowing a metaphor from the world of electric information), provide insight into process.

The finger-print which is on the right-hand page, opposite the aphorisms, symbolically becomes a visual whirlpool or vortex. This symbol involves a number of suggestions about the McLuhan approach which he adapted from Poe and related to Poe's own image of a man at the centre of a vortex. Poe's technique for artistic control was to work backwards from effects, a strategy which McLuhan seems to use for probing media, and which created the techniques of symbolic poetry and the detective story. An interest in Poe's image of the vortex, and in his relation to popular culture and to symbolic poetry, goes back to *The Mechanical Bride* and even further to McLuhan's early literary criticism "Footprints in the Sands of Crime." The last major pictorial layout three pages from the end of the *Massage* picks up the Poe theme juxtaposed against a picture of a man surfboarding fully dressed and carrying a briefcase:

> In his amusement born of rational detachment of his own situation Poe's mariner in "The Descent into the Maelstrom" staved off disaster by understanding the action of the whirlpool. His insight offers a possible stratagem for understanding our predicament, our electrically-configured whirl. (MM 150–1)

Immediately preceding this full page layout is a reduced reproduction (printed in reverse, i.e. white on black) of the front page of the New York *Times* with the headline "Power Failure Snarls Northeast," and at the corner of the page a statement also in white against black (but in regular "book-type") about sense ratios and the electric age which concludes: "Were the Great Blackout of 1965 to have continued for half a year, there would be no doubt how electric technology shapes, works over, alters—massages— every instant of our lives" (MM 148). The observation is trivial, but the arrangement of the two double-page layouts combined with the use of the Poe material evokes a whole series of themes similar to the McLuhan treatment of television in *Understanding Media* where he claims that Poe was acutely sensitive to the significance of the telegraph as the beginning of the electric age and its mosaic transformation of American innocence into depth sophistication:

> Artistic rule-of-thumb usually anticipates the science and technology in these matters by a full generation or more. The meaning of the telegraph mosaic in its journalistic manifestations was not lost to the mind of Edgar Allan Poe. He used it to establish two startlingly new inventions, the symbolist poem and the detective story. Both of these forms require do-it-yourself participation on the part of the reader. (UM 323)

So *The Medium Is the Massage* works by what McLuhan felt to be Poe's technique of "offering an incomplete image or process [which involves] readers in the creative process."

This involvement with Poe as an artist is not a merely incidental portion of *The Medium Is the Massage*. One of its dominant themes has to do with the role of the arts in the new electric information environment. A complex layout running over a number of pages (132–36) develops the message that "Art is anything that you can get away with." The focus of these pages is a huge, grotesque, modern pop art statue (82 feet long and 20 feet high) found in Sweden of a bordello-dressed pregnant female in the position for delivery, or possibly sexual encounter. The statue is hollow so that people can walk between the legs into and out of the body by way of the vaginal opening, suggesting the dual motifs of return to the womb and sexual penetration. Consequently, it relates to the major topics of his essay concept.

Two such topics in *The Medium Is the Massage* (and one always has to grant McLuhan his potential criticism when forced to use ancient, space-oriented words like "topics" which might suggest some kind of arrangement in a visual structure, like the placing of items for memory in the traditional memory treatises which are involved with the arts) are: (1) The role of anti-environments; and (2) The nature of the electric information environment. The first of these is associated by McLuhan with the stance of the artist:

> Environments are not passive wrappings, but are, rather, active processes which are invisible. The groundrules, pervasive structures, and over-all patterns of environments elude easy perception. Anti-environments, or countersituations made by artists, provide means of direct attention and enable us to see and understand more clearly. The interplay between the old and the new environments creates many problems and confusions. (MM 68)

Humour and even amateurism become anti-environmental modes for McLuhan in the *Massage*. Humour and amateurism both apparently undercut the "official" and therefore take the present environment, which is invisible, and suddenly make it visible, the reason simply being that McLuhan sees art as creating a conflict which results in making things intelligible. He even suggests at one point that the environment is propaganda until dialogue begins, for dialogue, as a dialectical process between two rather than one, is of necessity involved in producing an anti-environment.

The real problem here is whether art is the anti-environment, or if it is the use of the anti-environment *with* the environment to produce a new synthesis. Traditionally in definitions, such as Coleridge's of the imagination, the artist has been viewed as the reconciler of opposites, not as the creator of one kind of new vision opposing the old. The question becomes whether the hateful contraries are *in* a work or whether a work *forms* a hateful contrary to reality. When the latter has been tried, as it was in the first version of More's *Utopia* consisting only of Book II, the possibility for misunderstanding is intensified and leads to further ways of encompassing the interplay of environment and anti-environment within the work.

McLuhan's view of the artist, which comes from Lewis who sees all great art as satire, necessarily provides an over-emphasis on the artist as enemy, a theme which is used in the *Massage* to suggest the "anti-social" nature of art. Linking it with the Poe theme, McLuhan suggests:

> The poet, the artist, the sleuth—whoever sharpens our perception tends to be antisocial; rarely "well-adjusted," he cannot go along with currents and trends. A strange bond often exists among antisocial types in their power to see environments as they really are. This need to interface, to confront environments with a certain antisocial power . . . is manifest in the famous story "The Emperor's New Clothes." (MM 88)

The child in the story, of course, is the anti-social creator of the anti-environment. The poet, the artist, the sleuth, the child create dialogue in McLuhan's terms, which is what he himself is trying to create. When critics like Kenneth Burke in *Language as Symbol* question McLuhan's writing as suggesting that he is in a dialogue, they perceive his method, but reject his premises. Yet McLuhan is fully aware of his position and wants to achieve precisely the effect that they condemn.

The difficulty is that McLuhan, even in the *Massage* and later, while making his theory of the anti-environment explicit, is unable to be dialectical in a sophisticated way. In a rare moment in the *Massage* he can say:

> All media work us over completely. They are so pervasive in their personal, political, economic, aesthetic, psychological, moral, ethical

and social consequences that they leave no part of us untouched, unaffected, unaltered. The medium is the massage. Any under-standing of social and cultural change is impossible without a knowledge of the way media work as environments. (MM 26)

But here in this admission of the way that media is part of the total life of man is also McLuhan's revelation of his own bias, for surely it is not unidirectional and therefore it is not only media that must be understood to understand change. It is precisely the interaction between media and change in other social and cultural processes that leads to an understanding of both.

McLuhan can speak of seeing the clash in our technological age so that the Theatre of the Absurd appears presumably as a con-temporary symbolic form similar to the Dance of Death. What he fails to see is that some conflict will always be present in human affairs producing the dance or the drama or whatever. Conse-quently, he insists on the close relation between conflict and the information age, which goes back to the closing of *Understanding Media*. Information, as McLuhan sees it, is the all-pervasive fact of this new electric environment. It is a phenomenon which pre-sumably causes us to abandon data processing and adopt pattern recognition. As such, it demands a knowledge of the humanities, eliminating specialism which is to be replaced by generalism. Again he makes the point in a pseudo-technological way, for in *Understanding Media* he suggests that light and electricity them-selves are non-specialist kinds of energy (UM 350): "The very idea of communication as interplay is inherent in the electrical, which combines both energy and information in its intensive manifold" (UM 354). The Bergson-Hulme terminology suggests the idealistic way McLuhan sees even his metaphors, but this is sufficient for him to assert that the electric age requires artists because of its nature, for "As artists began a century ago to con-struct their works backward, *starting with the effect*, so now with industry and planning" (UM 355). The end result is that the greater complexity of information processing and automation sys-tems actually makes things more general, thus requiring a new education—"paradoxically, automation makes liberal education mandatory" (UM 357).

With these themes, the appearance of information, and not TV, as central in *Massage*, is easier to comprehend, for it is ultimately the culmination of the electrical revolution as McLuhan sees it. Also, the centrality of art becomes clear; it is the only strategy for dealing with electrical instantaneity. The electric circuitry of information, according to McLuhan, is re-creating myth, returning man to a pre-verbal, pre-Platonic stage of sensibility—"Myth is the mode of simultaneous awareness of a complex group of causes and effects" (MM 114). It is today "our technology [that] forces us to live mythically, [while] we continue to think fragmentarily and on single, separate planes" (MM 114). This is what first leads Mc-Luhan to quoting the Balinese (a source he uses again and again): "We have no art; we do everything as well as we can" (MM 114). Such a concept fits well into McLuhan's Renaissance background, where art often seems to have extended to the whole art of living, the art of the courtier. The information revolution in this analysis is forcing man to return to such a view, for it eliminates any specialization, even specialization in the arts, and announces the return of the concept of the amateur—the Renaissance courtier in modern electric age guise.

However, information is not non-specialist. No matter how general the processes of programming and the way in which material is stored in a computer, it only goes there by the provision of the material from a variety of specialized sources. It could be argued that information only becomes relevant to the extent that it is differentiated, specialized material, for without differentiation there is no communication and no learning. McLuhan makes his notion of integration through information too amorphous by attending only to the fact that information in the broadest sense is a highly abstract and generalized notion with an abstract and generalized technology governing it. But the kind of information that is overpowering society is the huge quantity of specific detail that must be controlled and understood.

The Medium Is the Massage has moments of profound insight at particular points, but its general message is irresponsible and misleading. It suggests that there is no responsibility for finding modes of dialectical interplay between the specialist and the generalist, when this is precisely the most pressing matter in solving the information pollution of the world today. Similarly, there have to be ways to rediscover man as a relevant amateur in interplay with experts. But the process must occur continually within society and will not be achieved by some magical notion that electricity and information are mystical ways to recover the *participation mystique* of community, as McLuhan seems to imply in his discussion on myth (MM 114).

War and Peace in the Global Village, the next essai concrète, is different, though its general themes develop from *Understanding Media* and the *Massage*. It is centrally concerned with developing the strategy of conflict involved in the concepts of environment and anti-environment, with special reference to education, war, clothing, games, and a few of the other more promising aspects of the other books.

Some new themes also enter the McLuhan world in this work. While he discussed weapons in *Understanding Media*, now he turns directly to the problem of war. For the first time the problem of pain comes to occupy a central place in McLuhan's thought, developing from the idea that extensions which numb man can also create pain and suffering. The movement from the *Galaxy* to *War and Peace* is not one of increasing optimism.

Just as "media" in *Understanding Media*, and "massage" in *The Medium Is the Massage*, are used as organizing concepts, so in *War and Peace*, "war" occupies the same role. Games are mock-conflict; clothing becomes a kind of armour. The work, laid out as an essai concrète, employs many visual devices of counterpoint, though the overall effect is actually more conservative than *The Medium Is the Massage*. In its design, however, it is chiefly interesting for finally achieving a comprehensive use of the technique of marginalia which McLuhan wanted to use in the *Galaxy* and which he borrows from the "Triv and Quad" section of Joyce's *Wake*. This presumably enhances the manuscript character of the book, though the device is used rather more effectively in combination with cut-outs as in the April 1969 issue of the *Dew Line* on "Breakdown as Breakthrough."

The most remarkable thing about *War and Peace* is McLuhan's increasing insistence on bringing forth the artistic arguments implicit in the *Galaxy* and *Understanding Media*. The opening section of *War and Peace* dwells on art. The artist, McLuhan says, is the only person not to shrink from adapting to the global village, for the artist "glories in the invention of new identities" (WP 12). Again one finds the influence of writers whose concepts, like Pound's personnae or Yeats' "mask," seem to be possible sources for the emphasis McLuhan gives to role-playing. Pain comes to be emphasized because it is the "discovery of modern art" (WP 13). He has in mind the fact that the artists in trying to force attention to the coming new media on the audience created great pain, for new media being new extensions of man create a kind of "referred pain." In something resembling a contemporary aestheticism Mc-Luhan suggests that we must learn to savour the pleasure and pain of the newer aspects of our world, possibly in a semi-Taoist kind of way with "its art of being in the world" (WP 20). All this stresses a strange message, though, for art becomes adjustment:

> . . . the Oriental world is a world that was never dedicated to fragmented or specialist stress on the visual sense. Art has been considered the primary mode of adjustment to the environment. (WP 20)

But if, as McLuhan asserts in this discussion of art as adjustment, the importance is that the average man in the West becomes like the artist with a critical awareness of the "discriminations of sensory life as expressed in our environments," then he needs some method of critique and discrimination which McLuhan is overlooking.

War and Peace uses a strange mixture of Joyce and bits of history to examine the thesis that peace will come through the function of art in adjusting men to the environment and that this function is implicit in the action of the technology. The themes are not especially new, though the preoccupation with pain, war, and aggression is. As the poor man's art, fashion is seen as a form of aggression, as art itself is. In a "tribal or oral world," however, there are no fashions, for "all clothing and all technology is part of a ritual that is desperately sought to be kept stabilized and permanent" (WP 22–3). The essay is ultimately a work of technological mysticism, and mystification for that matter, which ends with turning the world back into a work of art as a means of defusing it:

> One of the peculiarities of an electric technology is that it speeds up this process of transformation. Instant and total rehearsal of all

pasts and all processes enables us to perceive the function of such perpetual returns as one of purgation and purification, translating the entire world into a work of art. (WP 183)

The man who writes this is not too surprisingly going to end with a quotation from Blake, for they share a very similar kind of mysticism. The only problem is that in achieving his vision McLuhan has somehow dealt with the horrors of the modern world—especially its intense pains, its violence, and its wars—while seeming to never have encountered unpleasant subjects. Such a way of operating leads to accepting the way of war because it is a mode of education and to accepting aggressive fall-out from education because it is a mode of war. Yet in McLuhan it is a conflict without conflict, for the realities of the strife are lost in the system of the dialectic, and the necessity of the conflict conceals the fact that the tensions might be maintained in very different ways, creative ways. The path of McLuhanesque integration leads to a state of adjustment which, if ever reached, would be beyond tension, beyond war and peace. That is one reading of some aspects of the arts of the nineteenth and twentieth centuries, but it is not the only one.

Though there are other ratios possible between the arts and man, especially in using the arts as ways of coping with the world about one, they rapidly disappear if the whole world becomes a work of art. To see the world under some guises as art, or to live in the world as an artistic act, is not the same as reducing the world itself to an object of art. There seems to be the tendency in this type of thought to turn conflict into a device for reaching a conflict-free integration and at the same time to forget that some of man's greatest achievements rise out of the creative control of conflicting interests. McLuhan ends up a romantic, celebrating with the German romantics the power of technology as a mystical way to salvation.

All McLuhan's work demonstrates a close interest in the arts, but he does not return to a work that is exclusively about the arts until *Through the Vanishing Point: Space in Poetry and Painting*, published in 1968, the same year as *War and Peace in the Global Village*. He gives a description of the central portion of *Through the Vanishing Point* as "a spatial dialogue," by which he means a series of paintings and poetic texts in juxtaposition which "provide a contemporary audience with the tools for discovery of a common ground among the manifestations of art in the world" (VP 2).

12

Through the Vanishing Point: McLuhan and the Sister Arts

In the early fifties McLuhan indicated in *Shenandoah* the central importance of Wyndham Lewis to his own theory of art. It is not surprising, therefore, that in the *Vanishing Point* the concepts of environment and counter-environment become central to explaining what art does. Lewis' dialectical theory of art suggested that art had to cause "the artist's public . . . to be brought to see its world and the people in it, as a stranger would" (LC 93), which explains why McLuhan argues that all the arts "heighten perception [and] might be considered to act as counter environments or counter gradients" (VP 2).

Given such a view, comparison and contrast are proper methods to use in coming to understand the arts, for they "have always been a means of sharpening perception in the arts as well as in general experience" (VP 238). Perhaps McLuhan follows the poet Ezra Pound, a collaborator of Lewis' in the Vorticist movement, in developing this principle, for the same use of comparison and contrast lies behind Pound's *ABC of Reading* and is outlined by Pound in "How to Read" (*Literary Essays of Ezra Pound* 15–41). In any case, the method follows the method of art itself, for all structures of art have been reared on a pattern of comparison and contrast, according to McLuhan (VP 238). The comfort with which his general analytical technique of dividing the world into environments and counter-environments meshes with the use of comparison and contrast makes this method appealing to him.

The ABC of Reading would certainly seem to have had a substantial influence on the development of this new kind of *essai concrète*, the *Vanishing Point*. The major portion of the aforementioned "spatial dialogue" consists of paintings and poems placed across the page from short verbal aphorisms which make comments, provide contrapuntal attitudes, or illuminate the material critically in other ways. It is as if Pound's technique of verbal exhibits used in *The ABC of Reading,* juxtaposed with each other and with Pound's own comments, were extended into the comparison of the sister arts of painting and poetry.

A typical example of how McLuhan creates a unit with this method is provided by Exhibit 39 where McLuhan juxtaposes a poem by e. e. cummings, "Chanson Innocent," with Klee's *Twittering Machine.* Across the page from "Chanson Innocent," these comments appear printed in a manner usually associated with poetic texts:

> A *myth is as good as a smile.* An alphabetic ballet
> of words in rite order—a dramatic order
> of language as jester.
> A jitterbug interface before the
> monolithic space of the Frug and Watusi with their
> sculptural inclusiveness.
> Emphatic rejection of the bureaucratic modes
> of the Establishment.
> The balloonman satyrized for the sake of
> the Rites of Spring? (VP 187)

On the next page, there is a black and white print of Klee's *Twittering Machine* and on the other page more comments:

> Preview of the TV aerial, electric configuration
> patterned to pick up nonvisual energy.
> Compare "Weed in the water am I."
> "Abstract" art signaled the end of visual space.
> The *Twittering Machine* is a kind of
> *sensus communis.* (VP 189)

This pattern of constructing a unit is used throughout and in many ways it provides the quintessence of the McLuhan mode:

discontinuous juxtaposition and witty aphoristic statements. This way of handling criticism is an art form in itself and is quite close to the type of standards for artistic activity that McLuhan sets down at the end of the *Vanishing Point* where he quotes *The Book of Tea* as part of a "Note on Tactility":

> In art the importance of the same principle is illustrated by the value of suggestion. In leaving something unsaid the beholder is given a chance to complete the idea and thus a great masterpiece irresistibly rivets your attention until you seem to become actually a part of it. (VP 266)

McLuhan uses this strategy to try to tease the reader into seeing the need for relating the Cummings poem with the Klee painting. In the process, he uses suggestive language such as "words in the rite order" (taken from Joyce's phrase "the rite words by the rote order" [FW 167]), or he suggests double-entendre through spelling "satyrized" with the "y" (suggesting historical dimensions of satire), or he uses his own particular language or jargon, such as "sculptural inclusiveness" and "electric configuration." The verbi-visual mosaic he creates links not only Klee with Cummings, but both of them with Joyce. Motifs move back and forth from painting to poem: the Klee is the work of a jester, the Cummings is verbal "abstract" art; the Klee is "jitterbug interface," the poem is an "alphabetic ballet"—a verbal correlative for the *sensus communis*. The interpenetrations provide considerable material for a contemplative exploration of both "cultural objects" and their role in McLuhan's vision.

Like many other McLuhan writings, *Through the Vanishing Point* seems to provide a curious combination of something Mc-Luhan does well with the development of some theories that do not seem to come off. But unfortunately, if the underlying theories have inadequacies, then obviously to some degree the exhibits will be vitiated by the same inadequacies. One thing that is weakened most certainly is the fundamental theory about which the book revolves—the crucial relevance of the "vanishing point" as a symbol of the transformation of the arts in the Gutenberg era.

The "vanishing point" refers to the phenomenon discovered in the Renaissance which allowed painters to provide a perspective which seems to infinitely regress, giving the viewer the sensation of looking into a picture as if he were looking through a window. Since it obviously had very substantial influence on the development of the art of painting, it came to be one of those extremely important technical points tying together geometry and painting. As any such major discovery, it not only relates to the actual change that occurs in painting, but it also becomes a much broader symbol.

Erwin Panofsky, an art historian McLuhan frequently quotes, developed this view in an article called "Perspective as Symbolic Form," where he argues that perspective is important in the Renaissance because it creates a systematic space which is mathematized. But Panofsky goes beyond the concept of space to suggest that perspective is actually a symbolic expression of new ideas, for the vanishing point creates a point of infinite regression. The discovery of Renaissance perspective, then, has to do with the discovery of ways of mathematizing infinity which, for the Renaissance mind, results in a simultaneous reduction of the sacred. The difference between Panofsky and McLuhan is that Panofsky sees new Renaissance ideas in the arts and in philosophy as having a reciprocal interaction, while McLuhan sees them in a deterministic manner in which the discovery of moveable type and the associated discovery of perspective determine certain new ways of acting and seeing.

For this reason, McLuhan has to create a history of attitudes towards space which is not consistent with any of the art historians he most frequently uses as authorities—Gombrich, Panofsky, Giedion. McLuhan's story of the development of space must naturally result in a return to an acoustic, pre-civilized concept of space in the contemporary period, for McLuhan does not have any theory of progress. It also must eliminate the possibility of relative realizations of perspective at earlier dates and consequently cannot accept Panofsky's contribution that the Greeks with their vanishing axis had some idea of perspective as it effected reality, though not an idea for mathematizing space such as the Renaissance discovered. But most important, it means that McLuhan has to overlook the embarrassment of the way that his theory of space is out of mesh with that which Giedion develops in *The Eternal Present*.

In the *Vanishing Point*, McLuhan does cite Giedion's *The Eternal Present* when discussing Hesiod's *Works and Days* in relation to the Zetlin painting *I Am That I Am*. He agrees that in *The Eternal Present*, Giedion says that "the Greeks no more managed to achieve the visual enclosure of space than did the Incas. The new space breakthrough was left for the Romans" (VP 225). But he does not apply the difficulties that Giedion's analysis might create for his own view of space, for Giedion creates three periods, none of which includes the Renaissance and its vanishing point or moveable type. As he says in *The Eternal Present: The Beginnings of Architecture*, the three major discoveries of different ways of conceiving space are related to:

1) The primitives, the Egyptians and the Greeks, who conceived of space as having "its freedom of all directions, and the absolute absence of compromise with which it placed objects in space with no regard to their limits or their relation with their neighbours . . ." (522).

2) Roman times until the present when "The dome of Hadrian's Pantheon at the beginning of the second century signalized the complete breakthrough of the second space conception. From that time on, the concept of architectural space was almost indistinguishable from the concept of hollowed-out interior space" (523–24).

3) The contemporary, in which there is some return to an awareness of the relation between architecture to sculpture in which architecture is approaching sculpture and sculpture architecture, but in which also "the modelling of interior space continues, but there is a profound change in the approach to its vaulting" (526).

If the argument is that McLuhan is talking about painting and not architecture, this will not work because his arguments about space are supposed to relate all kinds of activities to one another. In fact, in the *Vanishing Point* he uses Piaget and Inhelder, the Swiss psychologists who studied the child's conception of space; Edward Hall, the anthropologist who studies space relations in *The Hidden Dimension*; Robert Ardrey, the writer about Africa, and his controversial notion of territoriality; as well as artistic sources. McLuhan is trying to conceive some grand theory about the evolution of space which will cover all of his needs, but without the discrimination of the art historians who do talk about specific spaces related to specific problems, the theory is bound to be tenuous in the extreme.

Along with that theory go others of equally shaky adequacy about the physiological processes involved in the perception of space and visual experience. McLuhan's arguments about the eye and its involvement are based upon a superficial reading of physiology which suggests to him that since the fovea—the centre of the retina and point of greatest visual acuity—contains only cones and is therefore most sensitive to colour, while the peripheries contain only rods and therefore cannot distinguish colour, that colour is more tactile because it involves the whole retina (though he says eye). This is a perfectly mythical and non-existent physiological process, and the statement is so speculative as to be totally irrelevant, for there is not that much really known about the total participation of the eye in vision, and there is even considerable uncertainty about the nature and operation of colour vision.

If such theories seriously accompany the analyses and presentation of the *Vanishing Point*, potential for distortion is rather substantial. Yet the *Vanishing Point*, perhaps more than any other of his books, indicates why he has a certain power and insight without having any particularly interesting theoretical coherence or adequacy. In the first place, he chooses intrinsically interesting problems to ask questions about—the vanishing point, the nature of space, the nature of visual perception. And he parallels these questions with questions stemming from other human activities which most of us would assume are associated to a considerable extent—the nature of poetic presentations, the perception of poetic language, and the effect of the other arts on the verbal arts. This is neither very remarkable nor likely to be very important raised in just this way, for the questions might be better approached in a treatise on aesthetics, or psychology, or fine arts, or linguistics. What he does do is to go further and try to correlate these questions with the actual insights of practising artists. He takes the artist very seriously, something he has been telling his audience ever since he began writing. Could it be that he even takes the artist so seriously that he is quite prepared to use the strategy of pseudo-scientific or pseudo-academic treatment of problems in the "science of art" to provide a kind of positivistic respectability?

Taking the artists seriously, though, provides McLuhan with a vast fund of material which might be called introspective, but which has the advantage of being the body of insights provided by the practitioners themselves. For this reason he can use Joyce or Lewis as artist-theorists, borrowing their concepts as probes to examine the world around him. When these probes are transferred from being used on the world itself to being used with respect to works of art, then both the probes used and the object examined may well render forth insight into the creative process.

This is what makes the *Vanishing Point* so important for understanding McLuhan and so difficult to assess in terms of itself or McLuhan's other works, for it is to a large extent a work of art using a set of pseudo-theories to compare and contrast other works of art in order to give an intelligible vision of the present moment. Given the limitations of McLuhan's view of the visual and his prejudices about what is what at any point in the historical spectrum, it is impossible to imagine that the pursuit of this technique could be totally successful.

To allow the book to work at all, it is first necessary to recognize that the objects juxtaposed are not selected with the exquisite precision that many might demand. But McLuhan's own attack on good taste might prepare us for the way he can overlook such demands. Commenting on an International Silver ad he says:

> Good taste is a sin of omission. It leaves out direct awareness of forms and situations.
> Good taste is the first refuge of the noncreative. It is the last-ditch stand of the artist.
> Good taste is the anesthetic of the public. It is the critic's excuse for lack of perception.
> Good taste is the expression of a colossal incompetence. It is the "putting on" of the genteel audience as a mask or net by which to capture ambient snob appeal.
> (VP 213)

McLuhan is not following the path of "good taste" or of "adequate scholarship," but rather the intuitive selecting of exhibits from his and Parker's personal experience of the periods of history. He is allowing the principle of conflict to be of paramount importance in arriving at intelligibility, but the most powerful concepts in his work actually come from symbolism, from Pound, from Joyce, and from Lewis. His and Parker's selections often release interesting clashes which are mediated by the aesthetic materials he borrows from these sources. By removing the art works from their usual frame and placing them in conjunction with his aphorisms and other art works, he destroys their context and environment, allowing them to speak anew, at least according to his theory.

Fundamentally, the book becomes a complex argument for the type of artistic insight that he insisted people should have at the conclusion of *Understanding Media*, but here it is placed immediately in the context of the arts themselves. Consequently, to discuss the *Vanishing Point*, it is almost necessary to do it the violence of attempting to extract the argument from its "spatial dialogue," except that this seems fair enough in terms of the particular introduction, "Sensory Modes," and conclusion, "The Emperor's New Clothes," which McLuhan provides and which are themselves essays about the dialogue itself. The forty-nine exhibits, or presentations, in the "spatial dialogue" range from the primitive to the very modern, opening with a primitive song and a reproduction of a cave-painting and concluding with an exhibit in which the opening eighteen lines from Eliot's *Waste Land* are juxtaposed with one of the Hogarth series, *The Rake's Progress*.

Exhibit 37 is in many ways the fulcrum for the history that McLuhan presents, since it deals with Seurat, paralleling him with Hopkins and asserting of him:

> The Oriental moment of reversal—
> Seurat prophet of TV.
> Seurat is the art fulcrum between Renaissance
> visual and modern tactile. The coalescing of inner and
> outer, subject and object.
> Seurat, by divisionism, anticipates quadricolor
> reproduction and colour TV.
> (VP 181)

If Seurat is the fulcrum, then contemporary art moves away from the Western mode of perspective to an Eastern mode which sees space in its primitive manner. Hopkins serves as an accompaniment to this shift by emphasizing tactility, which according to McLuhan comes about from "minimizing syntax intervals." He anticipates modern ways of perceiving by "perceiving nature itself as an art form" (VP 179).

Quite apparently, the aesthetic history here is going to be accommodated to McLuhan's philosophy just as intellectual history is in *The Gutenberg Galaxy*, so that the history is chiefly an illustration of an aesthetic—and that aesthetic quite obviously is at one with the aesthetic of *Understanding Media, The Medium Is the Massage*, and *War and Peace*. Yet it should be apparent that McLuhan's aesthetic should not necessarily rule out many other writers and artists who treated nature itself as an art form—the Renaissance of Bacon, Donne, and Browne; the particular vision of neo-Augustanism of Pope; and certainly the vision of the Romantics. Somehow this insight into Hopkins seems open to question. In English poetry from Chaucer and Spenser to Joyce, the tendency to treat nature as an art form and to see the reciprocity between nature and art is so dominant as to leave very significant questions as to what McLuhan does mean. Certainly Hopkins does deal with new artistic ways of handling relations between man and nature, but his distinct contribution is not in the perception of "nature itself as an art form."

Reading the *Vanishing Point* as such an aesthetic treatise, one is immediately struck by the massive vocabulary from certain areas of early twentieth century literary theory: the "vortex," from Pound and Lewis; the concept of "participation," from Eliot; the concept of "epiphany," from Joyce; the concept of "matching and making," from Gombrich; the emphasis on metamorphosis, intimately involved with Pound, Joyce, Rilke, and Eliot as well as other practitioners and historically developed by Elizabeth Sewell; the concept of "multilevel exegesis," used by Northrop Frye and borrowed from traditions of scriptural exegesis; the technique of the haiku, introduced by Pound and Yeats; a use of parataxis as a fundamental concept, which is developed by Auerbach and many others. The catalogue indicates a wide acquaintance with contemporary theory concerning the arts, but with a particularly strong emphasis on symbolist and post-symbolist sources.

Taking McLuhan's own statements, this would appear a reasonable assessment, for he especially singles out Lewis and Joyce for attention. Now what seems most at stake here is that Lewis and Joyce, who had deep suspicions of one another, do not reconcile themselves at any level to provide a co-ordinated aesthetic. Possibly it might be argued that Joyce could subsume Lewis and perhaps McLuhan hints at this, but the fact is that in the aesthetic of the *Vanishing Point* it certainly does not happen. Lewis dominates, and in some ways Lewis' aesthetic is more satisfying than McLuhan's for the simple reason that McLuhan does not take the very specific stance with respect to the so-called time philosophy of Pound, Chaplin, Joyce, and others that provided Lewis with a very integrated basis.

A Lewis painting appears in Exhibit 40 of the *Vanishing Point* along with a Pound poem, "Portrait d'une Femme." Naturally the emphasis is strongly on aspects of their work which would relate to the Vorticist movement. On the page across from the Pound poem, McLuhan comments:

> Wyndham Lewis regarded
> Pound and Joyce as a Sargasso Sea, a vortex
> of historical debris.
> (VP 191)

The vortex, as an immediate manifestation of energy, was tied up with the industrial world, and of Lewis' painting McLuhan says:

> The sitter's mask as a vortex is a processing of personal
> energy by the new industrial environment.
> (VP 193)

Both Pound's poem and Lewis' *Portrait of an Englishwoman* (an angular construction of heavy girder-like elements and construction blocks) are described as "puppets," the first "not as extension of man, but as immediate manifestation of energy" (191), and the second as "a servomechanism of the environment" (193). But this is in a sense precisely the highly dialectical lead that McLuhan develops from Pound and Lewis, which is quite different from the aesthetics of Joyce—or for that matter the symbolists, the chief of whom, Mallarmé, Pound described as a poet marked by "mushiness."

Now obviously, there are two ways that a Joyce might subsume

176

a Lewis: one, by the strategy of denying the need for coherent reconciliation and incorporating him as a manifestation of the total view of the contemporary period, which suggests a kind of mystical embracing of everything within the Weltanschauung by the overriding spirit of the period; the other, by demonstrating that at a certain level the insights of Lewis are incorporated into the Joycean poetic vision because the particular analytical quality they provide is one, but only one, useful aspect of that vision.

The first is the path McLuhan chooses; the second is Joyce's. The first is the route of the individual trained as an intellectual historian within a certain period of the development of intellectual history; the second is that of a contemporary attempting, like the Bauhaus, to genuinely reconcile the analytical and logical with the intuitive. In *Finnegans Wake*, Joyce attacks Lewis, associating him with Shaun, the brother of the artist-twin Shem. Lewis appears as Professor Jones, a pedantic and somewhat over-categorical type, insisting on the primacy of space. Like other Shaun manifestations, this one is eventually amalgamated, or "reamalgamerged" in Joycean language, into the total man, but it is equally obvious that Joyce has very serious reservations about Lewis' approach. Throughout the *Wake*, take-offs on Lewis occur, e.g. treating the title of *Time and Western Man* as "Spice and Westend Woman" (FW 292). The new age, Joyce seems to be indicating, is going to appear because of an ability that we will develop to synthesize the analytical qualities of Gutenberg lineality with the intuitive qualities of the pre-Gutenberg (though naturally Joyce does not use such crude divisions as pre- and post-Gutenberg, since he sees the oppositions as inherent in the whole progress of man from the earliest days until the present).

This is just where McLuhan's views encounter genuine difficulty if he wishes to retain Joyce as his major authority. McLuhan argues that the basis of the analysis in the *Vanishing Point* is a concept of environment and counter-environment, a methodology which would seem to have a great deal to do with Joyce's constant use of opposed pairs in *Finnegans Wake*. But Joyce does not try to generate a simple view of history which uses these oppositions. He can see the way his work in *Finnegans Wake* is quite neo-classical, the way his theory of structure derives from Ben Jonson,

Pope, Swift, and Sterne. There is no need on his part to posit a period of rigidly dedicated orientation around print, and then somehow to forget it as McLuhan does when he tries to use *The Dunciad* to conclude *The Gutenberg Galaxy*.

What McLuhan opts for in the *Vanishing Point* is an eclecticism in which the insights of Poe and Mallarmé, Lewis and Pound, Valéry and Eliot and Joyce will work together into a mosaic. The strategy for achieving this is to use every one of these people as material for aphorisms to be counterpointed with poems, paintings, and McLuhan's own words. There is certainly nothing wrong with this type of borrowing since it is a well established feature of literary criticism that McLuhan could well have learned from Jonson, in *Timber: or Discoveries*; Coleridge, in his critical writings; or even Eliot, for that matter. But then such borrowing has usually not been carried on to give the synthesis the blessing of all the aesthetics from which the borrowings came or, for that matter, from any particular one. Yet McLuhan suggests in his *Playboy* interview this is precisely what he thinks he is doing. He is a mere voice passing on the deeper wisdom of the symbolists and their successors like Joyce or Pound.

The difficulty arises if their own way of handling things is incompatible with McLuhan's and compatible only with a theory of equal sophistication to their own. Joyce had an extremely complex way of reconciling the various aspects of his poetic vision and aesthetic. The eclectic borrowing of a phrase here or there would not really produce a Joycean view. Joyce did not see his work as very loosely structured and random in nature, a collection of aphorisms or memorable quotes, such as McLuhan's. He strongly emphasized the overall structural patterns that he created and he painstakingly wove material from each part of his work into every other part. He compared his activity to something as highly ordered as *The Book of Kells* and a comparison of it could be worked out in elaborate detail with reference to Henri Focillon's discussion of *The Book of Kells* in his *Life of Forms in Art*.

The McLuhanite will immediately answer that *The Book of Kells* is manuscript, pre-print, and go back to McLuhan's earlier discussions of it. But that does not escape the very simple fact that in his execution Joyce shows a fondness for grammatical play, and play with logical patterns, and intricate work with aspects of meaning which is quite contrary to the anti-linear spirit which McLuhan attributes to them. This does not preclude Joyce's being interested in large-scale patterns like those found in Freud, or Darwin, or Marx, as well as Vico and Bruno. Joyce, in fact, includes an awareness of some of the creative aspects of Marxism in his work, as Bernard Benstock has partly shown in *Joyce-Again's Wake*, and as any careful attention to the way his dialectic operates on a social and historical level might have suggested. Such an interest is ultimately what McLuhan calls linear and should prevent involvement, even though on the contrary McLuhan is using it as the basis of what should be new. Interestingly enough, neither a quote from Joyce nor a page from *The Book of Kells* appears in *Through the Vanishing Point*, even though Joyce is usually credited as his prime source for material about the arts, a point underlined by his extensive use of Joyce in *War and Peace in the Global Village*. Part of this may just be an oversight based on absence of such material elsewhere, but part of it may be that Joyce really does not fit well into McLuhan's total aesthetic, which such inclusions would complicate.

Joyce did not accept, any more than Klee or Moholy-Nagy, the selective view that McLuhan is unfolding. The device of multiple oppositions of which Joyce was so fond only worked for him because the oppositions coalesced. Then new oppositions occurred. McLuhan's view that the "arts and sciences serve as anti-environments that enable us to perceive the environment" (VP 242–3), may seem a little like this, yet it is quite distinct in that there seems to be no very careful way in which the unfolding patterns in McLuhan function in the same way.

McLuhan uses the view, instead, to argue that the artist serves as an "Early Warning System" (compare the title of McLuhan's *Dew Line* magazine) and that he is "a person who is especially aware of the challenge and dangers of new environments" (VP 238). Joyce would have agreed with this, but not with the corollary that McLuhan develops from it of the artist as the perpetual enemy. In McLuhan's view, art, as Wyndham Lewis argued, is subversive, a symbolic or parabolic action (VP 252), which means either throwing together or throwing against: the etymologies of parable and symbol, according to McLuhan. For these reasons, McLuhan can speak of Pop Art as nonart:

> Today what is called "Pop Art" is the use of some object from our own daily environment as if it were antienvironmental. Pop Art serves to remind us, however, that we have fashioned for ourselves a world of artifacts and images that are intended not to train perception or awareness but to insist that we merge with them as the primitive man merges with his environment. Therefore, under the terms of our definition of art as antienvironmental, this is nonart except insofar as the illumination of the interior environment of the human mind can be regarded as an artistic stance. (VP 243)

The repetition throughout McLuhan's works about the Balinese having no word for art is to remind us that art as a specialized profession is disappearing as the whole environment becomes a work of art: the machine has made nature a work of art; then electric circuitry made the machine a work of art; now the satellites have made the entire environment a work of art.

One difficulty in accepting McLuhan's confusing thesis is that it is not new. The Renaissance saw nature as the art of God and it was not just the book that created that view. It is easy and common to treat an environment, no matter how broad, as a cultural object and therefore as a work of art. But far more complex is the fact that McLuhan insists on art as something involved in being thrown against or thrown together, as an anti-environment, and rejects the possibility that Pop Art could be art. Yet this hardly seems like an adequate kind of definition, not only for the discursive portions of McLuhan's work, but even to cover all of the examples that he includes in his exhibits. The use of Herbert's "The Collar" is a good enough example. One of McLuhan's aphorisms reads: "A peripety at the end, the moment of truth or recognition/achieved by contrast." Here the conflict is within the poem and the poem achieves a reconciliation of opposites, as in fact McLuhan's next aphorism suggests: "A stepping up of visual values makes a new dichotomy/between the spiritual and the material" (VP 95). This remark is paralleled by another on the Caravaggio painting on the next page where the aphorism reads: "The contrast between low living and high thinking—the Caravaggio formula" (VP 97).

The relation of art form to real world or of anti-environment to environment is much more complex, for both are within the poem and within the painting, interpenetrating content and form, medium and message. To speak about either as a counter-environment, even at its own point in time, just does not evoke the full interplay of the artistic encounter. What McLuhan has done is to magnify his rather singleminded dialectics of "hateful contraries" into a fundamental aesthetic principle which may have been quite exciting when Lewis first conceived of the artist as enemy, but which somehow loses credibility over time. If the clown or jester is really the type of the artist, then the role of enemy is absorbed in a far more complex set of ratios.

The *Vanishing Point* reveals McLuhan in both his weakness and his strength, an excellent empirical critic but not a theorist—a true inheritor of the virtues and the vices of I. A. Richards and the new criticism. What results is a very serious myopia that clouds the most exciting points about the contemporary art scene. He seems to be supporting the spirit of Herbert Read when he suggests that Cézanne led the revolt against the exclusively humanistic conception of art (VP 258-9) and amplifies the point by suggesting that the new art is humanism in reverse, the corporate image of an integral society. And that *is* McLuhan, the new schoolman, celebrating the demise of humanism and the restoration of a mediaeval-like unity.

But just because formalistic art is here to stay, as Read puts it, that does not mean Read abandons humanism as McLuhan seems to do. In *The Forms of Things Unknown* Read says:

> My desire is to redefine humanism in the terms of sensuous apprehension of being, which apprehension can be as austere, precise and classical as you like. . . .
>
> A wealth of concrete insights—that is the point: humanism is the creation of such a wealth of such concrete insights. . . .
>
> A new humanism, therefore, may turn out to be the old humanism written in a new language, but we must not underestimate the difficulties of the task, for there is no one ready to teach us a new language: poets must be born who will invent its syllables. (177-8)

But is not this what McLuhan really wants to do, if he could find the language and the principles of order and the way to proceed?

Instead he chooses to be a demi-clown, playing the role of a humanistic broadcaster of implicit values as objective facts in a participational jazz version of an Addisonian middle style.

The *Vanishing Point* should demonstrate, in spite of its confusions, that art is important and that the critic's approach to culture and pop culture has a good deal to reveal. It should suggest various potentially important kinds of new languages mixing media, using aphorism and type arrangement, and developing new methods of critical comparison and contrast. As long as the reader can avoid the mystification of the overall movement and can rise above the immediate empiricism, there is present behind it all a fundamental awareness of what contemporary humanism ought to be about, even if the tone is that of a schoolman believing himself happy to see the decline of the humanistic.

The vortex is a familiar McLuhan image by now. It moves all the way from his early literary criticism about Poe, through *The Mechanical Bride*, right down until the publication of *Counterblast* (1969). The second Exhibit in the *Vanishing Point* is the juxtaposition of a Pound haiku, "In a Station of the Metro," with a Chinese written character (VP 36, 38). Across from the Chinese character one of the aphorisms reads: "In contrast to phonetic letters, the ideograph is a vortex that responds to lines of force. It is a mask of corporate energy" (VP 39). Later, next to Coleridge's "Rime of the Ancient Mariner," is a remark: "The ballad form was a new vortex. A corporate mask of the pastoral antique" (VP 135). In a more general way, he observes that "A new poetic, or musical, rhythm is a vortex of corporate energy" (VP 183).

13

***Counterblast:*
The Vortex in
Full Motion**

The term vortex comes to McLuhan from Wyndham Lewis and Ezra Pound and their poetic movement which produced Lewis' folio-sized magazine *Blast*. The image rather nicely linked Poe with Pound and Lewis because of Poe's literary use of the image in his "Descent into the Maelstrom." Fundamentally though, vorticism had to do with nodes of energy and nodes of energy concentrated about images. *Blast* presented the manifesto of the movement, not merely as print, but as headline and advertisement. The very nature of print (i.e. newsprint) became part of the artistic effect of the manifesto, a pronouncement pushing the role of the artist as enemy and the role of the arts as satire. *Blast* became a weapon, or in McLuhanesque terms, a counter-environment, to be used to make the audience aware of the environment. In creating *Counterblast* (1969) McLuhan takes particular care to point out that:

> The term *Counterblast* does not imply any attempt to erode or explode *Blast*. Rather it indicates the need for a counter-environment, as a means of perceiving the dominant one. (CB 5)

Counterblast continues the collaboration with Harley Parker, who worked on the *Vanishing Point*, as well as exploring some new aspects of the essai concrète, this time chiefly in the area of typography (colour, size, arrangement, layout, etc.). In it McLuhan continues his "creative" activity following the lead of a creative artist he greatly admired, Wyndham Lewis. In spite of this, *Counterblast* is a curious book, for it appears to have come full circle, returning to a very different position, in some ways, from that McLuhan has expressed elsewhere.

The differences are subtle, but still genuine. To some extent they are primarily differences of emphasis in dealing with certain media. Film, for example, is not treated as a "hot" medium: "The content of film is a collection of media within media. The 'message' is all of them at once" (CB 23). Not just the film but the book, too, receives a new emphasis in this treatment, for "the TV screen is close in form and immediacy to the book page. The movie screen was not" (CB 98).

But if books are not becoming obsolete and movies mix media, the treatment of words themselves is also more complex. Such complexity is symbolized by a declaration in various display typefaces that "Words are Multi-screened/faceted but simultaneous myths" (CB 24). Following this line even further he calls intricacy of language, a "mass medium" (CB 84) and considers words acoustically as "a complex set of harmonic relations as beautiful as a seashell" (CB 112). Then, adding the semantic and syntactic aspects, he says:

> From one point of view, words themselves are a kind of symphony of the sensorium, a cinematic flow which includes all of our "five and country senses." (CB 114)

At least this seems less dedicated to speech itself as part of a primal fall or fragmentation, which was his view in *Understanding Media*. Naturally, writing, "the power of fixing the flux of words and thought," is still linked to specialization and its effects treated with a remarkable ahistoricity:

> With writing came the power of visually enclosing not only acoustic space but architectural space. With writing came the separation of music from the dance, of both from words. Before writing, all these divisions were fused in a single "mythic" knowledge. . . . (CB 115)

Such a vision is itself "mythic," for it takes effects covering larger periods of history and makes them simultaneous with the discovery of writing. Examples of structure manifesting the type of architectural space that McLuhan talks about are found in ancient Rome, but examples of the divorce of words from music certainly do not occur in any even marked form before the Renaissance—McLuhan cannot mean instrumental music because he relates the drum to the tribal world. Nevertheless, the insights into words and speech are an interesting return to McLuhan the new critic, and even his examples seem to suggest this:

> *Four Quartets* of T. S. Eliot is a complete guide to our own recovery of acoustic modes of knowing our own and past experience. *Finnegans Wake* of James Joyce is a verbal universe in which press, movie, radio, TV merge with the languages of the world to form a Feenichts Playhouse of metamorphoses. (CB 115)

This kind of statement linked to the fact that printing is now entering a new phase—"Print would seem to have lost much of its monopoly as a channel of information, but it has acquired new interest as a tool in the training of perception" (CB 99)—would seem to suggest that McLuhan now sees Joyce and Eliot as using print in a new way to train perception and in the process as having metamorphosed the book. The only trouble with this, if it is true, is that McLuhan has gone through the creation of a misleading apocalyptic vision about media and electricity which was hardly necessary unless the major point was to sell the insights of the symbolists and post-symbolists to the businessman.

In any case, such motifs of change are joined to new ways of approaching the book about which it would be a mistake to suppose that it "is becoming obsolete" (CB 98). Is it possible that McLuhan shows a gradual evolution towards understanding that his way of seeing media is a rear-view mirror? For the essential point, just as implicit at the beginning as now, is that no form is obsolete, but that electricity and other technologies provide vast new combinatorial possibilities which clearly demonstrate how unimaginative our thinking in terms of such rigid categories as print, script, TV, and the like has been. What is really being dealt with is ways of combining image, sound, word, movement, symbol, and rhythm in a multitude of very different ways. McLuhan deserves great recognition for elevating the general awareness about this, for such cross-disciplinary activity is the type that is penetrating the modern arts and which really suggests the great value there would be in a return to a real awareness of what the actual artistic scene means.

Another note appears in *Counterblast* along with the more complex way of handling film, speech, and print. There is a genuine emergence of what might be called a moral concern for what will eventually happen. Part of it may be cynically concealed as in the statement:

BLAST

    BLAST

BLAST

    BLAST

The Viet Nam war as extravagant
pedagogical effort to
Westernize the East.

BLESS

    BLESS

BLESS

    BLESS

Expo 70 in osaka
as thrifty manoeuvre
to achieve the same end. (CB 58)

The concern may be a little more confusingly apparent in the fact that there is no simple historical return, but rather "By surpassing writing . . . We have evoked a super-civilized, sub-primitive man" (CB 16). It appears in the suggestion that "private consciousness" is an anti-environment for "the collective unconscious," though still stated in overly opposed terms. But this new note becomes much more overt when close to the conclusion of the work Mc-Luhan says:

> Even if we should wish to recover that older world we can do it only by an intensive study of the ways in which the media have swallowed it. And no matter how many walls have fallen, the citadel of individual consciousness has not fallen nor is it likely to fall. For it is not accessible to the mass media. (CB 135)

Admittedly, McLuhan's individual consciousness may be opposed to a social consciousness, yet even allowing for a social consciousness, this recognition that the individual is not the mass is of crucial importance for any ethical approach. What is surprising, however, is that this did not become a feature of McLuhan's position at any time between *The Mechanical Bride* and the present and that his analyses have never shown any way in which the individual consciousness deals with its milieu except through awareness and understanding—certainly the two basic qualities needed, but hardly the only ones. The appearance of an emphasis on the individual consciousness is accompanied by a very interesting and rather strangely inconsistent remark about a humanistic sense of balance:

> Writing was a visualizing of the acoustic which split off or abstracted one aspect of speech, setting up a cultural disequilibrium of great violence. The dynamism of the Western world may well proceed from the dynamics of that disequilibrium. If so, our present stage of media development suggests the possibility of a new equilibrium. Our craving today for balance and an end of ever-accelerating change, may quite possibly point to the possibility thereof. (CB 131)

The only difficulty is that, in spite of the recognition for the "craving for balance," the McLuhan mechanism swings immediately into action to create opposition rather than synthesis, since

McLuhan's only vision of a way out is transcendent, which fits well with his apocalyptic temperament.

In spite of these moments, McLuhan's major theme in *Counterblast* concerns the new media education, which is necessary because we have moved into an age of "post literacy" and "post history" where "our new culture is not going to lean very heavily on any one means of encoding experience or of representing reality" (CB 131). Therefore, the age must tune in on the "concert of the arts, of the sensuous channels of the media" to allow us to recover "the inclusiveness of our awareness." The glimmers of something more sophisticated may flicker in the typographical layouts of *Counterblast*, but the conception itself practically confines McLuhan to continue the same endless method of simple oppositions. Interpreted in this way, his "individual consciousness" becomes the root of the principle of opposition for the battle between the self and the non-self. This is no recent war, but one that he inherited from Wyndham Lewis, and Lewis inherited from the German romantics.

Blast is a vehicle in such an encounter; the view of the Vorticist school towards the juxtaposition of images is another. Pound's dialectic of the ideogram based on the Chinese written character, with Fenellosa's view that its meaning rose out of the radical juxtaposition of elements to create meaning, was paralleled by Eisenstein's view in *Film Form and Film Sense* which used an analysis of the Chinese written character to speak about montage. Pound as social creditist and part fascist, Lewis as authoritarian, and Eisenstein as Marxist are all equally rationalistic in the way they develop their "artistic visions." It is precisely this rationalistic and possibly authoritarian quality that the seemingly mystical McLuhan picks up from these sources. For McLuhan really wants a neatly ordered world, and *Counterblast* is against those who would obfuscate the way that this is being achieved.

Counterblast brings us full circle in the analysis of the good guys and the bad guys, the generalists and the specialists, the visual orientation and the tactile, the linear method and the mosaic method—all of these and many other such groupings run through it. But it also brings these to bear heavily on what McLuhan has always wanted, a marriage between education and the arts as the means of exploiting, for the individual consciousness, the maximum advantages of the new world: "We are all technological idiots in the terms of the new situation . . ." (CB 16). Continuing the themes of the *Massage, War and Peace,* and the *Vanishing Point* he reminds us that: "All arts, science and philosophy are anti-environmental controls that are ever merging into the environmental and losing their power to create an awareness of environment" (CB 31).

Such views come directly from the insights of people like Ezra Pound with his view that the arts, to communicate, must always "Make It New." The artist becomes a person creating art, that is, "specialist artifacts for enhancing human perception" (CB 32). All new media are art forms, because all new media "enhance perception" and "have the power of imposing, like poetry, their own assumptions" (CB 52). So the artist is the only person to whom the media can be entrusted (CB 53). In fact, just because our age has suffered an implosion as a result of the vast increase in information, it has been forced into a series of strategies which earlier ages did not have to adopt: "The bias of our culture is precisely to isolate the bias of all others in an effort at orchestration" (CB 64).

This attempt at "orchestration" produces anthropologists who are connoisseurs of cultures as art forms, and communications students who are connoisseurs of media as art forms (CB 64). The key is the statement that shows how McLuhan links the early aestheticisms of Pound, derived from the aesthetic period of Pater, to the present situation: "Our age is an esthete of all the methodologies of all other ages" (CB 64).

Whatever our partial reservation about McLuhan, his insight into this type of problem is always acute. Levi-Strauss, for example, has influenced the arts as much as, if not more than, he has anthropology; Riesman, Denney, or Goffman are as widely read by artists and critics as sociologists. Our age *does* look at everything as a cultural object and it translates all of the cultural objects back into its own world. The intermingling of arts from different times and different places, the wide variety and choices of fashions, the periodic resurgence of movements like Camp—all point to the perceptiveness of McLuhan's sense of what is happening.

Knowing this, McLuhan can see and recommend that it is all-important to create a new education in the arts and in media. But there is a basic contradiction between his utopian or apocalyptic vision that predicts that a new education will automatically come about, while at the same time, in order to maintain conflict, he must caution that we will be absorbed and lost unless we preserve the individual consciousness through an increase of awareness. Consequently, his advice about education in *Counterblast* as elsewhere always seems to contain the ambivalance of accepting the necessity that will be imposed and at the same time developing emergency techniques to avoid that necessity. Considering the information revolution and its impact, he claims that: "In the age of electricity and automation, the globe becomes a community of continuous learning, a single campus in which everybody irrespective of age is involved in learning a living" (CB 41).

This "global village" or possibly "global campus" is the result of an age of implosion in which everybody is involved with everybody else, and in which everybody has to participate. This "Age of Implosion in education spells the end of 'subjects' and substitutes instead the structural study of the making and learning process itself" (CB 37), for the age of implosion is the age of depth, and "Nothing studied in depth can remain partitioned off as a 'subject' in a curriculum" (CB 37). But this is exasperating as well as illuminating since it depends on a way of playing with words that filters out any except the most cliché meanings.

Yet McLuhan has even defended the pedagogical value of elevating the cliché to the level of awareness, something he seems to have developed from the study of Joycean pun. In the *Vanishing Point* (3) he says that to contemporary man "space is a cliché, an unexamined assumption." By examining such assumptions which are "environmental," it is possible to transform the action of the environment:

> A somewhat different approach to the problem of the transforming action of new environments upon older ones can be taken by the study of cliché and archetype. The world of the cliché is itself

environmental since nothing can become a cliché until it has per-vaded some world or other. It is at the moment of pervasiveness that the cliché becomes invisible. (VP 259)

Developing the point, he argues that the analysis by Stuart Hall and Paddy Whannel in *The Popular Arts* provides many illustra-tions "by which a world of cliché, by the art of enveloping an older cliché, seems to turn the older cliché into an archetype or art form" (VP 259). Transferred to the action of McLuhan's essays, this would seem to explain the strategy by which, in the face of entirely new demands for different approaches to knowledge, the cliché meanings of "subject" and "curriculum" expose the weak-ness of the system with which they are related. Confronted with the depth study of structuralism, the older modes of organization appear as an archetype of a bygone environment now only to be considered as a cultural object from the past.

However, the difference between this method and Joyce's is crucial, for McLuhan is constantly borrowing Joyceisms with a view towards exploiting this feature, as the marginalia of *War and Peace* amply illustrate. A Joyceism, when used by McLuhan, usu-ally becomes extremely reduced in meaning and intent. This is the difference we saw in the earlier discussion of the "charge of the light barricade" where McLuhan's flattening of Joyce's pun actually reduces the complexity of the observation on the kind of phe-nomenon McLuhan is interested in. In a similar way, he can trans-late the term "collideorscape" from Joyce to "collideorscope" and then to plain "collideoscope," losing in the process the particular richness of the original Joycean phrase with its use of the root "scape" (meaning "shape" and hence "form" as well as suggesting a kind of dream-like inner landscape). It is also suggestive of the vision to be seen in a kal*eidos*cope (Joyce's "-scape" among other things substituting for "-eidos" which means "idea" and hence, "form"), where there is a sorting out to create momentary unities, just as in the Joycean dream where shifting forms create new forms or shapes to which the term refers. McLuhan's use of language, instead, tends to work in simple opposition of the type that Pound used rather than the "dance of the intellect among meanings" that Pound always found a little suspect and that Joyce delighted in. Joyce dislocates language in such a way as to create a web of involvement among all the levels; McLuhan feels that culture shock should be blessed as a dislocation of the mind into meaning and restrains himself to the "shock" tactics that are more characteristic of *Blast*.

Nevertheless, McLuhan sees his way of handling language and metaphor as intrinsically educative:

> The handwriting is on the celluloid walls of Hollywood; the Age of Writing has passed. We must invent a *New Metaphor*, restructure our thoughts and feelings. The new media are not bridges between man and nature: they are nature. (CB 14)

The *Vanishing Point* and *Counterblast* together present a programme for combining education and the arts along such lines. The *Vanishing Point* calls for a study of the arts along a comparative basis:

> Therefore the question of whether art should be taught in our schools can easily be answered: of course it should be taught, but not as a subject. To teach art as a subject is to insure that it will exist in a state of classification serving only to separate art off from the other activities of man. (VP 238)

The artist is crucial as "early warning system," producing poems and paintings which are "teaching machines" and preparing the environment for human attention in the process. This, of course, plays back against the point from which we started in *Counterblast* where McLuhan condemns subjects and curriculum, while plugging study in depth. But there is the further ambiguity that the whole world is a classroom and that education is going on all over: "Pre-electric art and education were anti-environments in the sense that they were the content of various environments." Now they are environmental. With one of those McLuhanish twists, he argues that today it can be seen that older arts which were corporate have now become individualistic and educative. Music, for example, originally designed for presentation to a "public" was then "a corporate ritual." Now electricity has made it "more and more the concern of the private individual" (VP 248).

Whether we question that electricity has done this, or whether we recognize that a phonograph (being mechanical) does not really depend so much on electricity as McLuhan maintains (though obviously its ability to equal or surpass certain fidelity conditions does), the point still holds that there is a shift. Yet, by his usual method, McLuhan has blurred most of the interesting social complexities inherent in this shift. Was concert-going really all that corporate? If it was, was it so different from the "mass" art of film? If neither activity is ultimately "mass," because there is a dialectic between corporate sharing and individual participation in both, what difference does this make in the quality of the artistic and educative processes? McLuhan always misses in these ways because his sweep is far too broad, demanding too much repetition and therefore too little attention to the interesting features of detail. He is making the point, however, that the "members of the mass audience [as opposed to the public] are immediately involved in art and education as participants and co-creators" (VP 247). Such involvement results in a situation where art and education become new forms of experience, new environments rather than anti-environments. If he wishes to carry this a stage further he could argue that this is why the old conception of art is dead and why the new avant-garde are engaged in minimal art, conceptual art, and other such forms which are supposed to bring our attention once again back to the creative process as something distinct from our everyday life, so that like the Balinese we would cease to have a word for art.

The paradox at the heart of *Counterblast* and the *Vanishing Point* is the paradox that is at the heart of all McLuhan, and it is concerning this paradox that he never gives us a serious encounter or insight. The paradox is that he *seems* to say that we must strive for one mode, singleness (integration, unification, wholeness, call it what you will), to the entire exclusion of the other, division (doubleness, opposition, fragmentation, call it what you will). Though one suspects McLuhan's choice is theological, it is forbidden to mix the overtly theological, since it necessarily implies a value system, with the role as observer-participant at the centre of the vortex. Joyce attracts him because within Joyce there is an attempt to use theological material as a method of integration, though Joyce applies his theology to the profane world and finds a way of realizing a secular vision of what he desires. McLuhan leaves us with a state of schizophrenia in place of possible sacramental theology, for he insists on keeping his contraries contrary, though allowing them perpetually to merge and separate, metamorphose and return Proteus-like to original forms. There are ways of handling McLuhan's dilemma (as Joyce did) without confronting a problem of belief, since however we look at it, the phenomena with which McLuhan is dealing are earthly phenomena, though he seems apocalyptically to wish to give them a divinely ordained direction.

To fail to accept the necessity of distinctions as well as integrated wholes creates an impossible predicament of which *Counterblast* is the prime symbol, since the difficulty is inherent within the conception that eliminates the complexities of material reality, leaving an abstract and sometimes abstruse dialectic of large issues and sharp divisions. This very way of looking at it leads to the difficulty of comprehending contemporary tactility even when talking about it. It leads finally to the kind of flitting, momentary anality that McLuhan's work expresses, such as his treatment of Joyce's *Wake* as "Rire End Look" rather than seeing it as the mature union of eroticism, sexual and anal, polymorphously perverse as it is.

Finally it leads to the stance that Wyndham Lewis adopts as author: possessor of the "wild body," cop policing the artistic badlands, singing the songs of the "enemy of the stars," and leading the battle of the self against the non-self. This stance led Lewis into some very suspect positions where an authoritarian élitism replaced social analysis, and it resulted from a cosmic contempt for society and its objects which had to be approached with a "superior arrogance." Now this is not too far·from the type of portrait of McLuhan as author that has been unfolding. He chooses the stance of Lewis, just as he began his career with a book that most immediately develops the techniques of *Time and Western Man*. Lewis is the master of the type of dialectic that flowers finally when McLuhan develops the concepts of environment and counter-environment.

It is most interesting that once launched on his career as media expert, McLuhan did not frequently remind himself or his readers just how diametrically opposed Joyce and Lewis were. In *Time and Western Man*, Lewis attacked Joyce's work for being an example of the intellectual fad favouring a Bergsonian bias for a philosophy of temporal flux, as McLuhan previously in his role as literary critic had pointed out. Joyce retaliated by writing some choice passages of satire about Lewis in *Finnegans Wake* in which he made fun of Lewis' commitment to "spatiality" and referred to his satiric method in the passage:

> Johns is a different butcher's. Next place you are up town pay him a visit. Or better still, come tobuy. You will enjoy cattlemen's spring meat. Johns is now quite divorced from baking. Fattens, kills, flays, hangs, draws, quarters and pieces. Fell his lambs! Ex! Feel how sheap! Exex! His liver too is great value, a spatiality! Exexex! COMMUNICATED. (FW 172)

No one questions the perspicacity of Lewis as an analyst of art or of general culture. On the whole he has been seriously underrated for a number of decades. What does seem strange is to dress up Joyce in Lewis' clothing, for while Lewis, as his painting and prose suggest, was the master of the massively abstract (like McLuhan), Joyce's mode was *The Book of Kells*, the quiet meticulous elaboration of the life of forms and the forms of life. Perhaps it is for that very reason that McLuhan does not speak about Focillon in any of his works (though Herbert Read called Focillon's *Life of Forms* one of the four major aesthetic treatises of the modern world) since Focillon develops his theory of the "life of forms" partly from *The Book of Kells* and it applies rather directly to the infinitely detailed texture of Joyce.

McLuhan's commitment is rather to Pound and Lewis, the Vorticists, and their primary image dominates his mind and results in the production of *Counterblast*. But then his other major interest, apart from the marriage of abstractions, is playing with the actual visual presentation and shape of materials. This has always attracted him, for *The Mechanical Bride* is primarily involved with graphic materials—ads, newspaper layouts, comic books—and much less with popular novels, radio, and pop music. The visually and spatially oriented Lewis, therefore, is a far more attractive predecessor, as is Pound with his distrust of the "music of poetry" and the suggestiveness of words as against the hard image. Pound and Lewis experimented far more freely with type itself, especially in *Blast*. McLuhan's development of the essai concrète is another outgrowth of that influence. He frequently commented on the way Pound typed his letters, attempting to use graphic arrangement and telegraphese. Part of the aphoristic layout of the *Vanishing Point* goes back to Pound's *ABC of Reading*.

In a world of media though, and a post-Joycean world, McLuhan is able to carry the technique a great deal further. His *Counterblast* loses much of the simplicity of headline of the early Lewis manifesto, but it more than compensates for this by the interplay of typeface, colour, style, and arrangement. The arrangement is not all that casual either. Like *The Medium Is the Massage* it has a definite structure and an inevitable movement, from the opening display with the word "Blast" in black against a red background juxtaposed with "the printed page" printed on a white page partially divided by a series of red and black questions, to the closing page where in varied type faces the ending is announced: "The Ivory Tower Becomes The Control Tower of Human Navigation" (CB 143). At another point, a heavy black page blasting Sputnik for transferring the evolutionary process from biology to technology is paralleled by one about the new media being related to the new environment as species are to biology, a message presented in a series of ordered type faces, lighter in weight and mixed with some phrases printed in blue type (CB 84).

The totality of the book is a visual-verbal or "verbivocovisual" attempt at a poem, if it is anything. The conflicts and tensions within it, which cannot be resolved at an intellectual level, do take on a kind of intelligibility as fragments built into a new metaphor, a new way of handling the environment as suggested early in the book itself. Yet against this are the long passages about education and the need for a new Erasmus, about the analysis of the press as a symbolic art form, and other critical essays. It is as if McLuhan were not sure his creativity would work unless everyone is constantly reassured that he is really at heart being "intellectual" about the whole thing. In any case, the process results in an illuminating series of individual aphorisms, useful as empirical tools for critical approaches to poetry and painting and as devices for the generation and exploration of a new form. In all this, McLuhan is a pioneer (in the Poundian sense), not a master, since a master is hardly what someone dedicated to probes and experiments would want to be.

A final judgement on McLuhan's work while he is still writing is nearly impossible, for at any time his awareness may potentially be turned from the particular contours in which it now moves and he could adopt a totally new position on many of the same basic problems. His own statements to interviewers such as those in *Playboy* demonstrate that he regards his probes with a certain contempt and therefore feels free to alter them at will. There are still, at the moment, two major paths that might be pursued in arriving at a conditional evaluation of the McLuhan world. In the first place, given the very large weaknesses pointed out in the previous sections, why did the McLuhan *approach* work at all? Secondly, to what extent is McLuhan's problem dependent on the fact that he arouses promise of far more than he is actually able to provide? After these queries are considered, a basic question still remains: What is McLuhan's vision at the moment and in what ways is it a satisfactory or useful one?

14
The Medium
Is The
Rear View
Mirror

Arnold Rockman, in *Encounter* (November 1968, 28–36), tried to answer the first question chiefly in terms of the way in which McLuhan provided legitimacy for many people who would not otherwise have had it. Advertising men, media people, scholars in new areas associated with communications, and avant-garde artists all picked up a certain respectability from the general interest in McLuhan's work. Yet this respectability could only be effective providing his work could lay on them the hands of a proper representative of the academic priesthood. Considering that McLuhan, at the time of *Understanding Media,* had only written *The Gutenberg Galaxy* and received grants from Ford and NDEA, he was not one of the leaders of that priesthood by any means. Yet his style, his uncompromising intellectual manner, even his snobbism (a new snobbism) about his ability to cross Oxbridge with Madison Avenue, all provided a good deal of reinforcement to other aspects of his academic image. For just as outsiders wanted legitimating, so academia, uneasy about the changes around it, wanted bridges to help it understand the new culture.

Yet neither of these roles, one suspects, would have totally ensured that legitimating response if McLuhan had not also managed to relate an artistic revolution (a revolution that was having its own peculiar impact on the business and political community) to the most intellectual of the interests of the academic community. What McLuhan discovered for this purpose was the relevance of the Bauhaus as a bridge between industrial design on one hand and the avant-garde movements that surrounded Eliot, Pound, the symbolists, and Joyce on the other. Kepes and Gropius, Klee and Kandinsky, Le Corbusier and Giedion provided the bridge between the practical arts of architecture and design and the less practical sister arts of poetry and painting. In this context, the advertisement, and similar visually oriented, yet popular forms of pseudo-artistic presentation, provided a natural starting point for further exploration.

From the beginning McLuhan has always demonstrated a willing adaptability to what seems to be going on in the larger areas of his society. In the early fifties he became interested not only in Wiener's new cybernetics and its potential application as a general theory of communication but also in the economic history of Harold Adams Innis as it illuminated the relationship between certain technologies, and the effect of those technologies on the social and intellectual growth of different periods. Subsequently, he has managed to move with the times at least in a superficial way. When ecology became a matter of growing concern, his interest in media and then technology as extensions of man became an interest in environments and anti-environments. Like the adman and the news analyst, he developed a sophisticated sense of the proper packaging technique for the insights of the moment.

This adaptability, joined to what was a dominant theme in the arts—the orchestration of the arts and the resulting metamorphoses of form—was sufficient to provide that Poundian date-line immediacy which McLuhan always respected. His work could be all-involving because, at least in its concerns, it was aware in a way that the work of other art critics and literary people was not (particularly the work of those who could provide either the erudite and snobbish approach or the actual credentials that McLuhan could).

This is an important consideration and not something which should lead to a simple condemnation of McLuhan. He wished, if our hypotheses are right, to be a modern Addison or Steele and yet remain quite different from Addison and Steele in his general approach and technical execution. First of all, as he makes clear in *Counterblast*, he wishes to use the stance of a clown since that is an integral posture not like the equitone prose and moralizing of Addison and Steele. Second, as he demonstrates in the *Vanishing Point*, his message was quite the antithesis of manners, for in the contemporary world "good taste" must be solely an escape. The epigraph of *Counterblast* reads that "Good taste is the first refuge of the witless." His works were to teach people that what they liked might well be what they should like, and what they had been told to or taught to like was "witless." Couched in erudition, hedged by degrees, presented with wit, and announced with conviction, it could not help but be a very attractive reassurance.

Yet at the same time McLuhan could feel that he was right, since he had learned about the new culture from Wyndham Lewis, Ezra Pound, T. S. Eliot, and the new prophets of pop kulch like Gilbert Seldes. Eliot's writings alerted him to the fact that Marie Lloyd was an important cultural phenomenon on the British vaudeville stage, that the detective story was a serious form of writing, and that even baseball and cooking had things to do with culture. Seldes and others like John Grierson provided new insights into Chaplin and Hollywood.

For a new critic schooled against the Romantic movement and associating its growth with the growth of the bourgeois culture of Addison and Steele, it did not take much persuasion to encourage the realization that Lewis' discussion of Addison's sell-out of English art in the *Spectator Papers* had a great deal to do with what was wrong. After all, Addison, while reforming manners and morals, had sold out wit to genius, reducing the role of the laughing side of humanity and promoting the move to Arnoldian high seriousness. McLuhan's interest in the new culture could be given a theoretical justification in terms of his literary commitments and allow the pedagogue to assume the role of the prophet.

This situation provided McLuhan with a multitude of ways to be effective. Certainly a new culture was needed and writers endorsed this point of view. The new visual artists on one hand, the poets on the other, and still further the film makers wanted a new synthesis of the arts which would bring the world of image and image in motion into greater prominence. His formula could not help but work, for it allowed for a reversal of the formula of Addison and Steele while relating the most sophisticated insights of the avant-garde to the nature of the popular arts and the needs of social planning, and at the same time followed a scheme that the Bauhaus and symbolists shared for orchestrating the arts and reintegrating the studies of human nature. The very people to whom it was directed were most conditioned, directly or indirectly, by these sources and most in need of some way of asserting their aims.

Now none of this could be achieved without the existence of conditions desperately requiring a new value orientation, and also where a new psychological orientation to adapt to the cultural situation was needed. That is precisely the kind of setting in which McLuhan's work began to appear. It arrived just at the time in the late fifties when instability had built up to where it was generally recognized by the academics as well as by other educated members of the middle class. The accumulation of media experience had grown to the point where there was considerable panic about advertising and television. The War and the Bomb had begun to leave their mark on those who were in their thirties, and problems of pollution and poverty had begun to attract the attention of the more sensitive members of society. So socially, politically, and psychologically the time for McLuhan's appearance as a replacement for the high priests of the older values was ripe.

When he appeared, as we have seen, he adopted a role for the new age. Fortunately for him, it was quite Addisonian, since it was that of an observer, but it was also quite different because it was that of an *uncommitted* observer who was not willing to force his value system (a position highly attractive to the dominant liberal and moderate conservative groups in North America). Besides, as a stance, it avoided entering into discussions about religion and politics, therefore allying itself not only with the New

Criticism, but also with the general taboos about encountering such subjects of difficulty. For McLuhan it had yet another advantage: by flirting with a set of authors that were closely related to a religious point of view, it was possible to suggest a number of religious values while seemingly simply endorsing the status quo. Virtually all of McLuhan's language about participation, community, retribalization, and the like relates to the new sense of liturgy that especially marked the Catholic and Anglican Churches in the forties and fifties and that had lured T. S. Eliot and W. H. Auden into their position as "religious poets." Unlike the often controversial Auden or Eliot, McLuhan stood as an Addison against a Pope, a figure relatively uncommitted to anything but a quietly liberal engagement with the future.

All of these currents produced what McLuhan came to be—a veritable miracle of success in attracting the attention of just about everyone. Naturally, he offended the more doctrinaire liberals, but he did not offend the liberal faith; naturally he offended the more conservative believers, but he did not offend the real nature of contemporary belief; naturally he disturbed the scientists, but they were the very priests against whom he was insulating those interested in him. He attracted the avant-garde artists because he preached the leadership of art; the young teacher because he showed new ways to teach and made them acceptable. This is after all the most important lesson he himself learned in his foray to Madison Avenue: how to be an academic huckster while still retaining his academic self-respect.

But this would hardly be a reason for looking at McLuhan as anything except a sociological phenomenon in the sociology of propaganda and promotion, as many analysts have already demonstrated. His power was more extensive than that, for like Addison, he was spokesman for an important set of philosophic and aesthetic points of view, and to a far greater extent than with Addison these views were central to where these areas of society should go.

What this meant was that McLuhan seemed to promise a good deal. Here was someone who could link the best insights of the surrealists, the dadaists, and the symbolists to the analysis of the world around us and the nature of the culture that it was developing. In the process he could integrate the popular arts which

Gilbert Seldes had already argued for, and which Joyce and Cocteau, Lewis and Pound, and so many others had already realized were of value to the higher arts and their traditions. Since the discussion ranged from language and society to the individual person, it would involve the very nature of these entities (at present the province of the human sciences) with the arts and possibly provide for the arts some of the validity of the human sciences. All this is implicit in *Explorations,* as it was implicit in the range and scope of his early Ford seminar. But more important, there were abstract and practical aesthetics to endorse its validity —with things like the Bauhaus and the critical writings of Eliot on one side, and the practical works of Joyce in *Ulysses* and the *Wake* or Lewis in his writings on the other.

Such a vision, though, needs a very strong base and a strong theoretical orientation which would better come from the philosophic position of a Merleau-Ponty or the sociology of knowledge of Weber and Simmel than from the empirical literary criticism of Leavis, Richards, and the New Critics. Not surprisingly, McLuhan drifted into an interest (though merely a superficial interest) in the empirical aspects of the behavioural sciences or in the occasionally striking sociological study of some specific area, such as Goffmann's *Presentation of Self in Everyday Life* or E. T. Hall's *Silent Language.* But he developed no interest in the theoretical ways in which Marx, Weber, Simmel, and Mannheim might have aided the type of synthesis he wished to achieve. As far as Marx is concerned, he shows in none of his works any awareness either for the content of Marxism or its relevance to his particular kind of determinism. Remarks, as late as *Counterblast,* that Marx had never seriously studied causality are far from reassuring to any reader, and it is hardly forgivable that a writer who presumes to be interested in the way that techniques of production change people should have been totally unwilling to examine Marx. This leads to a bankrupt sociology, for, as C. Wright Mills has observed, it is impossible to understand contemporary sociological theory without a knowledge of Marx, or for that matter of Weber. This great lack is not compensated for by his occasional interest in Durkheim since he shows little knowledge of Durkheim's major contributions and none of more recent anthropology such as Levi-Strauss.

The result is that McLuhan fails to present his findings in terms of any comprehensible theory of social structure. The questions about why print comes to be, how it actually interacts politically at certain points of time, why it endorses on one hand the status quo in a *Faerie Queene*, while on the other undermining it in a *Mother Hubbard's Tale*, are never confronted. Even empirical facts from recent times, such as the interplay between small groups and mass media, never come to occupy a central role in McLuhan's discussions.

Perhaps this could be excused, except there is also no notion of what he is doing in the psychological area either. He dabbles in Freud and Jung, but he rarely goes deeply into psychoanalysis, existential psychology, or even more behaviouristically oriented psychology unless it is the particular experiments with Pavlov's dogs. Walcowicz, on paradox in human communication; most of the more interesting parts of Reusch and Bateson, on communications; Mead, on social psychology; Hebb, on behaviourism—all relevant to matters he discusses—never seem to occupy a role either. In fact, his account of the sensory system is often inhibited by his singleminded insistence on a five-sense sensorium, and his deepest psychological insight comes from Thomas Aquinas' doctrine of the *sensus communis* with no attempt to justify it in the light of today's discoveries. In these ways though, McLuhan is a typical Canadian humanist of his particular point in time, for he developed when sociology and psychology were still held in disrepute by most humanists and even many economists and political scientists. His work tends to reflect this heritage. The same forces drive him into an interest in philosophy but, like Wyndham Lewis', his way of approaching philosophy is through conservative sources. He is more likely to be engaged by the articles of the *Summa* or the writings of German idealism than he is to be involved in contemporary philosophical currents. His attraction particularly to late mediaeval and early Renaissance philosophy is confirmed by his interests in Joyce and in rhetorical studies. References to such sources show up more frequently in his writings than do allusions to other philosophical material.

Such a limited set of theoretical tools means that there must be a number of weaknesses in McLuhan's ability to fulfil what he seems to promise us. His ends are further compromised by other inadequacies. First of all, he has no knowledge about the limits of the empirical techniques that he uses for discussing art. Second, he has no theoretical framework which shows an awareness of the contemporary period other than what he extracts from earlier philosophers or contemporary artists. While stimulating, the writings of the Bauhaus fall short of what could be called full-scale theoretical works. As philosophies on which to found integrated approaches to society, Lewis and Pound leave a great deal to be desired. The result is predictable and McLuhan must develop a committed anti-intellectualism as far as theory goes and accept a stage by stage *ad hoc* device of using an essentially sceptically derived aphoristic style (with a strong component of implicit negativism in it) against its normal direction because of a fundamentally theoretic naïveté. He becomes much more likely to mention Heisenberg or Planck or Einstein than he does Heidegger, Husserl, Wittgenstein, or Jaspers.

McLuhan seems to share the contemporary suspicion of modern philosophy, something which is in a way a throwback to the New Criticism and its strictly empirical approach to literary texts. Yet he is engaged in trying to be a philosopher himself, for he is ultimately theorizing about man's role in the contemporary world. His failure to deliver what he seems to promise is fundamentally a failure to respect any of the theoretical orientations that he might have to develop in order to achieve it. McLuhan must remain the message that a magic medium is a master of the ad hoc.

But as his rapid rise and his more gradual descent in a very short time indicate, there are two major criticisms: even at the moment, the ad hoc cannot be a substitute for a philosophy of the role of the aesthetic in contemporary society; a do-it-yourself-creativity-kit runs out of impact when the same man is forced to return again and again to the same themes. Just as advertising palls, so does the adaptation of his type of rhetoric to the intellectual or the artistic world.

For many, McLuhan's activities seem to promise the creation of a whole new philosophy of communication. In this he fails, although he seldom seems to have rejected the title "philosopher" when it is applied to him. If he is really neo-Thomist, as one might guess from articles like "Joyce, Aquinas and the Poetic Process," he must accept a philosophical position as a foundation for his own activity as a thinker. It could be instructive to re-examine McLuhan with the assumption that his work depends on a prior acceptance of Thomistic philosophy. This immediately provides a "view of man" as implicit behind his work, though it is quite likely that in sociologizing this view he has actually removed much of its integrity within the neo-Thomist position. Such a position would at least account for McLuhan's optimistic eschatology, which implies the operation of the Holy Spirit within history.

Allowing that McLuhan assumes without comment such a backdrop for his own work (and this would certainly seem likely if one reads carefully some of his major disciples such as Walter Ong, s.j.), man as human person is still absent as a significant factor in McLuhan's theories. In fact, in certain ways his theories are the antithesis of those held by neo-Thomists, such as Maritain who sees some kind of evolution of the ego or the individual consciousness occurring through history. McLuhan's man, even in the sexual realm, must foresee a return to a more severe type of tribal discipline looming in the future of the electric age (*Playboy* 65). Marx had suggested in *Capital* that just as "Darwin has aroused our interest in the history of natural technology [so] the history of the productive organs of man . . . deserve equal attention" (*Karl Marx*, ed. Bottomore and Rubel 78–9). Yet Marx saw such attention resulting in an understanding of man by disclosing the way Nature is dealt with by "the process of production by which he sustains his life, and by which also his social relations, and the mental conceptions that flow from them, are formed" (ibid. 79). McLuhan reduces such Marxian concerns to a fetishism of the modes of reproduction themselves without seeing any method by which man can actually alter the onward movement of history through his own intervention.

Even allowing, therefore, that McLuhan actually assumes some view of man such as the neo-Thomist one, the problem is not only that it is not expressed in his works, but that his works implicitly deny any very rich view of man himself. The most telling sign of this in McLuhan's own work is the way that he does not deal with the most traditional and intimately human of the media—dance and drama. Kenneth Burke, commenting on McLuhan and his tendency to discuss topics such as "weapons," but not "war" (even the treatment of war in *War and Peace in the Global Village* emphasizes the techniques of conflict rather than the nature of conflict), remarked that McLuhan lacked a full understanding of the drama of human relations. Naturally, for Burke and his followers such as Hugh Duncan, in a philosophy of symbolic action, the traditional art forms and especially drama have a great deal to tell the student of society about the actual structure of society. Burke tells us that "McLuhan's great skimping on *drama* as a 'medium' necessarily leads to an overly simplified view of media in general and their role in culture" (*Language as Symbolic Action* 411). Fundamentally, Burke is right, for McLuhan's whole approach ultimately fails, largely because of his inability to realize the important foundation of communication in human action and human symbolic expression.

It is characteristic that McLuhan's only overt treatment of drama occurs in his discussion of "games," for "games" are more limited than drama. In the first place they are a highly structured phenomena akin to technology. The essence of games lies in their rules, which cannot be violated without violating the whole game. Drama, which is frequently called "playing," is more flexible, akin to the creative potential possible within play as opposed to the closed world of games. Yet the medium that McLuhan analyzes in *Understanding Media* is games, not either play or drama. This very fact betrays his failure in understanding Huizinga and others who emphasize the "ludic" or play element in man's culture, as well as Piaget who sees an intimate link between imitation, play, and dreams and hence drama. Yet McLuhan should hardly have missed this possibility since he himself emphasizes his debt to Joyce, and Joyce emphasizes constantly the close relation between drama, play, and dreams, particularly in *Finnegans Wake* II, i (sometimes called the Playroom or Nurseryroom section) where the play hour of the children of HCE and ALP is presented as a drama in Feenicht's Playhouse. While superficially it may seem paradoxical for McLuhan, the antagonist of linearity, to opt for a form circumscribed by rigid rules as against a more freely creative form, it is perfectly consistent with the way that he attempts to transform technology into a mystery and make a fetish of technological devices and the organization of the technological system.

Joyce linked his vision in the *Wake* closely to drama and dance, describing the action of the dream in the *Wake* as being "like your rumba round me garden" (309). Throughout the *Wake*, the dreamer stages dances, playlets, puppet shows, vaudeville dialogues, dramatized inquisitions, trials, and rituals, all of which emanate out of the dream which is about an encounter of a human person with his wife and bedmate, ALP, and his family re-encountered in a dream world as a kind of running dramatization. McLuhan's multifarious remarks about Joyce appear to lose all sense of this since he overstresses Joyce's relation to technology and media. Yet the very shift in emphasis is crucial because first, McLuhan claims that so much of his insight is really derived from Joyce and second, out of the failure to see the primacy of drama and dance in the arts rises his failure to realize the centrality of man to understanding human symbolic expression.

Drama involves humans (i.e. the actors) in interaction with one another in a setting or place and it involves the performers in interaction with an audience which responds and sometimes even participates. Consequently, there is human interaction and human feedback involved as well as a symbolic expression achieved through the imitation of human actions, the primary purpose of the whole being what Brecht said Aristotle demanded, "that it should entertain people" (*Brecht on Theatre* 181). The instruments of drama are those instruments which G. H. Mead, in *Mind, Self, and Society*, showed to be the foundations of human expression and communication—gesture, and language as an outgrowth of gesture— a fact McLuhan recognizes in his Joyce criticism. The body and the voice in conjunction with the brain and central nervous system create man's distinctive gifts of language and symbolic expression. These elements of the human person, though, are intimately involved with the person as a sensate, living totality and are not abstracted from total human experience which is the basis of human communication. Such human experience, though, allows for diversity between humans, it allows for dialogue as a means of coming to terms with this diversity, and it precludes the possibility of exhausting the study of human communications with a study of mass man. Does McLuhan allow for this in his theory?

McLuhan's whole assumption that media affect all human beings in a similar way, providing that they have received the same opportunities to learn to "read" the media, of necessity accepts many of the postulates about mass man. Yet this is not an uncomfortable position for McLuhan since the apparently contemporary with-it books that he produces have very little to do with man as a fleshly and erotic person. Superficially, such a statement may seem startling since his very subject matter is intimately involved with the intrusion of intense eroticism into modern life. Besides, his selection of authors which he emphasizes in works like *The Gutenberg Galaxy* are all masters of the fleshly and the erotic— Rabelais, Cervantes, Pope, and Joyce. But as soon as the question arises about the relation of McLuhan's theory of tactility to actual sensory experience, a vast hiatus appears in McLuhan's theory as opposed to Joyce's poetic visions.

Occasionally McLuhan moves beyond discussions of tactility and turns to the subject of multi-sensuousness in the human person, but it is interesting to see what happens when he does. In an article in *Look* magazine (on which George Leonard was a collaborator) McLuhan discussed how "Youthful sexuality is cooling":

> The more modern writers present sexual activity as a separate, highly defined, "hot" aspect of life, the more they hasten the death of SEX. Most "literary" novelists have not yet discovered the present, much less glimpsed the future; which is one reason why so many of the brighter college students have turned to anti-novels and, in spite of its questionable literary reputation, science fiction. Robert Heinlein's *Stranger in a Strange Land,* a popular underground book, tells of an attempt to set up Martian, rather than the usual human relationships here on earth. In these relationships, what we term sex is communal and multisensual. There is not sharp, artificial distinction between male and female roles. Sex blends with other activities that might be called mystical. And there is even the need for a new word (Heinlein calls it "growing closer") for this demi-erotic mode of relating. Many young people see something of their own aspirations in the Heinlein book and others similar to it.

Norman O. Brown (*Life Against Death* and *Love's Body*) strikes an equally sympathetic response with his thesis that civilized man has even fragmented his physical person. According to Brown, many people can feel sexual pleasure only in the sex organs themselves; the rich sensory universe of the rest of the body has been deadened. (*Look*, 25 July 1967)

Heinlein's term "grok" (the actual word he uses for "growing closer") became for a while a password among the youth, even ending up on a button, so that McLuhan is right in relating it to the hip culture of LSD, marijuana, and Oriental religion and philosophy. He would seem here to share the intimate emphasis on the multi-sensuous and communal of the youth, in spite of his reminder to a *Playboy* interviewer that he disliked change. But McLuhan's vision sees this only as a transition, for in the same *Playboy* interview he has something rather contradictory (or apparently contradictory) to say:

It's paradoxical that in the transition to a retribalized society, there is inevitably a great explosion of sexual energy and freedom; but when that society is fully realized, moral values will be extremely tight. In an integrated tribal society, the young will have free rein to experiment, but marriage and the family will become inviolate institutions, and infidelity and divorce will constitute serious violations of the social bond, not a private deviation but a collective insult and loss of face to the entire tribe. (*Playboy* 65)

McLuhan it turns out is against anything that "contributes to the schism between sexual enjoyment and reproduction that is so prevalent," and hence he is against the pill as "mechanical." But this is hardly Heinlein's view of a society which "groks," for there the whole problem of infidelity disappears in the communal, multi-sensuous ritual of "growing closer." Homosexuality, which McLuhan also rejects, in Heinlein's world (if it could be) would disappear since it, too, would be a natural part of growing closer.

Now the reason for digressing in this way is that McLuhan's discussion of the electric age's multi-sensuousness rising from "multitudinous communication aids" stresses that there is a "new desire for exploration within the self" as well as an extension of "the human nervous system outside the body." The relevant question, though, is how does this happen? If, as McLuhan asserts, we are entering the "golden age of the family," what role does intercourse, child raising, and other human activity play in this tribal communications world, for in many tribes family in our sense of the word does not exist. There is no bridge in McLuhan between the account of the human person, his inner life, his multi-sensuousness and creativity and the outer world that is presumably merely an extension of his central nervous system, an extension which he does not control but which controls him.

If McLuhan really meant that for him SEX is dead, then he would also mean that the "polymorphous sensuality" of Heinlein or Brown will become part of human love and that this would have a decisive role in man's future, as Brown, Heinlein, and in a way Huxley have all suggested. If he were in fact being less utopian than Brown and the others, he would be reasserting the totally sensuous domain of man as relevant to his ability to live creatively in the present. But then he would also realize that the drama of man *begins* with man in interaction with man and not with the interaction of media or machine with man. SEX, though, is something that McLuhan has seen from the first as mechanical, an outgrowth of the world of the mechanical bride. In his *Playboy* interview he borrows a fictive device from the science fiction story mentioned earlier, *The Big Ball of Wax*, where the machine which electronically induces entertainment experience into the brain is the centre of action and used for specifically sexual purposes. What results is something like Robert Russell described in his satire in *Take One* on a new computerized media, "Intersex." McLuhan's version in his *Playboy* interview, though, reflects vividly that he still sees SEX in our present society as linked to mechanistic modes, even if there is a greater degree of freedom: "Projecting current trends, the love machine would appear a natural development in the near future —not just the computerized datefinder, but a machine whereby ultimate orgasm is achieved by direct mental stimulation of the pleasure circuits of the brain" (65). But is McLuhan failing to fully comprehend the social change of the sixties in his desire to retain the traditional picture that is so essential to his own well-being? Implicit behind his whole discussion of this area seems to be a deeply Puritanical core masked by a superficial liberality.

Besides, his view of this "love machine" could be a little more serious than it might at first appear, for it is closely linked to Mc-Luhan's belief that in the electric age, language eventually will disappear, reintegrating man within himself. Yet somehow it leaves vast questions about the total role (dramatic, playful, and the like) involved in man as symbolic manipulator of parts of his physical body—the very aspects that are fundamental roots for drama, for dance, and for the arts of man. Joyce's *Wake*, it could be argued, celebrates marriage, kinship, family, erotic togetherness, and many other social bonds, but in Joyce they rise naturally out of the action and out of a dream. In McLuhan they become mechanical results of a technology which once man creates, he cannot control, so that if McLuhan's prophecy is right, the tight morality of the future will be a natural evolution of the present. Such visions naturally, along with their other nightmarish aspects, would threaten human diversity if they were to become self-fulfilling prophecies under the hypnotized co-operation of advertisers and media specialists.

War and Peace in the Global Village is more central to this problem perhaps than any other McLuhan book, for in his misunderstanding of conflict, violence, and war resides his misunderstanding of drama. Drama involves conflict, which is the only way that human development occurs. But conflict need not be equated with war since there is a vast difference between the two of them. Consequently, to play on the theme "education as war" rather than seeing conflict in education as a natural process (and war, therefore, as hopefully an unnatural one), McLuhan eliminates the conflict of human interaction out of which society and its products arise. He also rejects, at the same time, a comprehension of the dialectical interplay which would be necessary to make his perpetual pairs more useful as ways of speaking about the world. But the absence of such an interplay also robs his conception of the multi-sensuous from any ability to creatively interplay with nature.

To see the world as a mass of media manipulating men involves seeing the world in categories quite similar to the old literary genres—epic, tragedy, comedy, lyric, pastoral. Such categories exist as conventions and as such are part of the code by which we communicate. The wit of *The Rape of the Lock* is only apparent if we recognize its use of the epic convention to relate it to a certain historical category of experience that has been transformed in the present. If, though, we make epic a Platonic idea—a category with its own independent existence, we eliminate any possibility of creative interplay with it. At the next higher category, that of the classification of the arts themselves, the same situation exists. Categories such as painting or sculpture are proving to be inadequate today to describe the wide variety of artistic practices carried on within the arts, and artists are constantly stretching the previously accepted boundaries. The categories are useful, but we become more and more aware that they do not begin to cover the possibilities of forms that can be produced. In fact, the very nature of artistic activity requires the constant change of conventions in order to create new visions. Consequently, McLuhan's way of speaking of media which are technological modes of transmission parallels the problem of defining the conventions of art forms themselves. To speak of television and film as media which have their effects independently of how they are used to present something, and how the viewer receives what is presented, hypostasizes television into a platonic idea as well. This is the result of a social analysis where there is no genuine dramatic interplay between parts.

It has important ramifications beyond this, for it conceals the relevance of very contemporary developments in communications. Modern multi-media activity has developed out of the realization that film, slides, computers, and other devices are not just single media but ways of bringing together various elements and components. The Czechs, who are masters of multi-media activity, described what they were aiming at as LISODE—Light, Sound, Dimension, and Environment. This way of speaking of their future activities, which has grown out of presentations such as the Diapolyecran, the multi-cubed screen at Expo, parallels the more avant-garde arts in showing that the elements of communications are image, light, sound, space, word, and the like which can be combined in a multitude of manners. The concept of "medium" which McLuhan popularized has, with that acceleration characteristic of modern dialogue, itself become a rear-view mirror, useful but hardly to be deified in phrases such as "The medium is the message."

214

Yet this analysis cuts more deeply at the roots of McLuhan's problems. For what the Czechs are doing, and what media, art works, and multi-media depend on, is an awareness of the importance of fragmentation as preliminary to creation. Fragmentation is not the villain that it appears to be when McLuhan speaks about specialization, or the effects of the phonetic alphabet or of print. Fragmentation is basic to the way that humans come to know. If Brown or McLuhan really believes that people are going to forget their sex organs in a new awareness of the total erotic potential of the human person, then they are going to be sadly disappointed since awareness of the sex organ is hardly a post-Freudian, or a post-print, or even a post-alphabet manifestation. SEX, in the sense that McLuhan means when he capitalizes it, hopefully is disappearing, but that is rather different from our very appropriate preoccupation with the means by which the species survives. Far more important, though, is what this means for an understanding of the electric age, as McLuhan calls it. Our ways of knowing are built on paradigms which of necessity are fragmentations of a totality. Integration is not synonymous with totality and McLuhan is not very careful about preserving this rather important distinction. Yet in order to create at all there is the need for what Coleridge in the *Biographia Literaria* called the secondary imagination, which "dissolves, diffuses, dissipates in order to recreate" (202). In the process of its operation the Coleridgean imagination achieved a "reconciliation of opposites" through its poetic activity. In the same way that information will not create the revolution McLuhan thinks it will, without specialists to provide the information, new modes of expression will not arise without an interplay between fragmentation and reintegration. This is the difference between McLuhan's pairs and Coleridge's "reconciliation of opposites"—McLuhan's pairs are like the classification "bad guys" and "good guys" (ears and eyes, electric and mechanical, hot and cool), while Coleridge's doctrine links the opposed elements in a dialectic in which their interaction is crucially necessary to the generation of the next development.

McLuhan's failure to understand drama, and his failure to see how that led to his misconception about the role of human communications in the understanding of media, conceals a much more essential problem—his failure to see the dramatic dialectic out of which society emerges. In so doing, he fails to be true to the source he so often praises, Joyce, for Joyce had a fully developed understanding of how the process of communication rises from a human person through an interplay of fragmentation and reintegration, producing the dramatic dialectic that is society. A real reading of Joyce is one of the most valuable ways of evaluating McLuhan, for Joyce saw, in his use of Nicholas of Cusa and Bruno and Hegel and Marx, the importance of dialectic in producing the historical drama of man which Vico tried to write.

Among his many references to Joyce, McLuhan rarely seems to quote a passage close to the end of *Finnegans Wake* where Joyce's dreamer reviews the nature of the book—and by implication the way of creating such a work of art. Joyce embeds the nature of the work in the activity of human memory and its relation to word and gesture, the sources of human drama:

> What has gone? How it ends?
> Begin to forget it. It will remember itself from every
> sides, with all gestures, in each our word. Today's truth,
> tomorrow's trend.
> Forget, remember! (FW 614)

If "today's truth" is "tomorrow's trend," Joyce is recognizing the dialectical drama within the processes of art itself, for "truth" rises out of "making it new" as the present truth becomes the trend of the future. In this context, he goes on to describe his book as a "millwheeling vicociclometer, a tetradomational gazebocroticon," emphasizing its four part structure borrowed from the Viconian cyclical theory of history and set forth as a "gazebocroticon" (gaze / book / rote (memorization) / wrote / icon). The term calls attention to the use of sight and memory in the creation of the fictive symbolic form, the icon, which is the "tetradomational artifact" Joyce creates. His work, the dreamer continues, is "autokinatonetically preprovided with a clappercoupling smeltingworks exprogressive process," where the phrase composed of "kina" (motion) and "tone" (sound) used reflexively ("auto") produces the "exprogressive process." He describes this as being an outcome of receiving "through a portal vein the dialytically separated elements of precedent decomposition for the verypetpurpose of subsequent recombination." This naturally emphasizes the Coleridgean view of the operation where the "separated elements of decomposition" are returned to a "subsequent recombination," the "gazebocroticon." All things considered, the Joycean account with its emphasis on the dramatic, on the nature of the book, on the technique of the Coleridgean imagination, runs counter to McLuhan's. Joyce, in fact, sees his "gazebocroticon" like any symbolic form, a marriage of the past and the present, the purpose of "the subsequent recombination" being "so that the heroticisms, catastrophes, and eccentricities transmitted by the ancient legacy of the past" can be "anastomosically assimilated and preteridentified paraidiotically, in fact, the sameold gamebold adomic structure of our Finnius the old One, as highly charged with electrons as hophazards can effect it."

The "assimilation" of which Joyce speaks results in the work being "paraidiotically preteridentified," because the work operates dialectically like the movement of Nicholas of Cusa's dialectic in his *De Docta Ignorantia* (Of Learned Ignorance). The "subsequent recombination" which is the work resulting from the imaginative vision is achieved by transmission "type by tope, letter from litter, word at ward, with sendence of sundance." In other words, the work communicates through the operation of a code and conventions involving rhetorical and symbolic devices (types and topes) in conjunction with language which deals with the mundane, excremental nature of the world (letter from litter), creating a message (sendence) which is in fact an artistic presentation (sundance). The process depends on an interplay of detail and vision which fully respects the nature of the human mind and its perceptual processes.

Joyce, as Benstock and others have pointed out, sees the need for a movement to achieve higher levels of non-aggressiveness and social awareness, and along with it, the need to develop a realistic strategy for dealing with the conflict that is necessary to life. He chooses to use the family, as Freud did, as a model for this search. Yet the world that McLuhan presents as coming from Joyce's insights lacks any real interest in social units as the family, or any real commitment to the need for conscious change within society. In fact, McLuhan again and again seems to want to reduce social awareness of communications to the mystical operation of the electric age—an age where fragmentation and linearity disappear. Joyce, on the other hand, recognized the crucial importance of seeing language and other modes of human expressions as codes composed of elements which are susceptible of greater and greater understanding. He sees the value of looking at language and art forms as based on codes and can even quip that the Holy Ghost as giver of the gift of tongues is the "homely Codes" in the phrase "the farmer, his son and their homely codes" (FW 614). This suggests the new secular awareness of the root structure of the symbolic process. Joyce secularizes the mystical by showing clearly the possibility of Barthes' semiological approach to communication.

But this again marks the Joycean approach, a secularization, while McLuhan strives to re-establish transcendence by assigning an almost divine plan to the operation of technologies. His vision, if accomplished, might easily see the establishment of a Brave New World style of religion associated with media. Because of this difference, Joyce speaks of individuals, of the working class types, of socially differentiated roles, while McLuhan speaks of a homogeneous mass, all of whom are affected in the same way by the world around them. Even though he gives some simple nod in *Counterblast* to the individual consciousness, McLuhan is forced by his position to allow only that the individual consciousness, not a total person, is in control of one of many diverse roles in a complex society. Certainly Joyce's hero can be described as a radio transmitter, but he is also described as "receptoretentive patternmind, a paradigmatic ear," for in Joyce all communicative experience relates to the function of society and to the nature and structure of man. In *Understanding Media*, technologies take on a role as accidental products of man's probing which alter him through being extensions of his body, but which he cannot himself alter in the process that occurs. Admittedly, McLuhan usually argues that he wishes to understand media in order to control them, but he gives us little understanding of the process of control involved, even when he changes from extensions to the conflict of environments.

The reason why McLuhan's dilemma has not been recognized more clearly or widely is partly because it rests so solidly on a knowledge of the contemporary arts. His dilemma is that of Lewis and Pound confronted by Joyce. Both of them rejected Joyce's dialectical complexity, feeling that it would swamp their own simpler, rationalistic approaches. Lewis condemned *Ulysses* as a time book; Pound accepted *Ulysses* as an emetic, but rejected the *Wake* as a return to the Christian. McLuhan, while holding a position and using writing techniques closer to Pound and Lewis, tries to embrace Joyce as the all-encompassing contemporary writer. First of all, this deifies Joyce far too much, but even if such deification were possible, it would still leave the problem of reconciling what seems to be in conflict. McLuhan is attracted to Joyce because Joyce provides a whole world of ritual which is not present in the same way in either Pound or Lewis. By this means, McLuhan seems to discover a way of sacramentalizing the world of Pound and Lewis and therefore making it part of a larger world view where things will occur in the "rite order." Yet Joyce does precisely the opposite of what McLuhan seems to attribute to him; he secularizes the sacramental, providing a way that literature becomes an alternative for ritual. He even spoke of his role as a writer in terms of "transubstantiation," a view that has been inherent in the literary world for some time now.

The whole tone of *Finnegans Wake* moves towards a view of man as liberating himself within society, using his ability to read the codes that create the symbolic expressions which are intrinsic signatures of the social relations inherent in his world. The Master-Builder cannot be controlled, but will always surpass the inventions he himself creates. This is not to suggest that Joyce was over-optimistic, since all such creation involves conflict, and control of conflict, and even potential failure. But Joyce's vision was rich and diverse, while McLuhan does not give sufficient credit, either to the mundane ability of man to deal with "homely codes," the fragments of which are the only ultimate source of control that he has, or to man's ability to use his intellect to intuitively reach beyond the world that he has created.

M cLuhan's latest work, *Culture Is Our Business,* is a collection of ads, cartoons, and magazine and newspaper pages or covers accompanied by pithy, aphoristic comments and quotations from selected books. Consequently, the technique of this particular *essai concrète* is quite similar to the main portion of *Through the Vanishing Point,* although the material superficially resembles the type of material with which McLuhan was concerned in *The Mechanical Bride.* One of the most striking features of *Culture Is Our Business* is the self-consciousness of McLuhan about McLuhan. One whole exhibit is a cartoon about McLuhan juxtaposed with a page of aphorisms headed "Hello! Marshall McLuhan" (264). Another exhibit is an ad about Tom Wolfe juxtaposed against a page of comments entitled "Sheep in Wolfe's Clothing" in which McLuhan mentions an article by Wolfe:

> At the beginning of his very flattering essay on myself in *The Pump House Gang* (Farrar, Strauss & Giroux), Tom Wolfe has a drawing of me which at once suggests another title for his essay ("What if he's right?"), namely, "I'd Rather Be Wrong." At the end of his essay he confronts me with a waitress in a topless restaurant to whom I uttered the assurance: "The topless waitress is the thin edge of a trial balloon!" (I.e., the silicone bust.) (COB 212)

This self-consciousness about McLuhan as cultural object ranges from a concern with his various previous works ("My own book *The Mechanical Bride* records the effect of the hardware service environment on *sex*" [124]) to a revelation of the importance of his role in the media scene: "*Medea Mystery:* McLuhan's phone call from Roy Thompson (owner of the *London Times*) for a private chat about media. Chat blossoms (unbeknownst to McLuhan) into BBC show, also televised across U.S.A." (208). McLuhan has become such a cultural object himself that he has even attracted the attention of other successful Canadians (and this mutual awareness of Thompson and McLuhan as Canadians is certainly an in-group reference behind the more general one). There is, however, a real recognition of McLuhan about McLuhan as myth, which further contributes to the myth in the course of extending it. In a very literal sense this would be true if one looks at what he says as early as *The Gutenberg Galaxy* (226) that "myth is the mode of simultaneous awareness of a group of causes and effects" (GG 266), which associates myth with a vision of totality. McLuhan as prophet of the electronic age is part of the process he describes: "Since the electronic age inevitably drives us back into a world of mythic vision in which we put Humpty Dumpty together again . . ." (WP 185). In fact, McLuhan sees himself as a modern-day Vico providing a new science of man: "To the preliterate man of integral vision a fable (i.e. myth) is what we would call a major scientific truth, and the entire scope of the new environments as macroscopic enlargements of our own self-amputations can today provide the beginnings of a new science of man and technology" (WP 186). In the context of his exhibit "Hello, Marshall McLuhan" in *Culture Is Our Business*, the aphorisms play around the theme of "multi-sensuous involvement" or "360 degree involvement," which would easily allow communication with an oriental, nonvisual culture, so that communication with Vietnam would be easy "If literate newsmen and military beaureaucrats pulled out . . ." (264).

Culture Is Our Business completes this process of putting McLuhan into the myth, which begins in earnest with *The Medium Is the Massage*, the conscious playing with his own previous work. Tom Nairn in an essay on "McLuhanism: The Myth of Our Time" picked up on the role McLuhanism was coming to play as myth:

> It is more important to see the sense of the whole process than deprecate it. That is, to see that McLuhan's odd way of expressing himself and the social form his ideas have assumed amount to a kind of contemporary *mythmaking*: this would seem to be the appropriate semantic model. Then one must ask *why* such an important movement of thought, dealing with such central issues, should assume the guise of myth (and a new sort of myth, at that) in our time. Myth was once the natural way of making sense of the world, in spite of its limitations and conservatism; in the twentieth

century it has become a way of imposing such conservative limits on thought, a strategy of evasion as well as a way of grasping reality. (M:PC 141)

Nairn argues that McLuhan is the first mythmaker of the dilemma of the "loss of language and meaning," paralleling Becker, Godard, and other creators (M:PC 144). His argument says, similarly to the chapters of this book, that McLuhan at an intermediate stage between poetry and theory half expresses and half theorizes about this common, fundamental problem.

Culture Is Our Business so totally absorbs McLuhan into the process that he himself is mythicizing as to most dramatically reveal the actual dehumanizing activity inherent in the process. In a conclusion reminiscent of *Dr. Strangelove*, McLuhan uses an anti-Vietnam poster with the screaming copy "And Now The Bomb?" (335). The Bomb, though, in McLuhan's world is "electric software" that "inspires nightmares of population explosions in the old nineteenth-century minds" (334). Yet like Teilhard de Chardin, who McLuhan sometimes quotes, be believes such software is the new phase of evolution, for "When the evolutionary process shifts from biology to software technology the body becomes the old hardware environment" (COB 180). Electric software is the new process, the new stage of evolution, the process that McLuhan celebrates as myth. In *Culture Is Our Business* that process supposedly eradicates any lines between art and business. Opposite an ad by the Minneapolis *Times and Tribune*, pointing out that they had sponsored a poetry lecture by T. S. Eliot attended by 13,723 people, McLuhan presents a series of comments on the ad: "When an esoteric poet addresses 13,723 people in a sports stadium on a high-brow topic, is the title of the present book obvious?" (44). Repeating the motif of many earlier works he suggests: "Poets and artists live on frontiers. They have no feedback, only feedforward. They have no identities. They are probes" (44). This Eliot ad is grouped within a section entitled "Culture Is Our Business" that obviously comments on the book itself, reiterating the Pound principle that "Art is new perception" and that "Art is valuable only when new" (46). What seems a nostalgic backward glance at *The Mechanical Bride* and *Explorations* period suggests that:

The cave art of Madison Avenue has been by far the most innovative and educative art form of the twentieth century.

Ads outclass the programmed features in magazine, press and TV.

Like the art in the Altamira caves, ads are not intended to be seen but to produce an effect. The cave paintings were carefully hidden. They were a magic form, intended to affect events at a distance. They were of corporate, not private, origin. So with ads.

They are not intended to be recognized as new art forms of our retribalized world. They are not a means of self-expression.

(COB 48)

This kind of art naturally is not "intended to be recognized as new art forms," although it presumably has this quality of being a magic form.

Yet to return to myth-making, McLuhan is suggesting here as he has elsewhere that the return to a "magical" function in art is a return to myth. This magical function Wyndham Lewis had discerned in ads, in fashions, in pop kulch and business, in writings such as *Time and Western Man* where he attributed these new phenomena to the world of process of Bergson. It is this Bergsonian world that McLuhan celebrates and introduces in which the promotional presentation of a serious poet and the "cave art" of Madison Avenue become equatable phenomena, as providers of "new perception."

A critic might be tempted to say, therefore, that McLuhan in

Culture Is Our Business is returning to some of his earliest work and even some of his earlier attitudes. He selects ads, a technique he used in the *Bride;* he indulges more extensively in value judgements, a method he abandoned after the *Bride.* But such a facile reading is erroneous. In the first place, the materials that he uses in *Culture Is Our Business* come from different sources. Many of the ads and other materials used emanate from magazines about the media, or are more intimately involved in the media themselves than the illustrations of *The Mechanical Bride.* There are a number of ads for advertising agencies, for media outlets, and even for specific kinds of media, such as *The New York Review of Books.* All of this relates *Culture Is Our Business* much more closely to the culture business of advertising, media, book production, magazines, and the like. In one sense this is just a difference of emphasis, for the *Bride* contained such materials; but the difference of emphasis is important to the specific way that McLuhan sees himself in relation to the media world in the book and the myth that it unfolds.

Apart from the source of materials in *Culture Is Our Business,* the value judgements it contains are of a rather different kind from *The Mechanical Bride.* In *Verbi-Voco-Visual Explorations* (*Explorations Eight*), McLuhan had stated the reasons for avoiding such value judgements, which he later reiterates in the *Galaxy, Understanding Media,* and interviews: "These remarks imply no value judgements, no preferences. To distinguish the properties of these things avoids the confusion of moral clamor. Clarification permits co-existence, and resolution of conflict."

With *Counterblast* McLuhan again appears to be allowing more judgements and less avoidance of implications about preferences. This is more marked in *Culture Is Our Business.* By the second illustration of *Culture Is Our Business,* McLuhan is moralizing. Commenting on a Hertz ad, which shows a disgruntled traveller sitting on his suitcases with the heading "Traveling can take the fun out of going anyplace," McLuhan comments: "The present ad had a deadly aim. It voices the deadpan mutterings of a tribe of highly motivated somnambulists" (18–19). But the comment has been prepared for by an opening section with innuendoes about "hopped up suburbanites" under the influence of tranquilizers which "enable people to persist in their ordinary activities while leading lives of howling desperation" (16). This is followed by suggestions that the car is obsolete (22); that "Both the kid and the executive are victims of somnambulist decision-makers" (64); that decision-makers are totally out of touch with the world they live in (104); that ads such as one by Coffee of Brazil entitled "How to Make Your Husband Smile in the Morning" are "intended to transform people into docile hams" (136); and that "the pill is a gimmick to make man a nineteenth-century machine" (176). But all of these observations are made in a different way of seeing the issue from that in *The Mechanical Bride*, for in this latest book McLuhan is concerned with what he feels inhibits the process of moving in the direction of the new evolution of "software."

Brought together, such comments do not relate to a perspective or point of view about morality as *The Mechanical Bride* did, they rather assert a certain apocalyptic movement which can be made more or less difficult. In a deeper way this places them on the same level as most of the other value judgements, which are about whether or not specific media productions are good or bad. Of one *Good Housekeeping* ad the reader is informed that it "is as rich an example of media illiteracy as could be asked for" (208), and of an ad for a Canadian publication, *Saturday Night*, the reader is informed, "The ad here is a mortician's notice of interment of a medium. Caveat emptor" (268). At times general principles about the use of media are related to value judgements, such as when he observes of a Union Carbide ad that it "uses a mass of useless verbiage just as TV commercials use radio-like intensity of sound that destroys their effect" (292). These judgements seem consistent with what media should and should not do as outlined in *Understanding Media* and other works.

Consequently, while there is a reappearance of judgements and even some pontificating in *Culture Is Our Business*, it is not a return in any simple sense. The major moral issues that it involves are implicit in its examination of the media world, not explicit in terms of its own judgements about specific ads or events. The implications revolve around such areas as violence and society, the centralization of power, the black problem, pollution, and the atom bomb—all themes closely associated with the social and political issues of the moment. Because of his peculiar moral approach, which tacitly assumes that all decision makers are bureaucratic and all bureaucracy must reach the wrong solutions— "Surely, it is not unbelievable that decision-makers are totally out of touch with the world they live in?" (104)—McLuhan must reject virtually all apparent solutions. Sometimes this leads him to try to eliminate problems through paradox by asserting the natural superiority of black and woman in the new electric world. Either diverts attention from developing ways of handling problems of the moment.

As each new book appears, McLuhan seems to be fighting more and more desperately to preserve his presumed neutrality about the coming of the "electric age," and as he sees more and more of a struggle, greater and greater preoccupation with violence appears in the works. Partly this reflects a growing social awareness about violence, though as a central motif it enters as early as *War and Peace in the Global Village*. A set of observations on an ad for *Ebony*, "the magazine that gets to the heart of the Negro market" (COB 225) are entitled by McLuhan "Slum Clearance as Violence" (224). Taking a very ambiguous view towards slum clearance (and quite properly so in view of its usual methods for handling the social problems involved), McLuhan asserts, "It is only to the visually specialized man that there is disorder in a slum or junkyard. (On beautifying junkyards see Chapter 26)" (224). The problem in McLuhan's analysis is that slum clearance offers "a visually organized solution" in which the individual loses his "identity" through loss of neighbourhood and loss of the multi-sensuous life of the slum. Violence occurs in the struggle to recover identity and a new slum is made "as quickly as possible."

The analysis has considerable correspondence to the facts, though the facts, as usual, are reflected in a rather distorted way. The only alternatives leading to a solution are not a result of the basic opposition between visual and multi-sensuous which preoccupies McLuhan. Nor is this method of oppositions an implicit part of any attempt to solve the problem. McLuhan does not precisely suggest it is, yet he certainly does not suggest it isn't. The effect is somehow to imply that the black is happier in his slum, so leave him there. Yet even that is not entirely true, for McLuhan observes that "War is education." The return of Blacks from Vietnam has created a revolutionary situation, for "War is not only education, but political revolution":

> If the Negro could feel the equal of the white man when he is at the wheel of a truck, it is obvious that his ego is enormously enlarged when associated with a vast military team. (COB 224)

This analysis of the slum problem and black problem is characteristically not an analysis but a set of probes sparking off the reader's analysis. Aspects of the topic appear in Section 5 of *Culture Is Our Business* where the theme is "Violence Is the Quest for Identity" (63). As an epigraph for the section McLuhan provides the following:

> At seventy-three, Groucho Marx pities the poor parent of the permissive era.
> "What you should do with kids is slug hell out of them when they're small. Explain to them what life is about, and if they don't obey, give them the cat-o'-nine-tails."
> Groucho is merely anticipating what the TV kids will do to theirs. When identity disappears with technological innovation, *violence* is the natural recourse. (COB 63)

There can be little doubt that, with a recognition of this return to violence, McLuhan's *Culture Is Our Business* is considerably less optimistic than *Understanding Media*, and critics who rather immediately reacted by suggesting its similarity to the *Bride* are really reacting to what is a lessening of the apocalyptic optimism by a recognition that the process will be intensely painful; this awareness, always potentially present in McLuhan, has tended to become more and more explicit.

For this reason it is not surprising that McLuhan's metaphorical quest returns to the Bomb as a point of reflection. In Section 5, one set of aphorisms entitled "The Military Gap" is placed opposite an ad by The University of Chicago Press which illustrates a Henry Moore statue entitled "Power Contained." The text of the ad points out: "In art, in science, in all areas of intellectual adventure—nothing is so powerful as an idea that has come of age. This statue presents such an idea: the intertwined themes of embryo, mushroom cloud, and skull containing the cathedral-like vaulting of human hope" (COB 67).

McLuhan's comments on the Bomb and the military gap emphasize the Bomb as the beginning of a software revolution—it "is not hardware. It ends war as a means of international powerplay" (66). World War III, which is in progress, becomes "a guerilla information war with no division between military and civilian participation" (66). Loss of identity through technological innovation creates this situation, the way Vietnam is the result of "the loss of identity of the U.S.A. as a business civilization" (66) (a quote from Robert Theobald). The whole of World War III is a projection of the Easternizing of the West and the Westernizing of the East, which McLuhan has emphasized ever since *The Medium Is the Massage*.

The result of this is that the Bomb is inevitable. It is, in fact, as the closing illustration of the book suggests, a projection of the struggle between hardware and software, the ultimate symbol of the explosion of the information revolution. (Somewhere in the process of the later books, the concept of implosion disappears, for this is not mentioned in *Culture Is Our Business*.) There is a *Dr. Strangelove* quality above all this, for McLuhan intensifies the paradox of the Bomb and makes it just as ambiguous an event as the Henry Moore sculpture seems to do. In any case, *Culture Is Our Business* with its conclusion on the Bomb strongly stresses this as the symbol of our unconscious fears behind all the other present-day symbols of violence.

Perhaps the off-note in McLuhan's handling of these problems is his failure, while assuming a clown-like role, to grasp Kolakowski's concept that in the role of the jester there must be occasions when there is some moral consistency in order that he be consistently inconsistent. In his essay "In Praise of Inconsistency," Kolakowski stresses questions where it is essential to be consistent to be moral; in such cases the truly inconsistent clown-like humanist will be consistent. McLuhan seems to fail to recognize this and it leads to the ambiguities about War, Bombs, Slums, Blacks, and numerous other issues throughout this work. He may agree, as he seems to do at one point, that the clown is the symbol of the humanist attacking power:

Like the artist-priest Stephen Dedalus, the clown is a probe. Whether it's Al Capp, or Walt Kelly, or Pat Paulsen, or the medieval jester, the clown attacks power. He tests the tolerances for us all. He tells us where the new boundaries are on the changing frontiers of the Establishment. The clown is merciless, without conscience, yet he gets our sympathy because he is a scapegoat. He uses the language of gesture. . . . (COB 288)

Yet McLuhan, even in *Culture Is Our Business*, does not explore the theme with the type of depth that chapter 8 of this book suggests was necessary. In fact, in *Culture Is Our Business*, he sees "The whole TV generation is moving into the clown-scapegoat role. . . . They have been robbed of their old image" (288). He does not explore the difference between clowns that leads Lenny Bruce, Bob Newhart, and even the Smothers Brothers, to upsetting the establishment more than Rowan and Martin or Al Capp, ultimately resulting in their exile. There are obviously different kinds of clowns in the present era, which has an importance McLuhan does not discuss. He also sees the mark of all this in slang, which is "verbal violence," seeming to forget that slang has always been with us and that while perhaps the kind of slang used is possibly verbal violence, whether it be Hippie or New Left or New York Construction Worker, slang in itself need not necessarily be verbal violence unless there is a confusion between form and content, which in McLuhan's world there is. All innovation in speech, to the degree that it is some type of transgression or deviation from a generally accepted norm, violates the expected or normal speech, but to stretch this meaning of "violates" to the act of doing violence to language is to employ metaphor in a way which calls attention to interesting implications in the act of deviant speech, but which tells us little in a competent way about the actual speech used.

In any case, slang is the accepted speech of some groups for some purposes, while the activity of the clown that McLuhan suggests, of necessity violates or transgresses or transcends some group norms. Tom Wolfe, as McLuhan himself points out, can use the speech of youth with their put-ons as a kind of put-on against them:

"Like I mean, you know," says the Human Moon, "these kids are where it's at today, man, and they know it, and I know it, and like I'm with them, and if they love me, it's only because I love them, and like they know it, and I know it, and we're in this thing together, and I'm with them all the way." (Tom Wolfe, in *New York Magazine*, August 26/68.) (COB 288)

McLuhan himself is a violent writer. He constantly classifies those he opposes in phrases such as "technological idiots," "somnambulists," and the like. His employment of pop phrases, clichés, ad copy, and the products of journalists are purposefully disrupting and dislocate the original meaning. His own particular style compounded of many levels of literary and popular style is perpetually deviating from normal expectancies, yet it is hardly slang. It is only when he equates, which he seems to do, the potential creativity of slang, of style like his, of the function of art and the function of discovery by use of metaphor, that he can speak of slang in the way he does. If this is the way that he thinks, then he is himself a manifestation of violence about which he speaks.

It is not too surprising then that McLuhan comes to be preoccupied with violence as part of the myth that he is making and in which he includes himself as part of the process in the act of making. The very concept of *Culture Is Our Business* is purposefully violent, though not as violent today as when McLuhan first thought of it fifteen or twenty years ago. McLuhanese speaks of the senses being bombarded, of the person being numbed by extensions of himself—language which inherently recognizes some kind of violent operation on people, like a massage, a working over which is not consciously sought for.

Operating in this way often misleads McLuhan—and seems to mislead him more and more. His way of treating a theme such as the Black Problem in *Culture Is Our Business* is typical, if a little bit more striking than most. To wittily explain away the black problem by insisting that "Black is not a Colour" and that being black is an advantage on TV is to use partial verbal wit to disguise a really genuine unwillingness to engage a serious problem. Much of the treatment of black themes in *Culture Is Our Business* is potentially offensive to the blacks and to others, though perhaps unintentionally so. The problem does not begin here, but it becomes more clearly manifest. It begins in *The Gutenberg Galaxy* with the ways in which McLuhan uses African illiteracy in film culture and continues in the way that he twists the formula about East and West around to suggest that the blacks are being stupid in trying to become Western as the whites try to become Eastern. The richness of either culture or the mixture of cultures that results from the encounter becomes lost in the generalization, and in some way the blacks still stand as an inferior race (as in fact do the Easterners and the participants of the Third World) by only "catching on" to the electric age after the West does. The depth of wisdom that rises out of this is:

> As explained in the McLuhan *Dew Line* newsletter for July, 1968, *black is not a color*. White is all colors at once, but black is not in the spectrum. It is a gap. The Negro question is a red herring. (COB 220)

Somehow this misses the whole point that modernity is trying to find a way of preserving ethnic and cultural diversity—to recognize that a black culture exists which is separate and which should exist and which must find a way to continue to exist without suffering for its existence. McLuhan himself recognizes the need for cultural diversity in commenting on "Apologies to the Iroquois" (242) where he suggests that "Today there are nationalist movements in Quebec and Wales and Scotland and in every place that harbours tribal memories or acoustic resonance" (242). How much of this treatment of such questions is conditioned by works of Wyndham Lewis such as *Paleface*, where the strategy of defending white against black is to point out the advantage that the black has in an age which romanticizes the exotic or the different, is difficult to tell. But in view of the strong influence that Lewis has had on McLuhan, and on *Culture Is Our Business* which ends with a Lewis text exegeting the meaning of the atom bomb, is difficult to say. Yet for any who wish to read this way, the possibility is not only present, but open.

Similar treatment of other problems appears in phrases and headings like: "Dr. Spock's spooks—Yippie, Yap!" (64), "The Natural Superiority of Women" (28), and—on the Negro problem!—"The Leopard Cannot Change His Spots" (218). At best the technique extended this far leads to confusion, and at the worst to potential applications against minority groups. These are not areas for ambiguity between theorizing and artistic play, which leaves the reader with ambiguous insights into question of morality concerning violence, bombs, racial problems, and the youth rebellion.

Culture Is Our Business strongly illustrates that McLuhan's strategy, like Al Capp's, may have been more successful before the Television Generation came of age. In any case, confronted with a genuine breakdown in cultural consensus, McLuhan's method becomes a highly conservative and somewhat dangerous way of playing jester, rather than a fruitful or creative one. The references throughout this work indicate it really depends on a world where the *New Yorker* type of intellectual had a shared consensus which admitted the relevance of Pound and Eliot and Lewis and the training of the Oxbridge universities as a way of comprehending the general problems of society. This is not to suggest that even then it is a totally desirable method, but at least it has relevance to certain accepted meanings. Even the particular mode of mysticism fits better with Eliot's emphasis on participation and the flourishing periods of liturgical reform in the Catholic Church than with Ginsberg and the occult mysticisms of the moment.

Chiefly, *Culture Is Our Business* is not a new series of insights, although the insights are applied to a new series of problems. Presumably this creates entirely new probes, but actually it uses the same general opposed pairs and metaphors for illuminating the specific moment. It is when these are turned to entirely new ranges of problems that everything appears to be rather misleading, as with the black problem or the youth revolution. This is attributable in part to a lack of any effort to think critically about the actual terms "culture" and "business" that are used in the work. The sense of "culture" that is used seems very close to the use of "culture" in *The Mechanical Bride*, and the concept has changed little throughout the whole of McLuhan's work. Overtly, culture is a respect for all the symbolic expressions of man; covertly it is a respect for these expressions as reduced hierarchical forms of the higher arts which they reflect. Whether this is an adequate way of seeing the problem is not what is at question—it is rather that no adequate treatment of the problem appears in *Culture Is Our Business*.

Admittedly in the latest book, McLuhan does add depth to some of his probes. He recognizes, in the same way we suggested in the body of this book he should have, that Dickens presents a multi-sensuous slum world, though he seems to give it a rather different application, failing to see the significance of this for his historical distinction between print and post-Gutenberg eras. He realizes, as has also been suggested in the text, that Carlyle has relevance to his examination of clothing and fashion as anti-environment, yet again he does not seem to relate this to any implications of Carlyle knowing about or using such symbolism for his historical thesis. To an extent many of the concepts that grew up between the *Galaxy* and *Culture Is Our Business* are not strongly present in the book. There is little about extensions, less about environments and anti-environments (though the terms do occur) and practically nothing about hot and cool (apart from a very few fleeting references). Concepts such as high definition and low definition play a much lesser role, as they tended to do as he moved away from *Understanding Media*. Yet the basic method is the same, using the probes, the aphorisms, the essay technique, and even producing what can still be called an essai concrète, though a somewhat more conservative one than that of *The Medium Is the Massage* or *Counterblast*. For some reason, *Culture Is Our Business* is one of the less interesting of McLuhan's works, probably because it shows so clearly his weakness when confronted with the complexly polarized world of the present moment. To attempt a stance of neutrality while using a fundamentally artistic method at such a point in history is bound to fail, for none of his models were "neutral" in that sense, whether one chooses Erasmus or the four writers of Gutenberg satires (Pope, Cervantes, Rabelais, and Joyce) or Eliot or Lewis or Pound or Dickens. Clearly the movement of history is most rapidly de-mythicizing the myth that McLuhan made.

This creates some basic ironies playing about the title *Culture Is Our Business*, for it clearly makes the focal point of the book the artistic tradition. And it does focus here. The book opens with reference to an ad from Grove Press and concludes with an analysis of the forces behind the atom bomb based on Wyndham Lewis' *The Human Age*. In between, it discusses Lewis, Joyce, and Eliot frequently and other literary figures and ideas to a considerable extent. It introduces the theme of the poet as pioneer living on the frontier, engaged in "feedforward" *not* feed back. The poet, as the man on the frontier and in keeping with the problems of society, lacks an identity and engages in violence and experiment: "The poet dislocates language into meaning. The artist smashes open the doors of perception" (44). Pound and Huxley act as backdrops to the phrasing to suggest the "inner trip" which the arts provide, an "inner trip" which is the opening theme of the first section "Flip!" of *Culture Is Our Business*. The purpose of art is to provide new perception. Consequently new art, which when new is commercially "kooky and worthless," is the only valuable art in a cultural sense. McLuhan suggests that this gap is narrowing now. Such an aesthetic is rather obviously a restatement of what has already been discussed, though in *Culture Is Our Business* it receives a new futurist emphasis that is concealed in his emphasis on the poets' "feedforward." Even this, though less explicitly stated, has been an ever present aspect of McLuhan's aesthetic views.

If this is true, McLuhan is again urging that man only learns many things through the arts and to neglect art—"culture"—is a dangerous option at the present moment. Certainly his use of Henry Moore, whose sculpture of the Bomb explores the ambiguities of one important event of the century, makes this manifest (though there is an implicit question as to whether or not discrimination and critical acumen are present automatically in perception or not). In any case, McLuhan argues that "The artist of the modern movement is a savage . . ." quoting again Wyndham Lewis' *Blast* which he used so extensively in *Verbi-Voco-Visual Explorations*. Because of this, there is no role for "good taste" as he pointed out in the *Vanishing Point*. He discusses this in a careful satiric presentation of an ad in which a "modern Perseus" in a "worsted suit" (which is being advertised) holds a Giacometti statue. McLuhan declares: "Away with the role of art as shield of vision in which to view and slay the gangrenous monster of Good Taste" (COB 172), and describes the male figure of the ad, in words borrowed from Joyce, as "Flatchested fortyish, faintly flatulent and given to ratiocination by syncopation . . ." (FW 109). In his attitude towards the snobbish use of art or any of its misuses, McLuhan moralizes and attacks with ease. Yet against such concepts he poses Lewis and savagery and primitivism.

The major literary text used in *Culture Is Our Business,* as in *War and Peace in the Global Village,* is James Joyce's *Finnegans Wake.* Presenting a Revlon ad for "Blush-On—'the first and only can't-be-copied'/totally transparent blusher," McLuhan gives his comments the title "It's a Barefaced Lie," and observes that "Make-up is Metaphor. It translates one face through another via transparency: 'And so o'er that art which you say adds to Nature/ Is an art that nature makes'" (280), quoting Polixenes on gardening in *The Winter's Tale.* McLuhan generalizes from make-up as barefaced lie as metaphor to all art as deceptive, and then explains the relationship of *Finnegans Wake* to forgery:

> *Finnegans Wake* owes much to a nineteenth century play by Sir Charles Young, called *Jim the Penman.* Jim was a counterfeiter who was able to accommodate himself to all levels of society by his forgeries. Joyce saw the artist as a forger who moved through all levels of experience. He branded his own *Ulysses* as "an epical forged check on the public for his own private profit." To this end he, the artist, had practiced "how cutely to copy all their various styles of signature." His artist is Shem the Penman: "Shem was a sham and a low sham. The *sham* and the *shaman* blend artist and priest puffing truth and untruth together." It is by indirections that the artist finds directions out, overcoming the fruits of the fall that had put a "kink in our [*sic*—FW reads "his"] arts over sense." (COB 280)

McLuhan still interprets Joyce through a Lewis focus, for he reduces Joyce's conception of the artist to only one part of the split personality that must be "reamalgamerged" in order to produce the creative dream—the artist as *Here Comes Everybody.* Shem, as a Stephen Dedalus type of artist, is one aspect of the total producer-consumer of the dream, and the complexities of deception and reality are a perpetual part of the dynamic process in Joyce's dream world.

Yet McLuhan, who is a "make-up" artist who warns readers *Culture Is Our Business* is a book which is not about ads, but about "our times" and suggests that there is much "levity" in it, embraces the Shem-style art of deception. *Culture Is Our Business,* precisely because it confronts so directly the most pressing images of violence, unrest, fear, and tension of our time, illuminates most vividly the values of McLuhan in making manifest the theme of the times and his weakness in deceptively being all things to all men, a priest in jester's clothing.

The thesis that McLuhan is fundamentally an artist, a poet manqué, is complicated by the fact that if he is an artist he has created a new form, or at least contributed to bringing a new form to fuller development. Throughout the book it has been suggested that McLuhan is a modern essayist in the tradition of Bacon and Addison, a fact which he recognizes himself. His whole position, though, reverses the print oriented, eighteenth century bourgeois values of Addison, requiring a new mode of expression. Where Addison supports manners and taste, McLuhan suggests they have become irrelevant. Where Addison writes in an equitone prose, McLuhan uses the tone of headline and copywriter. Besides, McLuhan attempts to find a form of expression which blends print with the new electric age techniques of expression.

He himself calls attention to Mallarmé's *Un Coup de Dés* which can be regarded as an early form of *poésie concrète* and which he, in *Culture Is Our Business*, specifically associates— as he did in his early article on "Joyce, Mallarmé and the Press"— with this form:

> The newspaper mosaic is crammed daily with visual puns of this kind. The mere juxtaposition of items without connection, save by dateline, makes the press a huge time harp of *poésie concrète*.
>
> Long ago Mallarmé made a newspaper poem called *Un Coup de Dés* (One Throw of the Dice) using the spread-out sheets of the paper as poetic wings. (COB 146)

McLuhan adapts this technique to a prose form which mixes theorizing with expression and which has close stylistic relationships to the development of the essay form. His first development of this form probably depended as much on Wyndham Lewis' *Blast* and the collage form in the visual arts as on Mallarmé, but in both cases it was the use of arrangment and layout of type (or visual material) that was crucial to what he tried to do. The earliest experiments of this kind pre-date the publication of *The*

Gutenberg Galaxy, appearing during the *Explorations* period and especially in *Explorations 8,* which has recently been revised and published as *Verbi-Voco-Visual Explorations* by the Something Else Press (a group which has had specific interest in the development of *poésie concrète* and related forms).

The full blossoming of the form, where more of the potential suggested by collage is developed, occurs in the collaboration with Quentin Fiore and James Agel on the production of *The Medium Is The Massage.* This method has been copied in Agel's own work on *The Making of 2001* as well as on a recent collaboration of Fiore and Agel with Buckminster Fuller, *I Seem to Be a Verb.* McLuhan went on to collaborate with Harley Parker on two later varieties of the form, *Through the Vanishing Point* and *Counterblast* which used various type faces and typographical arrangements far more extensively. Both are described in detail in the main part of the text.

Concrete poetry (*poésie concrète*) is represented by poems using various patterns of type, colours of type, visual layouts, and the like to achieve a full effect. Emmet Williams has published an anthology of concrete poetry which contains a number of illustrations. The term, as Williams explains, evolved later than the form and seems to have appeared independently in different countries. While concrete poetry is an accepted English term, the French has been retained here partly because McLuhan uses the French term *poésie concrète* in describing the newspaper and partly because the French term *concrète* carries a much stronger sense of concrete as meaning "growing or adhering together" than does the English "concrete," although this is part of its etymology. Besides, the term *musique concrète,* coined by Pierre Schaeffer, is French in origin and there is some attempt in adopting this name to suggest the affinity that McLuhan is trying to have with a mixed media world of auditory and visual effects. Besides he has in one recording, again assisted by Agel, tried to extend the form into an oral rather than a written form and he has included some of Tony Swartz's "Sound Collages" on a disc in the *Dew Line.*

Essai concrète is meant to apply to either printed or oral or even mixed media forms as long as they have the same relationship to the combination of theorizing and expression inherent in the essay as well as some conscious relation to the dialectical process of weighing and juxtaposing of opposites implied in McLuhan's development and in the Baconian tradition. These issues are discussed in the text with respect to the essay.

A history of the form in the twentieth century would have fascinating affinities with avant-garde art, the development of posters, the use of collage in the visual arts, the use of aphorism by Pound, the development of poems in shapes, and many other features which are intimately connected to the newer arts. It is paradoxical that McLuhan, who is so media conscious, developed a major contribution to the group of forms which are most closely involved with the breakdown of media, though this is quite naturally in keeping with his persona as he presents it.

What has gone? How it ends?
Begin to forget it. It will remember itself from every
sides, with all gestures, in each our word. Today's truth,
tomorrow's trend.
Forget, remember!
Have we cherished expectations? Are we for
liberty of perusiveness? Whyafter what fore-
where? A plainplanned liffeyism assemble-
ments Eblania's conglomerate horde.
By dim delty Deva.
Forget!

Our wholemole millwheeling vicociclometer, a tetradomational gazebocroticon
(the "Mamma Lujah" known to every school-
boy scandaller, be he Matty, Marky, Lukey or
John-a-Donk), autokinatonetically preprovided with
a clappercoupling smeltingworks exprogressive process,
(for the farmer, his son and their homely codes, known
as eggburst, eggblend, eggburial and hatch-as-hatch can)
receives through a portal vein the dialytically separated elements of precedent decomposition for the verypetpurpose of
subsequent recombination so that the heroticisms, catastrophes
and eccentricities transmitted by the ancient legacy of the past,
type by tope, letter from litter, word at ward, with sendence of
sundance, since the days of Plooney and Columcellas when
Giacinta, Pervenche and Margaret swayed over the all-too-ghoulish
and illyrical and innumantic in our mutter nation, all, anastomosically assimilated and preteridentified paraidiotically, in fact, the
sameold gamebold adomic structure of our Finnius the old One,
as highly charged with electrons as hophazards can effective it, may
be there for you, Cockalooralooraloomenos, when cup, platter and
pot come piping hot, as sure as herself pits hen to paper and
there's scribings scrawled on eggs.
Of cause, so! And in effect, as? (FW 614.19)

In his works McLuhan has frequently mentioned the fact that Canada provides an early warning system for the United States and seems to suggest that part of his specific value as a prophet and media guru comes from the fact that his base of operations has been in Canada and that he is Canadian. To investigate thoroughly this whole subject would require an extensive study, since Mc-Luhan spent a great deal of his most productive period in Canada and also was influenced by his early Canadian education at the University of Manitoba. This early education and later success, among other things, instilled in him the interest that led to his attendance at Cambridge and his commitment to English studies there.

APPENDIX 4
The Influence of the Canadian University Milieu on McLuhan : A Speculative Note

None of McLuhan's major publications appeared until after he had been teaching in Canada for some time and until after he moved from Assumption University, in Windsor, Ontario (now the University of Windsor). Although he started the work which led to the *The Mechanical Bride* before returning to Canada, the important work connected with the Seminar in Culture and Communications that led to the production of *Explorations* and *The Gutenberg Galaxy* was done at the University of Toronto. His seminar involved two other Canadian professors—Carl Williams, a psychologist (now President of the University of Western Ontario) and Tom Easterbrook, an economist who is still at Toronto. The others involved in directing the seminar were Ted Carpenter, an anthropologist, and Jacqueline Tyrwhitt, a town planner (both of whom have now left Toronto). McLuhan's interest in Innis was considerably reinforced by Easterbrook, who introduced McLuhan to Canadian political and economic thought. These influences, except for Innis, however important they may have been in suggesting some of McLuhan's ideas, were secondary to the influence that the milieu of the humanities in Canada had on McLuhan at the time.

It could be argued that the development of Marshall McLuhan and Northrop Frye at the same university was not accidental.

Although in some ways they seem superficially quite distinct, there are really many similarities, and over a period of time McLuhan has come more and more to manifest an interest in the theory of archetypes which formed an important part of Frye's literary theories. Frye and McLuhan are both interested in broad historical patterns, in very generalized groups of images and in neutrally oriented ways of approaching the cultural objects that they wish to analyze. Both of them are interested more than might ordinarily be expected in the theoretical influence of James Joyce and the symbolist poets such as Mallarmé and Valéry. Although the early McLuhan did not seem to share Frye's interest in Blake, by the writing of *War and Peace in the Global Village* McLuhan seemed to share a considerable commitment to some of Blake's apocalyptic views. In very different ways, both of them wish to find methods to replace the *history of ideas* approach to culture, Frye by developing a scientific criticism, McLuhan by transforming the history of ideas into a *history of artistic techniques* and then into a *history of technologies*.

This deep interest in the historical approach, especially in Mc-Luhan, was obviously coloured by his involvement in the Toronto school of English studies fathered by A. S. P. Woodhouse, an eminent Miltonist and student of Irving Babbitt's, who emphasized the role of history of ideas in the development of the historically oriented honours English programme at the University of Toronto. Woodhouse, along with Arthur Barker and Frye, strongly emphasized the study of the Renaissance, an area which McLuhan had worked on at Cambridge and one in which he carried on a sustained interest because of the general Toronto milieu where its importance was large enough to make it the subject of four one-year courses in the English honours programme (Shakespeare; Spenser and Milton; Renaissance drama; and Renaissance literature from 1500–1600). Although McLuhan's interest in humanism obviously dated back to his early days at Manitoba and developed through his early teaching at the University of Wisconsin and attendance at Cambridge, its peculiar development in *Explorations* and *The Gutenberg Galaxy* is apparently related to the way that he reacted against the history of ideas approach and developed an extensive interest in the importance of style and technique in literature and then the effect of techniques prevalent in society on literature.

His early interest in the American New Criticism manifested in articles such as "Aesthetic Pattern in Keats' Odes" or "The Analogical Mirrors" and subsequently linked to social theories about southern agrarianism (set forth in "The Southern Quality") made him a natural foil for the historian of ideas.

Yet the Canadian influence had also led McLuhan to try to counterbalance American scholarship with the humanist traditions of the United Kingdom. It led to his intense interest in Leavis and in the important themes inherited from Arnold and others concerning the relationship of culture and society. Along with an interest in the Renaissance, these formed an intrinsic part of the University of Toronto programme in English which, in addition to the four Renaissance courses mentioned above, required courses in Romantic literature, Victorian literature, and nineteenth century thought. As a student of Babbitt's, Woodhouse was interested in the thought of Arnold and he developed a strong emphasis on Burke, Ruskin, Carlyle as well as Bentham, Coleridge, and Mill. Since these were in keeping with McLuhan's own youthful interest in late nineteenth century literature, especially Meredith, and reinforced the traditions in which he had studied in England, the Toronto atmosphere kept the issues about culture and society centrally present in his mind. It provided an extremely solid tradition to react against and, given McLuhan's own particular vantage point, made him the type of critic peculiarly equipped to understand Raymond Williams' thesis in *The Long Revolution*.

The writings published in McLuhan's collection of literary criticism ("Coleridge as Artist," "Tennyson and Picturesque Poetry," "The Aesthetic Moment in Landscape Poetry," etc.) provide further confirmation of his commitment to an interest in this area as well. It is important to see the role of both Renaissance and Victorian studies in McLuhan's general milieu to grasp his particular awareness of the importance of a historical perspective. Yet implicit in his reaction to the specific source of this interest among the historians of ideas are the factors which form that side of him which some critics seem to find peculiarly ahistorical. Some of the same paradox between background and critical position is present in the work of Northrop Frye. This highly specialized programme of undergraduate study quite exceeded in intensity of specialization any similar programme in the United States, and provided the unique quality of Canadian education in the literary field. It meant that McLuhan, no matter how intrigued by popular culture and media, was constantly enmeshed in a world of intense literary emphasis.

This theme should some day receive an extensive examination as a sociological illustration of the way that the interplay of a specific milieu with an individual at a particular point in time may generate specific developments in apparently unrelated areas. The presence of Frye and McLuhan at Toronto and the major significance they have had would seem to suggest that such a study would be justifiable. It would also indicate ways in which—because of Canada's location between England and the United States, and the peculiar intermingling of British, Scottish, French, and American traditions, coupled to an entirely different way of seeing the trip to England and attendance at Oxbridge (or as a suitable substitute, Harvard)—the influence of environment had an important conditioning effect on the way that Canada synthesized academic thought.

Whether McLuhan, as he is, could have developed in the United States is an interesting question. Certainly one component would be that to be as acutely aware of literary values as he is, it would have been necessary to have been involved in a world where intense literary specialization began at a very early level of the university curriculum. Yet England could not produce a McLuhan, because it required some remove from the commitment to the preservation of a received cultural tradition which prevailed then, and which, as Wyndham Lewis argues, inhibited the U.K. from seeing some of the values of the United States. McLuhan, above all this, is representative of characteristics of a peculiarly Canadian culture which is able to accept greater diversity without the need to synthesize or metamorphose it and has at the same time a greater tolerance for the preservation of ethnic differences and other pluralistic modes.

The area of English studies is one of the two major influences at the University of Toronto which deserve investigation. The second is the influence of St. Michael's College (the Roman Catholic college within the University), which housed the Pontifical Institute of Mediaeval Studies, a department of religion, a seminary, and eventually a school of theology. McLuhan came to Toronto a Catholic convert of some years, interested in the history of the patristic, mediaeval, and early Renaissance periods as well as in questions concerning contemporary theology and related subjects. The Institute provided an ideal milieu for confirming his interest in these areas and placing them in the context of contemporary problems. From time to time Jacques Maritain visited St. Michael's, and off and on Etienne Gilson served as director of its Institute of Mediaeval Studies. Their writings are referred to in various McLuhan works, along with references to Thomistic philosophy.

McLuhan's intense interest in this area is particularly reflected in literary writings such as "Joyce, Aquinas and the Poetic Process," as well as in his references to Thomism in *The Gutenberg Galaxy* and other works. The Institute provided a milieu which, taken in conjunction with the English programme, counterpointed mediaeval scholasticism with Renaissance humanism, a theme that had engaged the interest of the younger McLuhan in his thesis on Nashe and in articles such as "An Ancient Quarrel in Modern America." Besides, the resources of the Institute provided McLuhan with a much deeper and more extensive knowledge of Thomism, as reflected in his interest in the doctrine of analogy which appears even as late as *Culture Is Our Business*. He most certainly participated in the constant debates about the concept of analogy which are referred to in the works of Gilson and Maritain and were the subject of lectures by Armand Maurer, c.s.b. that McLuhan attended during the early fifties at the same time that he was becoming involved in the Culture and Communications Seminar.

Also at this time St. Michael's College was a central focus for liturgical reform in Canada, a subject which again recurs throughout McLuhan's work. References to such works as *Liturgical Piety* by Bouyer indicate the degree to which his thinking about participation is coloured by the particular emphasis on participation with Catholic sacramental theology and liturgical speculation. His continuing interest in such an area is quite apparently manifested in his references to the Vatican's difficulty in understanding the liturgical role of the church in the new society.

The counterpoint of the milieu of St. Michael's College with the University of Toronto Department of English provided a way of continually thinking about historical differences between Protestant and Catholic, puritan and anti-puritan themes, which enter into McLuhan's thought. Quite obviously the peculiar shape and character of the collegiate structure of the Canadian university, with its theological as well as secular colleges, had considerable sociological significance to the way that McLuhan has developed. Very little of his specific interest can be attributed solely to Toronto, yet the continued engagement with subjects in these areas, even after becoming extensively involved in media studies, was obviously largely a result of the particular milieu.

The present book has not attempted to be a study of influences in a detailed or complex way. Such a study would require a very extensive consideration of some of the themes suggested here and would link them to the broader significance of McLuhan's having grown up in Canada. They certainly would suggest why the man who laid such heavy emphasis on the artistic and critical approach towards the study of social and cultural objects was a Canadian and not an American, even though, as H. D. Duncan has suggested, this kind of approach is implicit in so much of the American tradition of James, Dewey, and G. H. Mead. The United States may have developed a more profound theorist in Kenneth Burke, but he was not a pioneer in the same way as McLuhan in trying to extend these insights into the general area of popular culture and everyday life.

Other influences at Toronto also have some importance. The case for Innis is frequently made—perhaps too frequently since it tends to overstress the importance of Innis in McLuhan's thought. Innis confirmed McLuhan's insight about the importance of a history of technique and the extension of that to technology in a broader sense, but McLuhan had started in this direction before Toronto and certainly long before encountering Innis. Innis, however, has a role which is discussed in some detail by James W. Carey in *McLuhan: Pro and Con* as well as McLuhan's own introduction to *The Bias of Communication.* Another Toronto figure of this period mentioned by McLuhan is Havelock, who was a professor at Victoria College, although McLuhan's chief interest in him appears to have come about through his book published after leaving Toronto, *Preface to Plato,* rather than the type of personal contact in which the themes outlined here are involved.

One interesting aside on Canada has to do with McLuhan's extremely close relationship with Wyndham Lewis, as well as his major commitment to Lewis' thought. Lewis for a brief time actually taught in Canada, a period of his life which forms part of the backdrop of his novel *Self-Condemned.* McLuhan found in Lewis' peculiar sensibility a way of seeing new values in North America while approaching it from the perspective of a British and European tradition. Lewis, unlike most English critics of his period, had a unique feeling for the type of popular culture which was growing up in the United States as well as an appreciation of some of its peculiar technological preoccupations and their significance in the twentieth century. For McLuhan this became a way of uniting a tradition which had consciously rejected the United States with an interest in that particular world, while still preserving a way of making the traditions of the English world and English life relevant.

Most advertisers and businessmen turned on by the McLuhan method would be surprised and shocked to meditate on the roots that it has in the particular kind of university milieu represented by Toronto; and most Americans might be a little less surprised if they understood more of the distinctness of McLuhan's Canadian background. One could go on to speculate—the same country that produced McLuhan, developed the National Film Board, launched Expo 67, and created the Canadian Broadcasting Corporation as well as contributing extensive impetus to newspaper publishing in Great Britain—and open up a whole new area of investigation quite beyond the very specific and limited suggestions of this note.

BIBLIOGRAPHICAL INDEX

ADDISON, JOSEPH. *The Spectator*. Edited by Ernest Rhys. 4 vols. London: J. M. Dent & Sons, 1945. **2, 3, 37–38, 201–3**

BACON, FRANCIS. *The Advancement of Learning*. London: J. M. Dent & Sons, 1950. **98, 100**

———. *Essays*. London: J. M. Dent & Sons, 1947.

BARTHES, ROLAND. *Elements of Semiology*. Translated by Annette Lavers and Colin Smith. New York: Hill and Wang, 1968. **80, 83, 96, 115**

———. *Mythologies*. Paris: Editions du Seuil, 1957.

BENSTOCK, BERNARD. *Joyce-Again's Wake*. Seattle: University of Washington Press, 1965. **179**

BLAKE, WILLIAM. *The Poetry and Prose of William Blake*. Edited by Geoffrey Keynes. London: Nonesuch Press, 1948.

BLOOMFIELD, LEONARD. *Language*. New York: Harcourt Brace, 1933.

The Book of Kells. Described by Sir Edward Sullivan. London, New York: The Studio Publications, 1952. **178–9, 196**

BOULDING, KENNETH. *The Image*. Ann Arbor, Michigan: University of Michigan Press, 1966. **41**

BRECHT, BERTOLT. *Brecht on Theatre*. Edited and translated by John Willett. New York: Hill and Wang, 1966. **209**

BROWN, NORMAN O. *Life Against Death*. New York: Random House Inc., 1959. **61, 108**

BURKE, KENNETH. *Language as Symbolic Action*. Berkeley: University of California Press, 1968. **12, 160, 208**

CAMPBELL, JOSEPH. *Hero with a Thousand Faces*. Princeton: Princeton University Press, 1968. **62**

CARLYLE, THOMAS. *Sartor Resartus*. Complete Works, Vol. 1. London: Chapman, 1897. **130**

CARPENTER, EDMUND. "Eskimo Space Concepts." *Explorations Five* (Toronto: University of Toronto Press, 1955), pp. 131–45. **65**

———. "Eternal Life." *Explorations Two* (1954), pp. 59–65. **65**

CERVANTES, MIGUEL. *Don Quixote De La Mancha*. Translated by Samuel Putnam. 2 vols. New York: The Viking Press, 1949. **106**

COLERIDGE, SAMUEL TAYLOR. *Biographia Literaria*. Edited by J. Shawcross. London: Oxford University Press, 1949. **178, 215**

COMPTON, NEIL. "The Paradox of Marshall McLuhan." (*New Amer-*

ican Review.) Reprinted in Raymond Rosenthal, ed., *McLuhan: Pro and Con*, pp. 106–24.

DENNEY, REUEL. *The Astonished Muse*. New York: Grosset & Dunlap, 1964. **56**

DRUCKER, PETER F. *The Age of Discontinuity*. New York: Harper and Row, 1969. **19, 93**

DUFFY, DENNIS. *Marshall McLuhan*. Toronto, Montreal: McClelland and Stewart, 1969.

DUNCAN, HUGH D. *Communication and Social Order*. London, New York: Oxford University Press, 1968. **109**

———. *Symbols and Social Theory*. New York: Oxford University Press, 1969.

EISEN, JONATHON, ed. *The Age of Rock*. New York, Toronto: Random House, Vintage Books, 1969.

EISENSTEIN, SERGEI. *Film Form*. New York: Harcourt, Brace and World, Inc., 1949. **188**

ELIOT, T. S. *On Poetry and Poets*. London: Faber and Faber, 1957.

———. *Selected Essays*. London: Faber and Faber, 1932.

ELLMANN, RICHARD. *James Joyce*. New York: Oxford University Press, 1959.

ERASMUS, DESIDERIUS. *The Praise of Folly*. Translated by Hoyt Hopewell Hudson. Princeton: Princeton University Press, 1941. **32, 102–6, 112–19**

FEKETE, JOHN. "Marshall McLuhan: A Study in the Determinist Fetishism of Technology." M.A. thesis, McGill University, 1969. **86**

FELLINI, FEDERICO. *Fellini's Satyricon*. Edited by Dario Zanelli and translated by Eugene Walter and John Matthews. New York: Ballantine Books, 1970. **146–7**

FENELLOSA, ERNST. *The Chinese Written Character As a Medium for Poetry*. Translated by Ezra Pound. Washington, D.C.: Square $ Series, n.d. **188**

FERKISS, VICTOR C. *Technological Man*. New York, Toronto: Mentor Books, 1969.

FINKELSTEIN, SIDNEY. *Sense and Nonsense of McLuhan*. New York: International Publishers, 1968. **35**

FOCILLON, HENRI. *The Life of Forms in Art*. Translated by Charles Beecher Hogan and George Kubler. New Haven: Yale University Press, 1942. **178, 195**

FOWLIE, WALLACE. *The Clown's Grail*. London: Dennis Dobson, 1947. **147**

FREUD, SIGMUND. *Wit and Its Relation to the Unconscious.* London: Kegan Paul and Co., 1922. **157**

FRYE, NORTHROP. *Anatomy of Criticism.* Princeton: Princton University Press, 1957.

————. *The Modern Century.* Toronto: Oxford University Press, 1967.

FULLER, BUCKMINSTER R. with JEROME AGEL and QUENTIN FIORE. *I Seem To Be A Verb.* New York, London & Toronto: Bantam Books, 1970.

GIEDION, SIEGFRIED. *The Eternal Present.* 2 vols. New York: Pantheon Books, Bollingen Series xxxv.6, 1962–64. **67, 170–1**

————. *Mechanization Takes Command.* New York: W. W. Norton, 1969.

————. *Space, Time and Architecture: The Growth of a New Tradition.* Cambridge, Mass.: Harvard University Press, 1954.

GILSON, ETIENNE. *History of Christian Philosophy in the Middle Ages.* New York: Random House, 1955.

GOFFMAN, ERVING. *The Presentation of Self in Everyday Life.* Garden City, New York: Doubleday, Anchor Books, 1959. **204**

GOMBRICH, E. H. *Art and Illusion.* New York: Pantheon Books, Bollingen Series xxxv.5, 1960.

GRIERSON, JOHN. *Grierson On Documentary.* Edited by Forsyth Hardy. London: Faber and Faber, 1966. **201**

HALL, EDWARD T. *The Hidden Dimension.* Garden City, New York: Doubleday, Anchor Books, 1969.

————. *The Silent Language.* New York: Doubleday, 1959. **82, 204**

HALL, STUART, and PADDY WHANNEL. *The Popular Arts.* New York: Random House, 1964.

HART, CLIVE. *Structure and Motif in Finnegans Wake.* London: Faber and Faber, 1962.

HAVELOCK, E. A. *Preface to Plato.* Cambridge, Mass.: Harvard University Press, 1963.

HEBB, D. O. *The Organization of Behavior.* New York: New York Science Editions Inc., 1961. **12**

HEINLEIN, ROBERT A. *Stranger in a Strange Land.* New York: Putnam, 1961. **210–12**

HOGGART, RICHARD. "Mass Communications in Britain." In *The Modern Age,* edited by Boris Ford. Baltimore, Md.: Penguin Books, 1964, pp. 442–57. **70, 76**

————. *The Uses of Literacy.* London: Chatto and Windus, 1957. **18**

HUIZINGA, JOHAN. *Homo Ludens.* Translated by R. F. C. Hull. Lon-

don: Routledge and Kegan Paul, 1949. **51–2, 94, 114, 132–4**
HUIZINGA, JOHAN. *Men and Ideas.* Translated by James S. Holmes and Hans van Marlo. New York: Meridian Books, 1959. **114**
————. *The Waning of the Middle Ages.* Garden City, New York: Doubleday, Anchor Books, 1954. **94**
INNIS, HAROLD. *The Bias of Communication.* Toronto: University of Toronto Press, 1951. **38–9, 52**
————. *Changing Concepts of Time.* Toronto: University of Toronto Press, 1952.
————. *Empire and Communications.* Oxford: Oxford University Press, 1950.
JOYCE, JAMES. *The Critical Writings.* Edited by Ellsworth Mason and Richard Ellmann. New York: The Viking Press, 1959.
————. *Finnegans Wake.* London: Faber and Faber, 1939. **25–6, 29, 31, 41, 52, 68, 71, 87, 91, 94, 106–13, 125–6, 130, 141, 144–5, 163, 177–9, 191, 194–5, 208–9, 213, 216–19**
————. *A Portrait of the Artist as a Young Man.* New York: The Viking Press, 1964.
————. *Stephen Hero.* Edited by John J. Slocum and Herbert Cahoon. New York: New Directions, 1963.
————. *Ulysses.* London: The Bodley Head, 1949. **69, 111, 141, 219**
JOHNSON, BEN. "Timber, or Discoveries." In *Ben Jonson,* edited by C. H. Herford Percy and Evelyn Simpson, vol. VIII, 555–650. Oxford: Oxford University Press, 1947. **21, 178**
KEPES, GYORGY. *Education of Vision* (Vision + Value Series). New York: George Braziller, 1965. **85–6**
KLEE, PAUL. *The Pedagogical Sketchbook.* Translated by Sibyl Moholoy-Nagy. London: Faber and Faber, 1953. **150**
————. *The Thinking Eye.* New York: George Wittenborn, 1961. **67, 150**
KOESTLER, ARTHUR. *The Act of Creation.* London: Pan Books Ltd., 1964. **14, 25**
KOLAKOWSKI, LESZEK. "The Priest and the Jester." In *Toward a Marxist Humanism,* translated by Jane Z. Peel. New York: Grove Press, 1968, pp. 9–37. **105, 113–14**
————. "In Praise of Inconsistency." In *Toward a Marxist Humanism,* translated by Jane Z. Peel. New York: Grove Press, 1968, pp. 211–20. **105**
KROEBER, A. L. *Style in Civilizations.* Berkeley: University of California Press, 1963.
LANGER, ELINORE. "Inside the New York Telephone Company.1." *The New York Review of Books,* 12 March 1970, pp. 16–24. **127**

LANGER, ELINORE. "The Women of the Telephone Company.2." *The New York Review of Books,* 26 March 1970, pp. 14–22. **127**

LEE, DOROTHY. "Lineal and Nonlineal Codifications of Reality." Reprinted in *Explorations in Communication,* edited by E. Carpenter and H. M. McLuhan. Boston: Beacon Press, 1960. pp. 136–54. **65**

LEWIS, WYNDHAM. *The Art of Being Ruled.* London: Chatto and Windus, 1926. **60**

————. *Men Without Art.* London: Cassell & Co., 1934. **2**

————. *Pale Face: The Philosophy of The Melting Pot.* London: Chatto & Windus, 1929.

————. *Time and Western Man.* London: Chatto & Windus, 1927. **45, 52, 56, 59, 177, 194–6**

————. *Wyndham Lewis the Artist.* London: Laidlaw & Laidlaw, 1939.

LOEWENSTEIN, OTTO. *The Senses.* Baltimore, Md.: Penguin Books, 1966. **36**

LUKACS, GEORGE. *The Historical Novel.* Translated by Hannah and Stanley Mitchell. Harmondsworth, Middlesex: Penguin Books, Peregrine, 1969. **91–2**

MCLUHAN, HERBERT MARSHALL. *Counterblast.* New York: Harcourt, Brace and World, Inc., 1968. **110–11, 183–98, 204, 218**

————. *Culture Is Our Business.* New York: McGraw Hill, 1970.

————. "The Future of Sex." *Look,* 25 July 1967. **108, 210–11**

————. *The Gutenberg Galaxy.* Toronto: University of Toronto Press, 1962. **21–3, 32–5, 51–6, 63–95, 99–104, 109, 112, 118**

————. "James Joyce: Trivial and Quadrivial." Reprinted in *The Literary Criticism of Marshall McLuhan 1943–1962,* edited by Eugene Macnamara. New York: McGraw Hill, 1969. pp. 23–47. **116–17, 121**

————. "Joyce, Aquinas, and the Poetic Process." Reprinted in *Joyce's Portrait: Criticisms and Critiques,* edited by Thomas E. Connolly. New York: Appleton-Century-Crofts, 1962. pp. 249–65. **85, 206**

————. "Joyce, Mallarmé and the Press." *Sewanee Review,* Winter, 1954.

————. *The Mechanical Bride: Folklore of Industrial Man.* New York: Vanguard Press, 1951. (Boston: Beacon Press, 1967.) **8, 61–75, 79–80, 130–32, 139–40**

————. *The McLuhan Dew Line.* New York: Human Development Corporation, first published June 1968. **1, 6, 60, 106, 114, 129, 155, 163**

MCLUHAN, HERBERT MARSHALL. "*Playboy* Interview: Marshall McLuhan." *Playboy*, March 1969. **26, 27, 45, 55–6, 61, 63**

———. "The Psychopathology of Time, Life and Fortune." (*Neurotica.*) Reprinted in *Scene Before You: A New Approach to American Culture*, edited by C. Brossard. New York: Rinehart, 1955, pp. 147–60. **59, 113**

———. *Report on Project in Understanding New Media*. National Association of Educational Broadcasters, 1960. **119, 121–3**

———. *Understanding Media*. New York: McGraw Hill, 1964. **35–42, 119–65**

———. *Verbi-Voco-Visual Explorations*. New York: Something Else Press, 1967.

——— and E. S. CARPENTER. *Explorations in Communication*. Boston: Beacon Press, 1960.

——— with QUENTIN FIORE. *The Medium Is the Massage*. New York: Bantam Books Inc., 1967. **154–66**

——— with QUENTIN FIORE. *War and Peace in the Global Village*. New York: Bantam Books Inc., 1968. **13, 155, 163–66**

——— with HARLEY PARKER. *Through the Vanishing Point: Space in Poetry and Painting*. New York: Harper and Row, 1968. **167–82, 192–93**

MARCUSE, HERBERT. *Eros and Civilization*. New York: Vintage Books, n.d. **61**

MALLARMÉ, STÉPHANE. *Oeuvres Completes*. Paris: Librairie Gallimard, 1945. **239**

MARKS, J. *Rock And Other Four Letter Words*. New York: London, Toronto: Bantam Books, 1968.

MARROU, H. I. *A History of Education in Antiquity*. Toronto: Mentor Books, 1964.

MARX, KARL. *Karl Marx: Selected Writings in Sociology and Social Philosophy*. Edited by T. B. Bottomore and M. Rubel. Harmondsworth, Middlesex: Penguin Books, 1967. **207**

MEAD, GEORGE HERBERT. *Mind, Self, and Society*. Edited by Charles W. Morris. Chicago: University of Chicago Press, 1934. **12, 57, 209**

MEAD, MARGARET. "Vicissitudes of the Study of the Communication Process." In *Approaches to Semiotics* ed. by T. A. Sebeok et. al. The Hague: Mouton, 1964, 277–87. **96**

MEAD, SHEPHERD. *Big Ball of Wax*. New York: Ballantine, 1956. **135, 212**

MEYER, LEONARD B. *Emotion and Meaning in Music*. Chicago: University of Chicago Press, 1956.

MILLS, C. WRIGHT. *The Sociological Imagination.* (New York: Oxford University Press, 1959.) New York: Grove Press, 1959. **10–12, 43**

MOHOLY-NAGY, L. *Vision in Motion.* Chicago: Paul Theobald, 1947.

MORE, THOMAS. *Utopia.* Oxford: Clarendon Press, 1904. **102–5**

MULLER-THYME, BERNARD. "The Common Sense: Perfection of the Order of Pure Sensitivity." *The Thomist* 2, no. 3 (July 1940).

ONG, WALTER. *Ramus: Method and the Decay of Dialogue.* Cambridge, Mass.: Harvard University Press, 1958. **65–6, 100**

PANOFSKY, ERWIN. *Gothic Architecture and Scholasticism.* New York: Meridian Books, 1960. **87, 143**

———. *Perspective as Symbolic Form.* New York: Institute of Fine Arts, New York University, n.d. **170**

PASCAL, BLAISE. *Pensées.* London: J. M. Dent & Sons, 1948.

PIAGET, JEAN. *Play, Dreams, and Imitation in Childhood.* Translated by C. Gattegno and J. M. Hodgson. New York: W. W. Norton, 1962.

———. *Psychology of Intelligence.* Paterson, New Jersey: Littlefield, Adams & Co., 1963.

——— and BARBEL INHELDER. *The Child's Concept of Space.* London: Routledge and Kegan Paul, 1956. **115, 171**

PIKE, KENNETH L. *Language in Relation to a Unified Theory of the Structure of Human Behavior.* Part I, II, III. Glendale, California: Summer Institute of Linguistics, 1960. **115**

POHL, FREDERIK. *Drunkard's Walk.* New York: Ballantine, 1969.

——— and CYRIL M. KORNBLUTH. *Space Merchants.* New York: Ballantine, 1969.

POPE, ALEXANDER. *The Dunciad.* Edited by James Sutherland. London: Methuen, 1953. **70–6, 178**

———. "Peri Bathos." In *Selected Poetry and Prose,* edited by W. K. Wimsatt, Jr. New York: Holt, Rinehart and Winston, 1961, pp. 306–60. **76**

POUND, EZRA. *ABC of Reading.* London: Faber and Faber, 1951. **16, 167–8, 196**

———. *Guide to Kulcher.* London: Peter Owen Ltd., 1952. **70**

———. *The Literary Essays of Ezra Pound.* Edited by T. S. Eliot. London: Faber and Faber, 1954. **167**

RABELAIS, FRANÇOIS. *Gargantua and Pantagruel.* 2 vols. London: J. M. Dent & Sons, Everyman, 1946.

READ, HERBERT. *A Concise History of Modern Art.* New York: Praeger, 1959. **124**

READ, HERBERT. *The Forms of Things Unknown*. London: Faber and Faber Ltd., 1960.

RICHARDS, I. A. *The Philosophy of Rhetoric*. The Mary Flexner Lectures, 3. New York: Oxford University Press, 1965. **12**

———. *Practical Criticism*. London: Kegan Paul and Co., 1929. **17**

———. *The Principles of Literary Criticism*. New York: Harcourt, Brace and World Inc., 1961. **120**

RIESMAN, DAVID J. with REUEL DENNY and NATHAN GLAZER. *The Lonely Crowd*. New Haven: Yale University Press, 1950.

ROCKMAN, ARNOLD. "McLuhanism: The Natural History of an Intellectual Fashion." *Encounter* 31 (1968): 28–36. **199**

ROSENTHAL, RAYMOND, ed. *McLuhan: Pro and Con*. Baltimore, Md.: Penguin Books, 1968. **20, 30, 32, 107, 146**

RUSSELL, ROBERT. "Intersex." (*Take One*, August 1967, pp. 7–8.) Reprinted in *Architectural Design*, 9/69, pp. 471–72. **265**

STEARN, GERALD, ed. *McLuhan: Hot & Cool*. New York: Dial Press, 1967. **10, 16, 28, 43, 46, 47, 63, 64, 68, 106–7**

SVITAK, IVAN. *Man and His World: A Marxian View*. Translated by Jarmila Veltrusky. New York: Dell, Delta Books, 1970.

SYPHER, WYLIE. *Literature and Technology: The Alien Vision*. New York: Random House, 1968. **86**

STEINER, GEORGE. *Language and Silence*. Harmondsworth, Middlesex: Penguin Books, Pelican, 1969. **117**

THEALL, DONALD. "Here Comes Everybody." *Explorations Two* (Toronto: University of Toronto Press, 1954), pp. 66–77. **71, 76–7**

———. "Pope's Satiric Program: The War With the Dunces." Report of ACUTE, 1960, pp. 11–16.

VALÉRY, PAUL. *The Art of Poetry*. Translated by Denise Folliot, introduction by T. S. Eliot. New York: Random House, 1961.

VICO, GIAMBATTISTA. *The New Science*. Translated by Thomas G. Bergin and Max H. Fisch. Ithaca: Cornell University Press, 1948. **133**

WHITE, LESLIE. *The Science of Culture*. New York: Grove Press, n.d. **84**

WILLIAMS, AUBREY. *Pope's* Dunciad. Baton Rouge, La.: Louisiana State University Press, 1955. **100**

WILLIAMS, EMMETT, ed. *An Anthology of Concrete Poetry*. New York: Something Else Press, Inc., 1967.

WILLIAMS, RAYMOND. *Communications*. Harmondsworth, Middlesex: Penguin Books, 1966. **18**

WILLIAMS, RAYMOND. *Culture and Society 1780–1950.* (New York: Columbia University Press, 1958.) New York: Doubleday, Anchor Books, 1959. **18**
———. *The Long Revolution.* London: Chatto and Windus, 1961. **18**
———. *May Day Manifesto.* Harmondsworth, Middlesex: Penguin Books, 1968. **48–9**
WIMSATT, WILLIAM K., JR. and CLEANTH BROOKS. *Literary Criticism.* New York: Alfred A. Knopf, 1957.
WOELFFLIN, HEINRICH. *Principles of Art History: The Problem of the Development of Style in Later Art.* New York: Dover Publications Inc., n.d. **119**
YOUNG, J. Z. *Doubt and Certainty in Science.* Oxford: Oxford University Press, 1961. **83**